Harosheth hagoyim

-Smithy of nations

S. Kalyanaraman

Sarasvati Research Center

2012

Library of Congress Control Number LCCN: 2012915515

Printed in the USA
First paperback printing, September 2012

ISBN-13: 978-0-9828971-4-0

ISBN: 0982897146

Lebensraum (living space) of Ancient Near East

During the 3rd millennium BCE, a veritable revolution in the history of civilizations was unleashed with the invention of the smithy supported by the crucible and the forge. The ability to identify metallic minerals, to smelt them, to alloy them to create new metals provided for the next stages of casting ingots and forging metal tools and weapons including ploughshares for the plows, axes, harrows, sickles, swords, knives, linchpins to hold the hubs of axles of spoked-wheels of carts and chariots. These resultant technological developments led to the establishment of state power using improved mobility of troops engaged in warfare, issues of coins from mints and development of markets involving improved seafaring and rapid land-transport of surplus products in bulk for trade activities by caravans of manufactory artisan guilds, merchants' guilds. Social institutions got transformed beyond recognition as cultures evolved from the chalcolithic era into the bronze-age. The invention of smithy was thus developed further as a trans-state institution of smithy of nations, a development recorded in the Old Testament of the Bible, calling this Harosheth hagoyim. The smithy guilds operating in a variety of new corporate forms, extended their reach beyond state boundaries to become the smithy of nations to meet the demand for metals, metallic tools and weapons produced in the smithy and merchandising them across an expansive interaction area of Eurasia. This development, together with the associated invention of writing systems for bills of lading and other trade transctions, transformed the *lebensraum* (living space) of bronze-age civilizations of the Ancient Near East. A profound cultural consequence was the formation/evolution of linguistic areas (language unions or *sprachbunds* such as the Indian *sprachbund*) with free exchanges of semantic clusters and other language features.

El-Ahwat (Translation: Arabic, 'the walls') discovery in Biblical Archaeology of Israel, identified as Harosheth hagoyim, 'smithy of nations'

University of Haifa and University of Cagliari in Sardinia set up teams headed by Professor Adam Zertal to excavate the archaeological site of El-Ahwat.

The excavation done from 1993-2000 led to the discovery of a fortified place of the late bronze age (ca. 13th-12th centuries BCE). A detailed account of the excavation is provided in: *El-Ahwat: a fortified site from the early iron age near Nahal 'Iron, Israel*, edited by Adam Zertal (ISBN 978-9004176454; 485 pages), Brill. 2011. An overview of the book is at Sardinians in Central Israel? The excavator of El-Ahwat makes his final case by Jefff Emanuel on March 5, 2012.[1]

The indications derived from the archaeological finds are that there was international trade in bronze artefacts. The name harosheth-hagoyim and the semantics of the phrase hold the key to unravel the interactions involved in such trade. This unraveling takes us far over time and space of woven cultural threads of exchanges and contacts among the seafaring people -- of bronze-age and earlier chalcolithic eras -- who constituted the smithy of nations – Harosheth hagoyim.

I have provided an explanation for the presence of inscribed pure tin ingots in a shipwreck at Haifa.[2] It is likely that the traders/artisans who created these tin ingots and inscribed them with Indus script were also the traders/artisans involved in the international trade at El-Ahwat, which could be related to Harosheth hagoyim mentioned in the Old Testament of the Bible.

El-Ahwat excavations in Israel identify the location as Harosheth hagoyim. The original word is: חֲרֹשֶׁת The word is pronounced khar-o-sheth.[3] The place is mentioned in Judges 4.2 of the Bible, Old Testament. Bronze-age contacts extended from El-Ahwat on Kishon river to Rakhigarhi on Sarasvati River. Seafaring merchants traded across the Persian Gulf and from Mt. Mustagh Ata of Tocharian speakers of Turkmenistan who traded in *ancu* 'iron' (cognate *amśu* 'soma') to Caspian Sea across many regions of Ancient Near East including Haifa. This Harosheth hagoyim, 'smithy of nations' also evolved early writing systems like Indus script, cuneiform, Aramaic and kharoṣṭī. This is a multi-disciplinary account of cultural contacts – discovered in archaeological, metallurgical and language studies -- with inventions in smelting, alloying, chariot-making and writing systems, in an extensive region of 2nd millennium BCE with links between Harosheth hagoyim and Proto-Indian speakers/artisans/traders of the smithy of nations. The *raison d'etre* for this account is to call for more studies to unravel the nature and chronological evolution of the smithy of nations spurred by contacts among traders, artisans and technology innovators of ancient civilizations surrounding the Ancient Near East.

The enquiry begins with the word harosheth and etymological cognate: *kharoṣṭī* which is a term used in Proto-Indian languages of Indian *sprachbund* as referring to a writing system. It will be established that both harosheth and kharoṣṭī are semantics related to smiths' work. One interpretation is that haroshet is a noun meaning a carving[4]. The word *kharoṣṭī* occurs in *Lalitavistara* (10.29) and interpreted as a kind of written character or alphabet. A variant spelling, excluding the dental -*st*- in Ardhamāgadhi is *kharoṭṭhi* in Jaina texts. *kha-rehu-sten* is a proper name in a Tibetan literary text, the name of a Khotan sage. *Kharoti* (Pashto: خروټی) is a Pashtun tribe in Afghanistan.

"The basic idea is cutting into some material, e.g. engraving metal or plowing soil." Sanskrit cognates are: *karṣá* m. 'dragging'; 'agriculture'; *kṛṣṭi* 'ploughing'. The semantics of *kharoṣṭī* as the name of an ancient writing system are strikingly similar. The word kāru in Sanskrit connotes an artisan. This is cognate with Kashmiri word khār 'blacksmith'. The suffix *oṣṭī* relates to -*ōṣṭh* 'lip'.
The second part of the phrase hagoyim in harosheth hagoyim also finds a cognate in Proto-Indian. In Prākṛt the word *goyā* connotes a community, guild, comparable to the semantics of –goy in Hebrew meaning 'nation'. Hence the phrase harosheth hagoyim is interpreted as 'smithy of nations' which is the cognate semantics of *kharoṣṭī goyā* meaning 'writing/engraving community of smiths'(Prākṛt).

Judges 4.2 refers to Harosheth hagoyim: "2 And the LORD gave them over into the hand of Jabin king of Canaan, that reigned in Hazor; the captain of whose host was Sisera, who dwelt in Harosheth-goiim." (Variant spelling: Harosheth-hagoyim).
ב וַיִּמְכְּרֵם יְהוָה, בְּיַד יָבִין מֶלֶךְ-כְּנַעַן, אֲשֶׁר מָלַךְ, בְּחָצוֹר;
וְשַׂר-צְבָאוֹ, סִיסְרָא, וְהוּא יוֹשֵׁב, בַּחֲרֹשֶׁת הַגּוֹיִם.

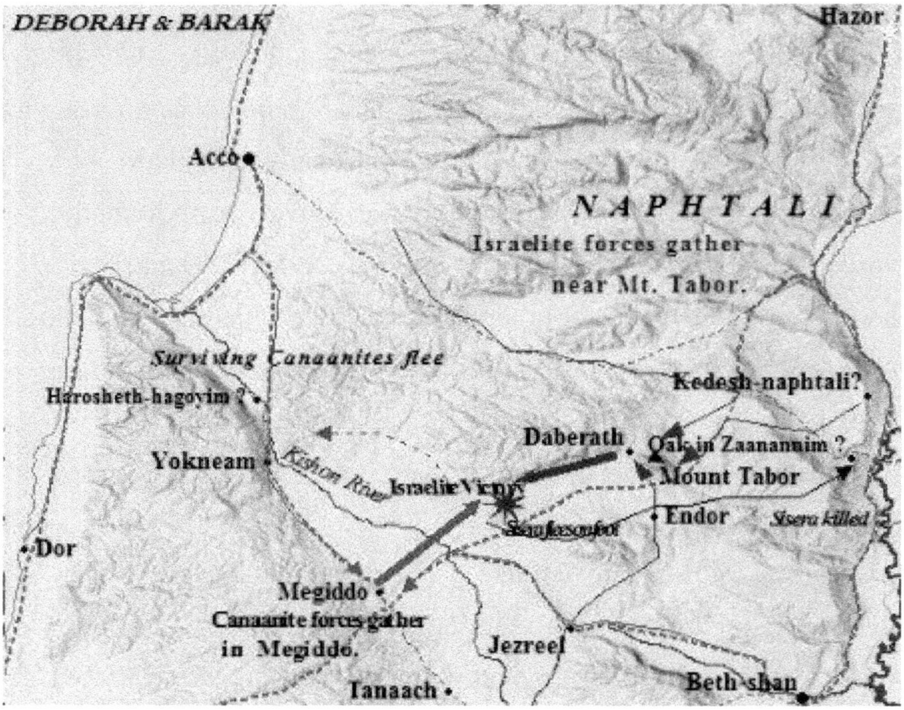

After Holman Bible Atlas.[5]

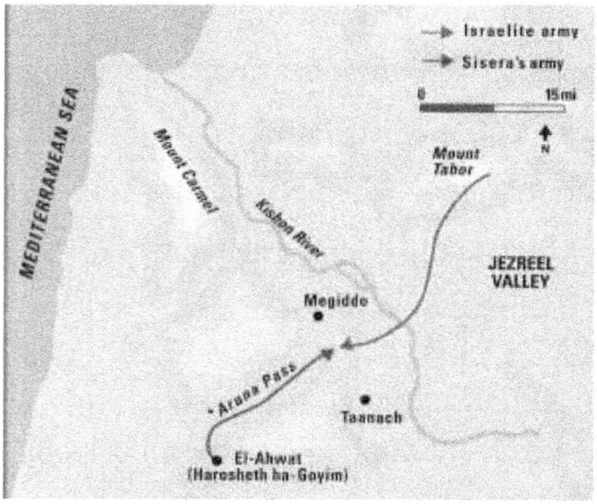

A remarkable find of El-Ahwat excavation which justified its identification as Harosheth hagoyim, ‘smithy of nations’, was a bronze shard with the relief of a female head. (It is unclear if Harosheth hagoyim refers to a particular settlement, as the archaeologists surmised or to a large area containing many settlements). The shard measures 2 cm. high, 1.6 cm wide and 3 mm thick. The relief showed the 'face of a woman wearing a cap and earrings shaped as chariot wheels.'

Chariot linchpin of El-Ahwat (Harosheth hagoyim), circa 13th century BCE.[6]	Bronze Head in High Relief. From the Gandhara culture, circa 3rd century CE. Northern Pakistan Comparable to the woman's head on chariot linchipin of El-Ahwat (Harosheth hagoyim).[7]

Archaeologists located the find in what they called the 'Governor's house'.The bronze piece is part of a linchpin which should have been used to hold the wheel of a battle chariot, with the axle-hub of the chariot wheel. "Such an identification reinforces the claim that a high-ranking Egyptian or local ruler was based at this location, and is likely to support the theory that the site is Harosheth Hagoyim, the home town of Sisera, as mentioned in Judges 4-5," says Prof. Zertal.

A report on the locus of this find reads as follows: "But the real surprise came to light in the excavation of the northeastern, higher area of the site. On a flat terrace supported by a long retaining wall, we found a large building we call "the governor's house." It is 75 feet long and 36 feet wide, with walls 6 feet thick and a stone-paved courtyard in front. Most of the walls had been dismantled, but the floor had survived, along with many artifacts—including more Egyptian scarabs of the XIXth Dynasty, a small bronze statuette of a woman's head (a goddess?) with a cap and large earrings, a square seal of black stone incised with a soldier on one side and a horse on the other, rings, large gold earrings, and silver, bronze and Carnelian beads. A particularly remarkable find was a beautiful ivory ibex head that closely resembles ibex images adorning vessels that often appear in Egyptian reliefs depicting Egypt's diplomatic and trade relationships with its colonies or rivals. This ibex head, which is of unusually high quality, together with other artifacts found at the site, lead us to believe that the building had functioned as an administrative center with some connection to international trade." [8]

'Dancing Girl,' the iconic bronze figurine of Mohenjodaro.	Bhirrana. Potsherd with engraving of 'dancing girl' in a posture comparable to the Mohenjodaro bronze figurine.

El-Ahwat near kibuts Katsir-Harish Iron smelting furnace.[9]	Circular clay furnace (damaged), comprising iron slag and tuyeres and other waste material stuck with its body, exposed at lohsanwa mound, Period II, Malhar, Dist. Chandauli.[10]

"The origins of Iron-working in India: New evidence from the Central Ganga Plain and the Eastern Vindhyas" By Rakesh Tewari: "Recent excavations in Uttar Pradesh have turned up iron artefacts, furnaces, tuyeres and slag in layers radiocarbon dated between c. BCE 1800 and 1000. This raises again the question of whether iron working was brought in to India during supposed immigrations of the second millennium BCE, or developed independently." Does the circular iron furnace in Malhar (Ganga valley) compares with the circular iron furnace of Harosheth hagoyim?

"(El-Ahwat) The city's uniqueness - its fortifications, passageways in the walls, and rounded huts - made it foreign amidst the Canaanite landscape." It is notable that the site of Bhirrana[11] on the banks of River Sarasvati also yielded discoveries of circular dwelling units.

El-Ahwat near kibuts Katsir-Harish Ivory ibex head.[12] Was this a hieroglyph connoting damgar 'artisan/trader'? [*tagara* 'ram' (Marathi); *damgar, tamkāru* 'artisan/trader' (Sumerian/Akkadian)]

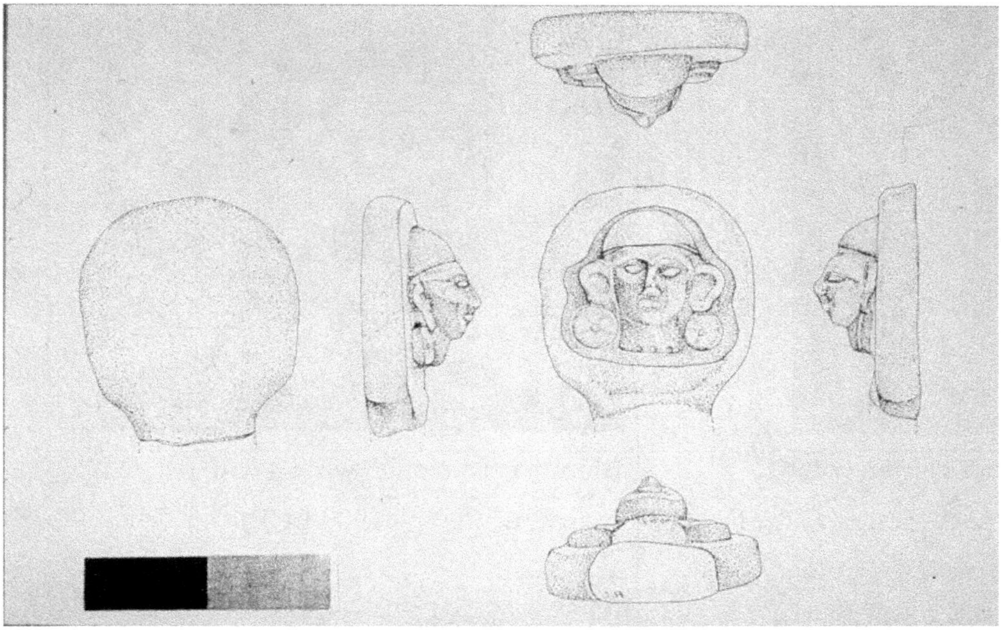

Chariot linchpin decoration.[13] [A hieroglyph? *mũh* 'face'; rebus: *mũha* 'ingot' (Santali)].

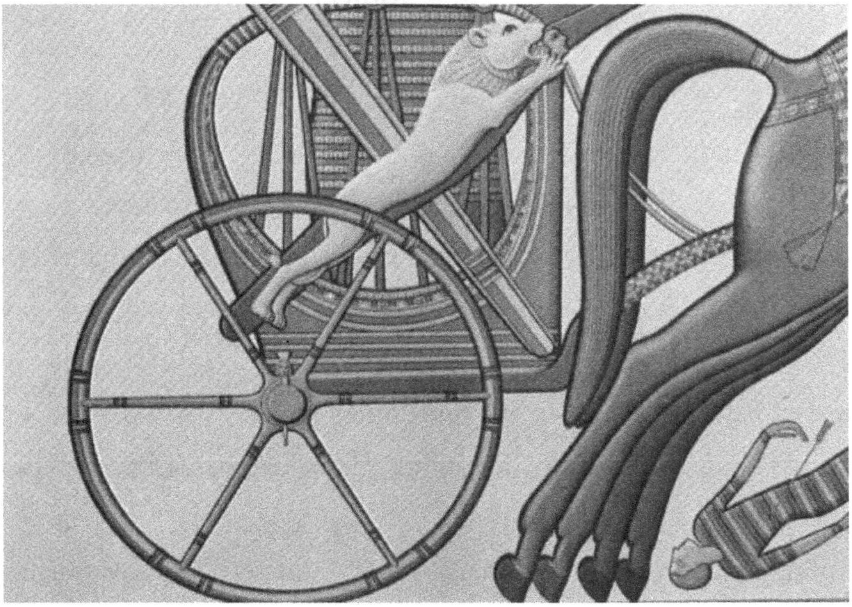

(After El-Ahwat near kibuts Katsir-Harish Egyptian reliefs showing battle chariots and engraved linchpins.[14]

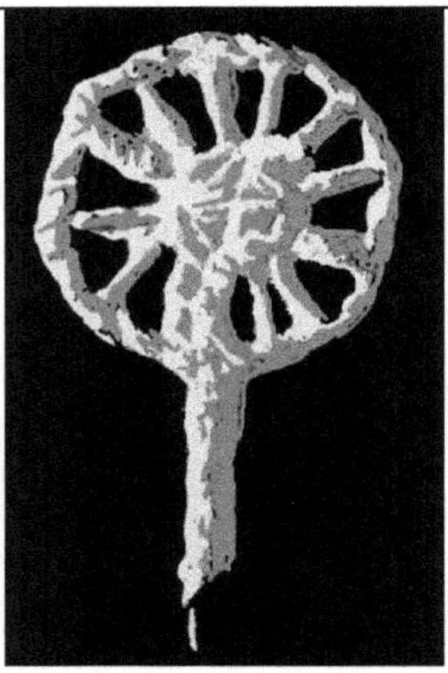	
A bronze hairpin with "cartwheel" design as the head from Tepe Yahya, Iran (note the incised circled cross or "X" in the center).[17]	Bhirrana. Terracotta wheels with painted spokes, (c. 2500 – 1900 BCE).[18]

As to how the Aramaic traders spread the idea of a writing system which evolved into the syllabic script of kharoṣṭī is yet to be unraveled by archaeological studies and further researches. Use of Aramaic from 2nd millennium BCE stretched from Syria in the west to India in the east. The indications of the find of a linch-pin of a figure-head of a woman wering chariot-wheel shaped earrings points to some contacts with metal-work artisans/traders (who were Proto-Indian speakers) and who later evolved and used kharoṣṭī.

This inquiry further evaluates the presence of Proto-Indian sememes in the contact areas which can be broadly termed 'smithy of nations', harosheth hagoyim with the following indicators:
Including in this report are identification of soma: *ancu* (Tocharian), *amśu* (Indian *sprachbund*), *asem, asemon* (Egyptian) and concordant morphemes: *ta'anach* (Biblical), *ṭaṅka* 'mint' (Indian *sprachbund*).

Proto-Indian in *harosheth hagoyim*, 'smithy of nations' is a provisional review of the contact areas of speakers of Prākṛt and other ancient Indian languages. The challenge is to outline the structural features of Proto-Indian from ca. 4th millennium BCE. A *sememe* [Greek: σημαίνω (sēmaino), "mean, signify"] is a language unit of meaning, correlative to a morpheme. A sememe for key component of soma yields the clue to identify soma as a metallic mineral. The sememe is *ancu* (Tocharian); cognate *amśu* (Indian *sprachbund*). Bronze-age evolution of languages with technical, metallurgical terms matches the cultural evolution of the bronze age with focus on glosses for and smithy processes involving minerals, metals and alloys. These identifications reinforce the over 1200 semantic clusters of an *Indian lexicon*. Tocharian-Indo-European lexical isoglosses (with some loan words from one of the lost sources), point to Proto-Indian (with some loan words from one of the lost sources, such as Language 'X') as a language with two dialectical forms: Vedic, the literary form and Mleccha, the vernacular form. Louis Renou noted: "Toute le RV est present in nuce autour des themes du soma."[19] (Trans. All the *Ṛgveda* is present in a nutshell around the topics of the soma.) About 120 hymns out of a total of 1028 hymns or a thousand verses and almost the entire ninth book (with 114 hymns) deal with soma. The number of hymns used to Soma are next only to those to Agni and Indra as devata-s. Indra and Varuna gain anthropomorphic status as divinities, but Soma is generally represented in reference to physical nature of Soma, though metaphorically. Chāndogya Upaniṣad calls soma as rājā.

The gloss *asem, asemon* (Egyptian) is cognate with soma (Indian *sprachbund*).. Early Vedic is attested in what is perhaps one of the oldest documents of mankind, the *Ṛgveda*. Mleccha as a language is attested in Manusmṛti (and as Meluhha in Mesopotamian cuneiform texts). Ta'anach 'cult' stand dated to 10th century BCE has hieroglyphs comparable to Mesopotamian and Indus artifacts which yield a link with *ṭaṅka* 'mint' (Indian *sprachbund*) and in the context of *damgar* 'mint-merchant' (Akkadian). Warka vase with Mleccha hieroglyphs is dated to ca. 3200 BCE. Glosses of Indian *sprachbund* hold the key to unravel the semantics of hieroglyphs/homonyms in Indus script inscriptions and of hieroglyphs of Ta'anach stand from Tell Taannek/Tiinnik and Warka vase from Sumer. Both Tiinnik and Sumer could have been mleccha (Proto-Indian) contact areas. The apparent semantic links between Tocharian and Indian *sprachbund* call for a rethink on roots and evolution of Proto-Indo-European (PIE) and of PIE Urheimat.

***ātmā yajñasya* (*raison d'etre* of sacred Vedic offering)**

Hermeneutics is the science of discovering new meanings and interpretations in 'all those situations in which we encounter meanings that are not immediately understandable but require interpretive effort.'[20] Such an effort can explain the semantics of *amśu* (Rigveda) as 'metllic mineral', by relating it to the meaning assigned to *ancu* (Tocharian), a cognate which means 'iron'.

yajña (root: yaj); yajati 'The act of offering something with reference to some deity; द्रव्यदवताक्रियार्थस्य यजतिशब्देन प्रत्यायनं क्रियते | ŚB. on MS.4.2.27.'

(Apte.lexicon, p. 1297). *Amśu* is the very *raison d'etre* of the offering, for example, in agniṣṭoma (fire-offering). There are seven soma samsthā: अग्निष्टोम,

अत्यग्निष्टोम, उक्थ, षोढशी, अतिरात्र, आप्तोर्याम and वाजपेय

Soma yajña is the soul of the *Ṛgveda* (*ātmā yajñasya*: RV. IX. 2,10; 6,8). Within soma, *amśu* which is a component, is *ātmā yajñasya*

Within soma ore-block complex, *amśu* is the key metallic-mineral ingredient which is offered in soma samsthā. With the identification of *amśu*, soma gets identified. The process is reduction or purification (*pavitram*).

In an extraordinary process described eloquently in Vedic chants (chandas), soma was purchased, and went through a process kept secret from the seller. Soma was washed in water (*yad-adbhih pariṣicyase mṛjyamāno gabhastyoh-* : RV. Ix.65.6), then pounded either with stone or in a mortar (RV. 1.83.6; RV. 1.28.4); it had amśu (RV. Ix.67.28); it yielded andhas, rasa, pitu, pīyūṣa or amṛta; it was filtered through a strainer (*antah- pavitra āhitah-* : RV. Ix.12.5). It was not 'drunk' by mortals. Soma was the product of an activity using intense fire, and involving the participation of the entire household for days and nights. Soma was wealth.

"If Soma was really a precious possession, as the singers praise it, then it was hardly likely that it was a *publici juris,* and its habitats must have had their rightful or pretened owner who guarded his property. No matter whether the owner was an Aryan or not, whether it was a mountain chief who ruled over the peaks and valleys where the Soma grew particularly well, or it was a tribe, traders must have, in any case, taken off from there in order to offer the precious produce of their homeland to their neighbours for sale. However, this would not suffice to answer the question why then this trade, with all its details, found a place in the ritual of the Adhvaryu. Its inclusion there has a deeper symbolic meaning."[21]

Without indulging in speculation on why the Adhvaryu refers to the purchase of soma from a seller in the text, it may be hypothesized that the name of the 'product' purchased could be found in lexical isoglosses of Proto-Indian. Indeed, the ancu of Tocharian and amśu of Rigvedic constitute isoglosses, as this monograph will demonstrate.

Nicholas Kazanas[22] notes one of the most baffling isoglosses shared by Tocharian in the east, Hittite and Phrygian in the centre, Italic in the south and Celtic in the west. "This is the marker –r- found in the medio-passive aspects of verbs in these brnches (and to a minor extent in Sanskrit) – e.g. dadhi-ré/ dadh-ré 'they have placed'). It would have been impossible for the speakers of Tocharian, Hittite, Phrygian (near Greek, Albanian and Anatolian), Italic and Celtic to have co-existed

I close contiguity and apart from the others at the centre which was the Kurgan culture so as to have developed this –r- isogloss. South is the Black Sea. East is the Caspian and, in any case, Tocharian would have to double back across the central Kurgan region. If the place was north, then the Hittites and Phrygians would have to double back southward across the central region. But if they all moved northwest from Saptasindhu, then the Tocharians would move north and the others westward. No problem. These simple linguistic facts show that Vedic is anterior; more so, if we consider the Vedic has a muchmore obvious system of dhātus (like √sṛ, bhū, dhā etc) giving verbs and nouns, primary and secondary derivatives. But the periphrastic perfect is conclusive. Avestan has only the acc. fem. with perfect auxiliary of ah-. Sanskrit has this auxiliary as- in the perfect but this is a later format (as is also the common bhū-) of Brāhmaṇa times. In Vedic texts there is first in the Atharva Veda the perfect of kṛ(cakāra) as auxiliary. If the IAs had left Iran they would have with them as- first and then kṛ-, not the reverse. This shows that Avestan left when kṛ- passed in relative desuetude and as came into use...The new picture may well come to be as follows: –In one of the older hymns of the RV, addressed to the goddess and the river Sarasvatī, it is said: 'She, the holy follower of Universal Order, [Sarasvatī,] has spread us all [the five tribes of the Vedic people (stanza 12)] beyond enmities, beyond the other [seven] sister-rivers, as the sun spreads out the days' (6.61.9)4: *sā́ no víśvā áti dvíṣaḥ svásṝ anyā́ ṛtā́varī/ átann áheva sū́ryaḥ//* 4. The river Sarasvatī was in those ancient times regarded supreme and the "seven sisters" (sometimes, daughters or young ones) are the other rivers, which are in fact more than seven; but seven is an auspicious mystical number."

Map (from Nicholas (2010)[23]) showing distant sites with Harappan artefacts (after Lal 2009: 77); the seven rivers and Sarasvat.; larger Saptasindhu and 5 Vedic

peoples with Purus etc; expansion by āyu eastward and by Amavasu west and north (to Tocharian speakers) from Bactria. Isoglosses accommodated also.

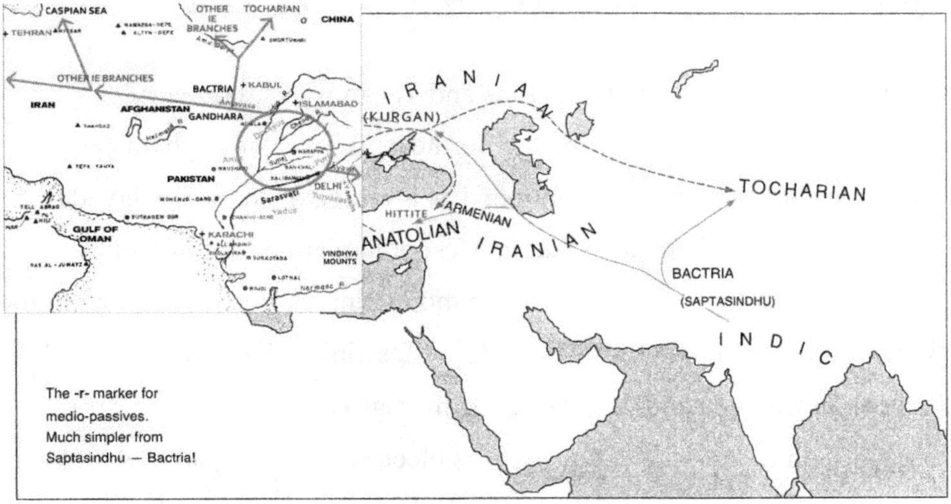

Evaluating the position of Tocharian among the other Indo-European languages, Douglas Q. Adams[24] investigates phonological, morphological and lexical isoglosses. This evaluation leads Douglas Q. Adams to group Tocharian with Meillet's 'Northwestern' group with close ties with Germanic. In his view, the ties Tocharian has with both Greek and Indic outside of the Northwestern group reflect later contacts on the part of the pre-Tocharians with the pre-Greeks and pre-Indics as the pre-Tocharian moved progressively eastward in the late Proto-Indo-European world.

Pinault (2006) identifies *amśu* of Rigveda with *ancu* of Tocharian. Tocharin language as an Indo-European language has revealed a word *ancu* in Tocharian which meant 'iron'. It is likely that this is the word used with the semantics of metallic mineral for soma in Rigveda. Processed in yajña, are elaborated by the *kavi-* 'smiths'. (The key is in the proto-indic lexeme: kavi, semant. 'smith, poet'. Cognate, *kayanian.*)[25] cf. S. Kalyanaraman (2000).

Muztagh Ata of Kyrgystan (close to both Oxus and Tarim rivers, border of Tajikistan and China's Xinjiang – beyond the northeast frontier of Afghanistan) could have been named Mt. Mujavat (mentioned as a source of soma in Rigveda). It is Avesta: Muṣā, Yt.8.125. It is notable that in Mesopotamian legend of Ninurta, god of war and agricultural fertility hunts on the mountains, Anzu which is the lion-headed Eagle with the power of the stolen Tablet of Destinies. The 'eagle' is identified as śyena in Rigveda and Avesta (saena meregh) as the falcon which brought the nectar, Soma. It is likely that soma as electrum (silver-gold ore) was bought from the traders who brought*anzu* from Mt. Mujavat. Comparable to the Anzu myth is the rescue of Atri from a fiery burning pit (RV V.78.4).[26]

Atri saved from a fiery pit

Saving of Atri from the pit (fiery cavern) and Atri discovered the light, Soma

Atri is one of 9 brahma rishis. Bhrigu, Pulastya, Pulaha, Kratu, Angiras, Marichi, Daksha, Atri, and Vasishtha: these are the nine Brahmas (or Brahma rishis) celebrated in the Puranas (Vishnu Purana 1.7)

3 Ye freed sage Atri, whom the Pañcajanāh (Five Groups) honoured, from the strait pit, ye Heroes with his (RV 1.117) Or those of the Five Groups of men, bring quickly all that help to us. (RV 5.35) [RV 1.108.8 identifies five groups of people: Yadus, Turvasas, Druhyus, Anus, Purus (I.108.8).] Anus lived on the Parushni (Ravi) river. Yaska's Nirukta (9.26) refers to Iravati or Ravi as Parushni river. On the former course of this river is the archaeological site of Harappa. Was Harappa called Hariyupiya in RV? At Hariyupiya he smote the vanguard of the Vrcivans, and the rear fled frighted. (RV 6.27.5) *Baudhāyana Śrautasūtra* (18.44) records two movements of people from Saptasindhu: *Prān āyuh pravavrāja; tasyaite kurupañcalāh kāśi-videhā ity etad āyavam pravrājam; pratyan amāvasus tasyaite gāndhārayas parśavo 'rāttā ityetad āmāvasavm* (Trans. Āyu migrated eastward; his (descendants) are the Kuru-pañcalas and the Kāśi-videhas: this is the Āyava migration. Amāvasu (migrated) westward; his (descendants) are the Gāndhāris, the Parśus and the Āraṭṭas: this is the Ām*āvasa migration.*)

Agni saved Atri in the fiery cavem (RV 10.80.3)

(Aswins) Ye rescued Atri from distress and darkness (RV 7.71.5)

Aswins. for Atri caused the pit heated with fire to be a pleasant restingplace (RV 10.39.9)

As from great darkness ye delivered Atri, protect us, Visvedevas (Chiefs), from danger in the conflict. (RV 6.50)

[1300236] High in the midst of heaven may we behold thee whom men call Savitar, the bright red Eagle, Soaring and speeding on thy way, refulgent, unwasting light which Atri erst discovered. (Atharva Veda 13.2)

Rajasuya. Atri was the son of Brahma, the creator of the universe, who sprang from the lotus that grew from the navel of Narayana. The son of Atri was Soma 1 (the moon), whom Brahma installed as the sovereign of plants, of Brahmans, and of the stars. Soma celebrated the Rajasuya sacrifice, and from the glory thence acquired, and the extensive dominion with which he had been invested, he became arrogant and licentious, and carried off Tara, the wife of Vrihaspati, the preceptor of the gods. In vain Vrihaspati sought to recover his bride; in vain Brahma commanded, and the holy sages remonstrated; Soma refused to relinquish her. Usanas, out of enmity to Vrihaspati, took part with Soma. Rudra, who had studied under Angiras, the father of Vrihaspati, (Vishnu Purna 4.6)

The sons of Kadru Nagas, the son of Vinata, the Gandharvas, the lords of the creation, and the seven great Rishis, viz, Bharadwaja, Kasyapa, Gautama, Viswamitra, Jamadagni, Vasishtha, and the illustrious Atri who illumined the world of old when the Sun was lost, all came there (Kadru's naga yajña). (MBh.1.123.6648)

Kadru told Suparni 'Verily I have won thine own self. Yonder is Soma in the heaven' she said. 'Fetch him hither for the gods and thereby redeem thyself from death'. 'So be it' (said) Suparni and created the metres. Speech indeed, is Suparni and from vaak (speech) the metre are born. From among them (the metres) Gayatri fetched soma. That soma was concealed in two golden vessels. These (vessels) were having their sharp-edged (lids) closing together at every moment (at every twinkling of the eye). These two foresooth are consecration (diksha) and penance (tapas). Him (Soma) these Gandharvas guarded. They are these hearths (dhishnyas), these Hotrs (fire-priests). The Gayatri tore off one of the two vessels and brought it. Thus was consecration (dikshaa). By that, the gods consecrated themselves. Again she took off (to the heaven) and tore off the other vessel and brought it. That was penance (tapas). Therewith the gods underwent penance. They are 'the Upasadas'. Again she flew (to heaven). She took (consumed) soma by means of a Khadira-wood-(piece). Since she ate (achakaad) with it, it is named Khadira. Hence the yupa (sacrificial stake) is of Khadira wood. So too the wooden sword (sphya) (is of Khadira wood). She took it (soma) away when the Acchaavaaka was protecting it. That is why Acchaavāka fell from grace.[27]

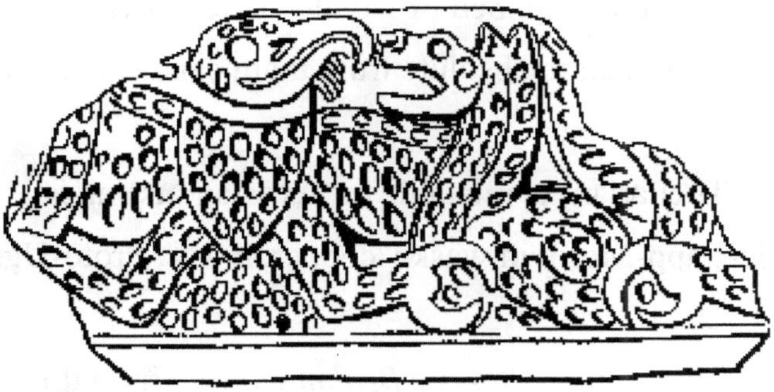

The struggle of the eagle and the serpent found on a soapstone bas-relief in Nippur, ca 2500 B.C.E.[28]

Nippur vessel with combatant snake and eagle motif. Istanbul Museum. The design is raised above the base; the vessel of chlorite was found in a mixed Ur III context at Nippur in southern Mesopotamia.[29] In a variant Assyrian-Babylonian legend, when the eagle and the serpent swore an oath to Shamash and when the eagle broke the oath, Shamash cut the eagle's wings and left him to die in a pit.

A remarkable explanation of 'myth' NOT as poetic imagination, but as Itihāsa 'historical truth', 'the nearest approach to absolute truth' is provided by Ananda Coomaraswamy[30]: "Like the Revelation (śruti) itself, we must begin with the Myth

(Itihāsa), the penultimate truth, of which all experience is the temporal reflection. The mythical narrative is of timeless and placeless validity, true nowever and everywhere: just as in Christianity, 'In the beginning God created' and 'Through him all things were made,' regardless of the millennia that come between the datable words, amount to saying that the creation took place at Christ's 'eternal birth.' 'In the beginning' (agre), or rather 'at the summit,' means 'in the first cause': as as in our still told myths, 'once upon a time' does not mean 'once' alone, but once for all.' 'The Myth is not a "poetic invention" in the sense these words now bear; on the other hand, and just because of its universality, it can be told, and with equal authority, from many differnet points of view...It is in the marvels themselves that the truth inheres. 'There is no other origin of philosophy than wonder, ' Plato, Theatetus 1556. And in the same way Aristotle who adds 'therefore even a lover of fables is in a way a lover of wisdom, for fables are compounded of wonder' (Metaphysics 982B). Myth embodies the nearest approach to absolute truth thatn can be stated in words."

The *haeus- in *haeusom- 'gold' (Tocharian) is relatable to: Avestan: ušā and Rigveda Uṣas. Proto-Balto-Finnic-Lapp-Mordvin waske 'copper, brass', Proto-Ugric was 'metal, iron'.[31]

What was processed in soma yajña was *amśu*. *Aitareya Brāhmaṇa* confirms this. The *amśu* were pressed and processed almost like a religious act. The adhvaryu takes the skin (carma or tvac) and puts on it *amśu*. He then takes two boards of adhiṣavaṇa, puts one on top of *amśu* and beats with the stones (grāvāṇa). Then soma is put between the two boards. Water is poured on them from vasatīvarī pot. Soma is taken in the hotā cup (camasa), wetted again with vasatīvarī water and put on a stone. Laying grass on them, they are beaten so that juice (rasa) runs out into the trough (āhavanīya) and strained through the cloth (pavitra or daśāpavitra) held by the udgatā. The filtered soma is caught in another trough (pūtabhṛt). Libations are poured from two kinds of vessels: grahas or saucers, and camasas or cups.

[Adapted from Haug's notes from Sāyaṇa's commentary on *Aitareya Brāhmaṇa*]. The précis on soma/amśu processing provided by *Aitareya Brāhmaṇa* is substantiated by many Vedic texts: Soma pavamāna. Soma in the process of passing through the refining instrument (potṛ). [The actors are: Hotṛ, connected with Indra; the Potṛ connected with the Maruts (Potṛ is the purifying priest; also the 'cleaning' insrument); the Neṣṭṛ linked with Tvaṣṭṛ; the divine wives, Agnīdh with agni, the Brahman with Indra and the Praśāṣṭṛ with Mitra-varuṇa]. ulūkhala (mortar) is used to press Soma (RV. I.28,1,5; grāvan is rendered as a 'press-stone'). This is a reference to the pounding of the ore block to pulverize the ore. In Yasna (XXIV.7; XXV.2) hāvana (hu = to crush) is 'the utensil in which the twigs of the haoma plant are pounded'. Another method refers to the grāvāṇah (press-stones) are placed on the'ox-hide', held by the hands and with ten fingers and activated through two boards. (RV. X.76,94 and 175). Dhiṣaṇā (RV. X.17,12) is perhaps a reference to a hollow in which the press-stones work. This may be a reference to a hollow covered with ox-hide specially prepared on the sacrificial ground. The ox-hide is refered to in RV. IX.79,4; IX.66,29; IX.101,11 and was used to catch the drops of Soma (apparently, the pulverized bits of the electrum ore block). The later rituals state that the pressing-boards are adhis.avan.a phalaka and are also laid across a sounding-hole dug beneath (See Hillebrandt, VM. I.148). A reference to the sacrificial ground with the hollow is mirrored in the term: r.tasya yoni (RV. IX.64,11,22): the home of the yajna. The reference to r.tasya dhārā (RV. IX. 63,14,21) is a reference to the process of flowing through the wool strainer. Indra's outward appearance flowed away from his semen and became suvarn.am hiran.yam when he had drunk Soma that was exposed to witching. (ŚBr 13,1,1,4: S.Br. 12,7,1,1: retasa evāsya rūpam asravat; tat suvarṇam hiraṇyam abhavat.[32] [Note: ŚBr. 12,7,2,10: lead (śīsa) is 'a form of both bronze and gold'; ahi is a snake; nāga is a snake; nāga = lead (Skt.)] RV. 4,17,11 relates how Indra gained cows, gold, troops of horses. When Soma purifies itself, Soma wins cattle, chariots, gold, the light of heaven, and water for them (RV. 9,78,4). The river Sindhu is rich in excellent horses, good chariots, good garments, rich in gold (RV. 10,7,5,8). RV.

9,112,2 recounts how the blacksmith searches for a customer who possesses (much) gold. Gold is described as śukram hiraṇyam (RV. 8,65,11) or shining with a light of its own. "He who buys the (Soma) with gold buys it as sa s'ukram" (Taittirīya Samhitā: 6,1,10,1). Even the sun is equated to gold: hiran.yam prati sūryah (RV. 1,46,10: sun is equivalent to gold). Agni is called hiran.yaru_pa (RV. 4,3,1: gold-like). Apām Napāt (the Child, Descendant of the Waters) has a terrestrial form of the earthly fire and is theociated with gold (RV. 2,35,10: hiraṇyarūpah; RV. 2.35,9: hiraṇyavarṇāh). Indra and Vāyu's chariot (which is 'heaven-touching') is made of gold (RV. 4,46,4). RV. 2,35,10 reports that Apām Napāt in his earthly manifestation as the sacrificial fire, comes out of the golden yoni (yoni hiraṇyaya which is Soma's seat (RV. 9,64,20). References to electrum may be noticed in RV. 8,45,22 where the metal silver is called 'whitish hiraṇya'; rajata is used as an adjective to mean 'whitish, silver-coloured'. [See ĀpS. 5,29,2 which states that rajatam hiran.yam should not be given as a daks.iṇā.] Pūs.an has golden ships which sail in the sea (RV. 6,58,3) and bears an axe made of gold (RV. 1,42,6).RV. 9,86,43 refers to Soma as hiraṇyapāvāh which can be interpreted as 'purified golden Soma.' Soma was poured through through a sieve made of wool. Every hymn of Book IX of the Rigveda refers to the filtering through the strainer. (pavitra = sieve, means of purifying, filter; pū = to purify; pavate = he cleanses himself; pavamāna = self-purifying). References to filtering are in : RV. IX.1, 1 and 6; IX.28, 1,2,6. 'Soma while filtering himself, flows thousand-streamed, across the wool' (RV. IX.13,1). In this filtering process, Soma is tawny in colour; and sounds like the thunder of the sky or the bellowing cattle. In RV. IX.97,33 the word 'karman' is used to denote the toil involved in the sacrifice. Soma is mixed with milk (gavāśir = addition of milk to Soma), curd and grain. These are intended to stoke the burning embers and to act as oxidizing agents to remove the baser metals.

Alchemical tradition is documented in a text dated to the mid-second millennium BC in Mesopotamia; this is reminiscent of the Rigvedic agniṣṭoma which lasts for days and nights! "For 5 shekels of pappardillu stone you mix one-third mina of mountain honey, 10 shekels of TA, one sūtu of milk, 4 shekels of red alkali and one-half sila of wine...You test on glowing charcoal... you pour into a stone bowl of algamis'u-stone (steatite)...lute with dough...you heat it for a full day on a smokeless fire. You take out and..for five days, it is (not?) reliable. You soak it in (liquid)...You boil alum and...in vinegar. You steep (the stone) in lapis lazuli-coloured liquid and place it in the fire...Property of Nebuchadnezzar, king of Babylon."[33]

Map of ancient Persia.[34]

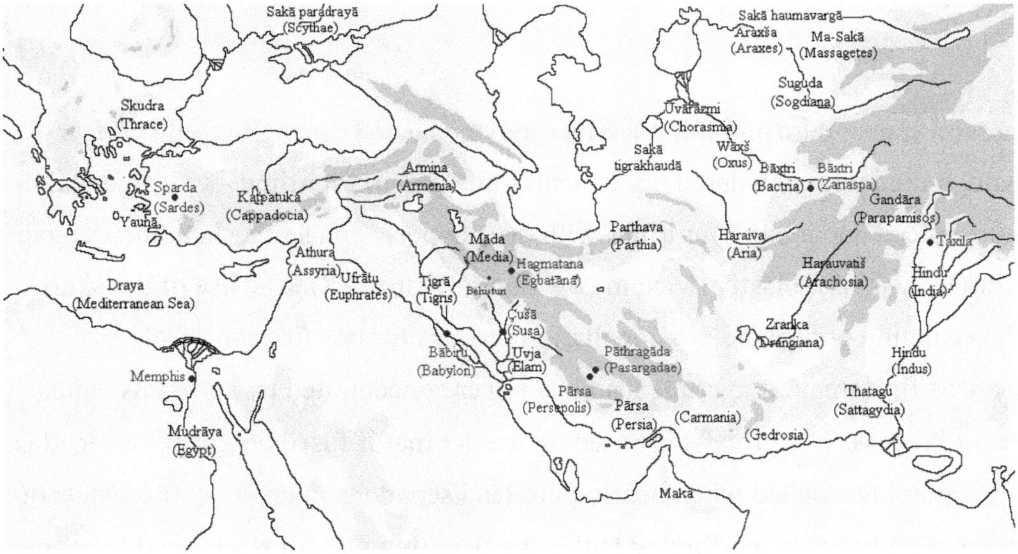

he gold dust obtained and carried by an Indian (brought in as a tribute to Darius 522-486) is depicted on a frieze in Persepolis. A man from India, carrying bottles with gold dust. Relief from the eastern stairs of the Apadana at Persepolis (Indians reportedly paid 360 talents of gold dust as annual tribute). Babylonian talents when reduced to the Euboean scale make a total of 9,880; and if gold is reckoned at thirteen times the value of silver, the Indian gold-dust will be found to amount to 4,680 talents. Thus the grand total of Darius' annual revenue comes to 14,560

Euboean talents – out of which 4,680 talents (32.14%) came from India.[35]

Arthaśāstra states: pure and impure silver may be heated four times with copper sulphate, mixed with powdered bone (asthituttha) again four times with an equal quantity of lead and again four times with dry copper sulphate (sushkatuttha), again three times in skull nd lastly twice in cow dung. (Stanza 88). The use of the skull which is calcium phosphate is a cupellation process for purification of silver. Galena was first smelted to crude lead and silver concentrated by a process called Pattinson Process. The process is based on the act that if fused argentiferous lead is cooled, a point is reached when nearly pure lead separates in crystals. If crystals of lead were withdrawn by perforated ladles the remaining liquid alloy would become increasingly rich in silver. About 7/8ths of the original lead is removed by this process and the rest of the lead is reoved by cupellation process. Separation of silver and other impurities from gold (electrum) was invented before Amarna age, possibly during or shortly after Ur III period (ca. 2200-2000 B.C.)

Arthaśāstra mentions salt among the articles necessary for purifying gold: KA 02.14.23 mūkamūṣā pūtikiṭṭah karaṭukamukham nālī samdamśo jongan ī suvarcikālavaṇam tad eva suvarṇam ity apasāraṇa mārgāh".[36] Agatharcides (2nd century BC) describes how in Egypt gold-bearing ore was found and washed until more or less pure gold dust remained. This dust was put "into earthen pots. They mix with this a lump of lead according to the mthe, lumps of salt, a little tin and barley bran. They put on a closely-fitting lid carefully smearing it with mud and heat it in a furnace for five days and nights continuously; then they allow the pots to cool and find no residual impurities in them; the gold they recover in a pure state with little wastage. This processing of gold is carried on round about the most distant boundaries of Egypt."[37]

"The procedure was tested in 1974[38] with an alloy of copper and silver containing 37.5% of gold. It was found that heating the pots filled with the alloy and salt gave the highest gold recovery rate of 93%. Including tin, lead or charcoal reduced the efficienty to less than 80%. Healy concluded that the account given by Agatharcides 'seems to be an example of the conflation of at least two processes'. Gold is used in the purchase of Soma; gold had exchange value: Śrautasūtras: Baudhāyana (6.12-13; 14-15); Bhāradvāja (10.16.2-18.14); Āpastamba (10.24.1-27.8); Kātyāyana (7.7.3-8.25): "After having handed over king Soma to the Soma-seller, the Adhvaryu should ask him: "O, Soma-seller, is your soma available for purchase? He should reply: "It is available for purchase." The Adhvaryu should (offer to) purchase it for ten (objects), (namely) seven cows and the three (objects, that is to say), gold, a piece of cloth, and a she-goat..." (Satyāṣāḍha, 7.2).[39]

Gold and silver are intertwined in the Adhvaryu's transaction: cf. Bhāradvāja Śrautasūtra, 11.1.1-9.3:"...(the adhvaryu should further put down) two sheets--(one) of silver and (the other) of gold. They should be each) one hundred manas in weight..." Lāṭyāyana Śrautasūtra (III.1.9 cited in Agniswami's commentary on Anandacandra vedāntavāgīsa) says that gold was obtained from the ore by smelting. "Gold is the first offspring of fire..." says a copper plate inscription of Raja Maha Sudevaraja.[40] Rigveda refers to hiraṇya 174 times (Atharvaveda has 91 references almost as as an adjective, golden); other synonyms used are: candra, jātarūpa, harita and suvarṇa.

How do we interpret Satapatha Brahmana verse (XIII.1.1.3): "Now, when the horse was immolated, its seed went from it and became gold; thus, when he gives gold (to the priests) he supplies the horse with seed"?

Gold was desired (RV VI.47.23, VII.78.9); Soma rasa was fountain of gold (RV IX.78.4).The place of sacrifice is also golden (RV. V.67.2; IX.64.20). Sindhu is rich in gold (RV X.75.8), it is path of gold (RV VIII.26.18). Even weapons are of gold. “The kanvas sing forth agni’s praise together with our maruts’ who wield thunder and wear swords of gold.” (RV. VIII.7.32). Gold is won from the earth, washed and cleaned and purified (RV. I.117.5).[41] Gold is won from the rivers; Sindhu was full of golden beds and hence is called ‘golden’ and ‘of golden stream’ (RV. X.75.8; VI.61.7; VIII.26.18). “Rich in good steeds is Sindhu, rich in cars and robes, rich in gold, nobly- fashioned, rich in ample wealth”. (RV. X.75.8). “This river with his lucid flow attracts you more than all the streams. Even Sindhu with his path of gold.” (RV. VIII.26.18). The path is golden (hiraṇyavartanī)(RV.I.92.18; V.75.2;3; VIII.5.11;8.1). Prajāpati is the progenitor of the universe and is hiran.yagarbha (the golden foetus): “in the beginning rose hiraṇyagarbha, born only Lord of all created beings. He fixed and holdeth up this earth and heaven what God shall we adore with our oblation.” (RV. X.121.1; Griffith, RV, Vol. II, p. 566). Gold (hiraṇyam) was the objective of the Vedic singers (RV. VI.47.23; VII.78.9). The prayers refer to gold that glitters (RV. X.107.7), that gives wealth (RV. II.34.11; VII.66.8), that is self-luminous (RV. V.87.5). The singers seek: “The Sea and all the Deities shall give us him with the golden ear and neck bejewelled. Dawns, hasting to the praises of the pious, be pleased with us, both offerers and singers.” (RV. I.122.14; Griffith, RV, Vol. I, p. 169) Gods Indra, Mitra, Varuṇa etc. were often described as golden in hue (RV. I.46.10; I. 167.3; I.139.2; II.35.10; IV.3.1; IV.10.6; VI.16.38; VII.45.2; X.20.9) driving from golden seats (RV. IV.46.4; VIII.5.28; VIII.22.9) in golden chariots (RV. I.30.16; I.35.2; 56.1; 139.4; IV.1.8; IV.44.4; IV.44.5; VI.29.2; VIII.1.24; VI.66.1; VIII.33.4; VIII.46.24), having shafts or poles (RV. I.35.4; 5; VIII.5.29), wheels and axles all bright as gold (RV. I.64.11; 105.1; 139.3; 180.1; VI.56.3; VIII.5.29) with golden reins for the horses (RV. VIII.22.5) who had golden manes (RV. I.122.14) and were bedecked with golden ornaments. Gods As'vins and Maruts and the asuras alike adorned themselves with magnificent jewellery using gold rings (RV. VIII.32.29) gold ear-rings (RV. VII.56.13; I.166.10; I.64.11; V.54.11; II.34.3; VI. 16.38) golden necklets and armlets (RV. VII.56.13; I.166.10; I.64.11; V.54.11; II.34.3; VI.16.38). "Your rings, O maruts, rest upon your shoulders, and chains of gold twined upon your bosoms. Gleaming with drops of rain, like lightning-flashes, after your wont ye whirl about your weapons." (RV.VII.56.13; Griffith, RV, Vol. II, p.55).

If Soma is electrum and Indra is burning embers (such as charcoal, indha, used in a furnace), the yajña can be interpreted, at the material level, as a process of reduction (or, pavitram, purification), using kṣāra, of a metallic ore compound (mākṣikā or quartz or pyrites) to yield the shining molten metals: (pavamāna, rasa-- raso vajrah, cf. RV 9.048.03, i.e. rasa, vigorous as a thunderbolt) gold and silver (hiraṇyam and rayi), after oxidising the baser metallic elements (in the unrefined pyrite ores) such as lead (nāga or ahi or vṛtra) and copper (śulba). Reducing agents include alkaline as well as combustible materials --vegetable andanimal products-- such as: herbs (kṣāra), barley--grains and cooked piṇḍa, milk,curds, clarified butter, viands (animal fat), bones (used in cupellation processes,and for making crucibles, during the bronze-age), sheep's hair or wool (reminiscedas golden fleece).

Soma is a material and also the only process elaborated in the *Ṛgveda.* The rest of the hymns related to Agni, Indra or other facets of vedic life will have to be concordant with this process which seems to constitute the very essence of vedic life, a process integral to the day-to-day living of the vedic seeker. What is Soma? Soma which was the 'soul' of the vedic sacrifice was put through three daily pressings, while worshipping all the gods. (Avesta Yasna X.2 mentions only two pressings). Soma/haoma literally means 'extract', from the root su – hu 'to press'.

Scores of identifications have been claimed as summarized by Harry Falk[42]: hallucionogenic plants: hemp, cannabis sativa, the mushroom amanita muscaria, or the wild mountain rue, peganum harmala, opium and mandrake; fermentable plants: rhubarb, common millets, rice, or barley, and grape; stimulant plants: ephedra, ginseng. Falk underscores "that ephedra was called *sauma already in the common ancestral Indo-Iranian language" [p.68]. Falk, however, notes that "there is nothing shamanistic or visionary either in early Vedic or in Old Iranian texts" [Falk, 1989, p.79]. David Flattery and Martin Schwartz (Flattery & Schwartz 1989), identify Soma/Haoma as peganum harmala, since "ephedra is without suitable psychoactive potential" [p.73]. Elizarenkova[43] is skeptical about the ephedra theory and notes that Soma as a plant is a ritual substitution.

Linking with Indra, Soma is called in RV. IX.85.3 the 'soul (ātmā) of Indra', the bolt (vajra) of Indra' (RV.IX.77.1) and even 'generator of Indra' (RV.IX.96.5). The reference to ṛtasya dhārā (RV. IX.63,14,21) is a reference to the process of flowing through the wool strainer.Indra's outward appearance flowed away from his semen and became suvarṇam hiraṇyam when he had drunk Soma that was exposed to witching. (S'Br 13,1,1,4:S'Br. 12,7,1,1: retasa evāsya rūpam asravat; tat suvarṇam hiraṇyam abhavat.)

Ṛṣi Agni cākuṣuṣa, devatā pavamāna Soma:

dhībhir hinvanti vājinam vane krīḷantam atyavim

abhi tripṛṣṭham matayah sam asvaran

RV 9.106.11 They send forth with their fingers the powerful Soma sporting in the water, passing through the fleece; praises celebrate him abiding in the three receptacles. [With their fingers: dhībhih = dhītibih; or, by their praises]. Alternative trans. : They send forth with their fingers [alt. translation, 'with their praises'] the powerful Soma passing through the fleece.

Amśu is soma, asu is haoma

Two attributes of tenderness and stringent taste are associated with asu (Avestan) or amśu (Veda):

Tasty asu (Gershevitch, 1974, p. 48); Soma is not sweet (madhu) but sharp, astringent (tīvra). Soma is described as having 'hanging branches bending down' (naicāśākha: RV. III.53,14) It is not necessary to interpret the term 'tīvra' (sharp) in the context of taste; tīvra connotes the sharpness of the metallic components of the ore blocks.

The texts of Avesta and Veda are not intended to be scientific characterizations. To try to match the attributes to botanical identifications tend to be speculative excercises. James Darmesteter[44] (1875) discussing Avesta referred to haoma: "...it comprises the power of life of all the vegetable kingdom...both the veda and the avesta call it the 'king of healing herbs'...the zarathustri scriptures say that homa is of two kinds, the white haoma and the painless tree (no doubt the source of the 'tree of knowledge' and 'the tree of life'...could it be that Soma is the tree of life? The giver of immortality?" This remarkable note is consistent with the lexical meaning assigned to asu as 'life principle'. The Being who evolved in the beginning is also the lord of the snow-clad mountains, the ocean and the river Rasaa...when the waters moved producing Agni, from the waters evolved the asu of divinities.

Amśu is the shape of, integral part of Soma according to Ṛṣikā Parucchepa Daivodāsi addressed mitrāvaruṇa who uses the phrase amśum duhyanty adribhih ('milking the amśu with stones'). This shows that amśu are extracted (milked) out of the product. This extracted material is Soma – Soma ā pītaye sutah. To assume that the milking is from a plant is to propound a theory not based on the text, nor based on the semantics of the word 'amśu'. That amśu refers to the shape of Soma is also seen from the phrase tigma śṛngo ('sharpened horns') used in RV 9.97.9 and from the phrase sahasra bhrṣṭi ('thousand knobs') used in RV 9.86.40: sahasra bhrṣṭir jayati sravo bṛhat. The metaphor of 'milking' also occurs in RV 8.9.19 (milking the swollen udders), RV 10.107.5 (milking the divine udder).

yad āpītāso amśavo gāvo na duhra ūdhabhih

yad vā vāṇīr anūṣata pra devayanto aśvinā

RV 8.009.19 When the yellow Soma stalks milk forth as cows from their udders, when the devout (priests) repeat the words of praise, then, O Aśvins, preserve us.

RV 8.9.19 thus provides the attribute of a teat (of an udder) to amśu, explaining how swollen amśu are milked like cow's full udders. The colour is pītāso, 'yellow'. The following citations from the Camakam (see seventh Anuvāka) point to the word amśu as a synonym of Soma using words like agumśu, upaagumśu as vessels for holding Soma.

The phrase used in RV 4.58.1 is upāmśu:

Ṛṣi Vāmadeva Gautama addressed agni or sūrya or āpodevatā or gāvah or ghṛtah:

samudrād ūrmir madhumān udārad,

upāmśunā sam amṛtatvam ānat;

ghṛtasya nāma guhyam yad asti,

jihvā devānaam amṛtasya nābhih

Translation a: RV 4.058.01 The sweet water swells up from the firmament; by the (solar) ray (man) obtains immortality; that which is he secret name of clarified butter is the tongue of the gods, the navel of ambrosia. [Yajus. 17.89-99; the sweet water swells up from the firmament: samudrād urmir madhumān udārat: the meaning depends on the variants of meaning of samudra: samodante asmin yajamānah, that in which worshippers delight, sacrificial fire; or, samudrād dravanti āpah, that from which waters rush, celestial fire, lightning; ūrmi = reward or consequence; second occurrence of ūrmi = rain; in the latter sence of ūrmi, samudra may mean antarks.a, the firmament; samudra may also mean the udder of the cow, whence flows milk, samudravati, from which come ūrmi, ghī or butter; another interpretation restricts the objects to two: ghī and agni, atra annādhyāsena ghr.tam stūyate prāṇā dhyāsena ca agnih; as a representative of food, ghī is here praised, as that of vitality, agni; samudra is the ocean of ghī, from which it rises as its wave, samudrād ghṛta-mayad madhumān rasavān ūrmirudagacchat, and, having so risen, it pervades immortality by Agni, as the life of the world with whom it is combined: udgatya ca sa ūrmir-ansunā jagatprān.abhūtenāgninā samaikibhūya amṛtatvān vyāpnoti; in both interpretations, agni is intended, with whom ghī, as the material of the oblation, is meant to be identified. That which is the secret name: ghṛtasya nāma guhyam yad asti jihvādevānām amṛtasya nābhih: i.e., the material of sacrifice commonly called ghī is, in the mantras of the Veda, designated the tongue of the gods, being used metonymicaly for Agni; also the navel or binding, that is, the means of securing immortality for him who offers it in oblations. Since the ghr.ta is intented to be the secret name, the reference intended may be to another principal oblation: the Soma].

Translation b: 'A honeyed wave climbs up from the ocean, and by means of this mounting wave which is the Soma (amsu) one attains entirely to immorality; that wave or that Soma is the secret name of the clarity (ghrtasya, the symbol of the clarified butter); it is the tongue of the gods; it is the nodus (naabhi) of immortality.'

Camakam is Vasordhārā homa, performed for Agni and Vishnu, recited for the stream of wealth, pouring ghṛtam (ghee) reciting from vājas'came mantra till the eleventh Anuvāka. The homa is performed during Rudra Ekādaśi. The homa is also performed in Agni Cayana (also called Suparna Citi, Agni Garuda Cayana). Cayana is 'making a stage for the altar'. The Agni Garuda Cayana is detailed in the 4th and 5th *Kāṇḍa* of Taittirīya Samhitā and in Kāṭaka Samhitā.[45]

Camakam is in the fourth Kāṇḍ*a* and Seventh *Prapātaka (Prasna*) of the *Krishna Yajur Veda*. In the fourth Anuvāka, together with *Rayi* : = gold ; *Rāya* : = with Nava ratnas (precious stones) ; many cereals are invoked such as yavā, mashā, tilā, mūdgā, khalyā, godhūmā, masurā, priyamgava, anava, śyāmaka, neevaara. The fifth Anuvāka invokes agni, āpah, vasu together with many metals, stones, sikatā, vanaspatayah. The sixth Anuvāka is titled Arthendram and invokes Indra together with other 20 divinities including Agni, Soma, Savita, Sarasvati, Pūsa, Bṛhaspati, Mitra, Varuṇa, Tvaṣṭha, Dhāta, Maruts, Viṣṇu, Aśvin, earth, antarikṣam, svarga, mūrdha, directional divinities, Prajāpati.

The seventh Anuvāka is a list of various vessels used in Soma yajña. Some of them are: agumśu (amśu vessel), raśmi (silver vessel), adābhya (big holder), upāgumśu (other Soma vessels).

The eighth Anuvāka is an invocation of various instruments used in Soma yajña such as: idhma (samiti or twigs), barhis (darbha dry, river-bank grass; cf. Avestan barsom, baresman 'bundle of twigs'), vedi (altar or yaña kuṇḍam), dhiṣṇya (platform for 7 Hotr), śruca (śruva, juhū, spoon made of ati wood using baked mud at the outlet hole, for pouring ghṛtam), camasā (for Soma), grāvaṇa (stones used to crush Soma), svarava (wooden knife), uparavā (four pits under Soma crushing point), adhiśavane (two planks to extract Soma liquid), droṇakalaśa (vessel for Soma), bhūtabhṛt and ādhavanīya (two water-pots used while extracting Soma liquid), āgnīndam (agni and indra maṇḍapa and to seat the ṛitwik agnidra with the agni pot), havirdhānam (maṇḍapa to keep havis and Soma liquid), Gṛhā (place for seating Yajamāna's patni, wife), sada (place for seating Hota and Sama vedin), purodāśa (havis offerings to Agni, prepared with rice-flour and cooked animal parts), pacatā (accompanied śamitra, fire used to cook animal parts), avabhṛta (holy bath taken at the end of the yajña), svagā kāra (recitation of śamyuvaka and firing the samits or holy twigs).

The ninth Anuvāka refers to yajñena kalpantām (emerging through performance of yajña using Ṛk, yajus, sāma, stoma – the Gāna and the counting), invokes the power of light and sound, power of tapas and dīkṣa (initiation to understand the power of mantra) and includes: Agni, dharma (pravargya for Soma yajña), arka (Indra as devata), Sūrya, Prāṇa, aśvamedha, pṛthivī, aditi, diti, dyau, sakvarī, angulya (finger of Virāṭa Puruṣa), diśā (four directions), ṛtu (time), vratam (ekastana vratam, vow), ahorātrayo (due to rains during day and night) for the plants to grow (vṛkṣtyā). The line is: bṛhadrathantaram ca me yajñena kalpetām, that is: using two sūkta, Bṛhat and Rathantara of Samaveda, the yajña is sought to be made productive and effective.

The tenth Anuvāka is an invocation of varieties of cattle, all biological species to perfect praana (energy), senses, mind and soul as jñāna yajña. The references are to: garbha (pregnant), vatsā (new-born calves), tryavī (one-and-a-half year male calves), tryavī (one-and-a-half year female calves), dityavād (2 year male calves), dityouhī (2 year female calves), pañcavi (2-and-a-half year male calves), pañcavī (2-and-a-half year female calves), trivatsa (3 year male calves), trivatsā (3 year female calves), turyavād (3-and-a-half year male calves), turyauhī (3-and-a-half year female calves), paśtavat (4 year male calves), paśtauhī (4 year female calves), ukṣā (breeding bulls), vaśā (virgin cows), ṛṣabha (5 year old bulls), vehat (aborted ones), anadvān (pullers, bullocks), dhenu (newly delivered cows). The refrain is 'yajñena kalpatām' (that is, let performance result in): āyur (life), prāṇa (life-breath), apāna (apāna-breath), vyāna (vyāna-breath), cakṣur (eyes), śrotram (ears), manas (mind), vāk (speech), ātmā (ātman), adding: yajño yajñena kalpatām (let this yajña make perfect many yajña).

The eleventh Anuvaaka is a benediction to Adhipati (the omnipotent), of odd numbers (human) and even numbers (divine) and invoke vāja (food), prasava (generation), apija (continuous food production), kratu (for use in Yajña), suva (Sun), mūrdha (sky), vyasnya (sky divinities), āntyāyana (divinity of praḷaya, birth at fag-end), antya (praḷaya, consummation), bhūvana (earth divinities), bhuvana (universe).

In thecontext of processing (refining or purifying or smelting) Soma electrum ore or quartz), charcoal is a vital component; since charcaol combines with the baser metals and oxidizes them leaving the residual potable, gold-silver compound which is electrum. When Soma is referred to as indrapīta or 'drunk by Indra (indav indrapītasya)(PB 1.5.4), the reference is indeed to the reducing action of glowing charcoal embers during the process of smelting the electrum ore. Naturally, Indra received the major share of Soma. (RV. I.2,3; II.41 indicate the sequence of offerings of Soma: vāyu, indra-vāyu, mitra-varuṇa, aśvins, indra, viśve devāh, Sarasvatī.) Thus, Indra, as the chief partaker of Soma, is linked with Soma from the mountains (the ore) and some on the earth (ground in pressing-stones): 'May heavenly drink exhilarate theee, Indra, and also what is pressed in earthly places'. (RV. X. 116,3).

An epitomy of this framework may be seen from the following selections:

pavamānā asṛkṣata somāh s'ukrāsa indavah
abhi vis'vāni kāvyā
pavamānā divas payar antarikṣād asṛkṣata
prthivyā adhi sānavih

9.063.25 The brilliant purified Soma-juices are let fall amidst all praises.

9.063.27 The purified (juices) are poured forth from heaven and from the firmament upon the summit of the ground. [The summit of the ground: i.e., the raised place, the place of divine sacrifice or yajña].

Ṛṣi nodhā gautama; devatā pavamāna soma:

uta pra pipya ūdhr aghnyāya indur dhārabhih sacate sumedhāh
mūrdhānam gāvah payasā camūṣv abhi śrīnanti vasubhir na niklaih

RV 9.093.03 And he nourishes the cow's udder; the intelligent Indu is associated with his stream; the cows clothe the elevated Soma in the ladles with their milk as with newly washed robes. [Nourish the cow's udder: the Soma entering the herbs, etc., nourishes the cow who eats them]. Alternative trans.: The udder of the cow is swollen; the wise juice is imbued with its streams the cows milk their milk with Soma, heaven's head.

Ṛṣi Kakṣīvān Dairghatamasa (auśija); devatā: pavamāna Soma:

divo ya skambho dharuṇah svaatata āpūrṇo amśuh paryeti viśvatah
seme mahī rodasī yaks.ad āvṛtā samīchīne dādhāra sam ishah kavih

RV 9.074.02 The supporter of heaven, the prop (of the earth), the Soma-juice who, widely spreading, filling (the vessels), flows in all directions-- may he unite the two great worlds by his own strength; he has upheld them combined; (may he) the sage (bestow) food upon (his worshippers). [The prop of the earth: cf. RV. 9.089.06; may he unite: yakṣat = samyojayatu; āvṛta= by its own unaided strength]. Alternative trans.: Amśu filled full moves itself everyway…

Ṛṣi Viśvāmitra Gāthina; devatā Indra:

pra yat sindhavan prasavam āpah samudram rathyeva jagmuh

ataścid indrah sadaso varīyān yad ī somah pṛṇati dugdho amśuh

RV 3.036.06 As the rivers pursue their course, the waters rush to the ocean like the drivers of cars (to a goal), so the vast Indra (hastens) from his dwelling (in the firmament), when the humble Soma libation propitiates him. [The comparison: as small rivers and scanty waters contribute to the vast ocean, so the Soma, however insignificant, contributes to the gratification of the great Indra]. Alternative trans.: Indra is farther than this seat (that is, Soma's seat) when the milked ams'u, the Soma, fills him…

Ṛṣi : saptaṛṣigaṇa; devatā: pavamāna soma:

pra soma devavītaye sindhur na pipye arṇasā amśoh payasā madiro na jāgṛvir

acchā kośam madhkṣutam

RV 9.107.12 You are fed with water, Soma, like a river, for the banquet of the gods; with the juice of your filament you go to the honey-dropping receptacle, exhilarating, vigilant.

Texts have no reference to priests getting intoxicated by Soma or Amśu.

There was no intoxication of the priests, there is a rca which refers to Indra getting intoxicated.

Ṛṣi agniyuta sthaura or agniyūpa sthaura; devatā indra:

mamattu tvaa divyah soma indra mamattu yah sūyate pārthiveṣu

mamattu yena varivaś cakartha mamattu yena niriṇāsi śatrūn

RV 10.116.03 May the celestial Soma exhilarate you, Indra; may that which is effused at terrestrial rites exhilarate you; may that exhilarate you through the influence of which you have bestowed wealth; may that exhilarate you whereby you scatter foes. Alternative trans.: Let the celestial Soma intoxicate you, Indra, let that intoxicate you which men press.

"Spiegel is not wrong when he maintains (*Arische Periode*, p. 177) that there was little mention of the intoxication of the singers and priests...these hymns, after all, occupy themselves more with gods than with men...Indra drank pure Soma which pressed forward again through all the openings of his body so that the gods had to cure him by means of the Sautrāmaṇī ceremony which was intended for this very purpose by the Brāhmaṇas' (cf. Av 3.3.2; TS 2.3.2; S'Br 5.5.4.9 ff.; 12.7.1.11).[46]

jāgṛvī as an epithet of Agni, is used to suggest rica-s which awaken, particularly during the atirātra yajña. The word occurs only once in each of *Ṛgveda* Mandala 1, 5, 6 and 10, and eight times in Books 3 and 9. Some claim that the epithet is also related to Indra and Soma in one or two occurrences. It is a leap of imagination to assume that the epithet refers to the stimulating properties of Soma (in pharmacological or psychic terms). RV 5.44.14-15 uses the term, jagāra, an apparent reference to vigilance needed during the process; Soma is referred to as abiding in the fellowship of Agni to whom the ṛca is addressed. The Ṛṣi of the sūkta is Avatsāra Kāśyapa offered to Viśvedevā. In RV 5.44.13, Sutambharā is referred to as a priest. The word means 'bearer of the Soma'.

RV 5.44.14 *yo jāgāra tam ṛcah kāmayante yo jāgāra tam u sāmani yanti*
yo jāgāra tam ayam soma āha tavāham asmi sakhye nyokāh

RV 5.44.15 *agnir jāgāra tam ṛcah kāmayante gnir jāgāra tam u sāmani yanti*
agnir jāgāra tam ayam soma āha tavāham asmi sakhye nyokāh

5.044.14 Him who is ever vigilant, holy verses desire; to him who is ever vigilant sacred songs proceed; him who is ever vigilant the Soma thus addresses, I am always abiding in your fellowship.
5.044.15 Agni is ever vigilant, and him holy verses desire; Agni is ever vigilant, and to him sacred songs proceed; Agni is ever vigilant, and him the Soma addresses, I am ever abiding in your fellowship.

The epithet mada (Somasya mada) used is an indication of rapture or bliss as in laba sūkta RV 10.119. The Ṛṣi is Laba Aindra. Laba is a bird perhaps as a metaphor for Indra, a bird whose wings touch and expand beyond the earth and the firmament. "The traditional explanation of the Laba-sūkta is the only credible one: a bird, assumed to be Indra in disguise, has drunk from the Soma offered and is thought to feel the same as the god in his usual, non-material form. Because all the proponents of Soma as a hallucinogenic drug make their claim on the basis of a wrong interpretation of the Laba-sūkta, their candidates must be regarded as unsuitable."[47] The refrain of the sukta is: *kuvi't so'masyāpām iti* (Have I drunk of the Soma? Yes, says Indra).

In the context of the poetics of the Ṛgveda which abounds in allegories, puns and metaphors, it is hypothesised that only Soma, and Soma alone was a product refined using Agni; all the other references to divinities are poetic degrees of freedom to invoke gods into artefacts used in the processing of Soma. RV 8.48.3 *apāma somam amṛtā abhūmāganma jyotir avidāma devān* ('we have drunk soma, we have become immortal, we have gone to the Light (of heaven), we have obtained the divinities.') *kim nūnam asmān kṛṇavad arātih kim u dhūrtir amṛta martyasya* ('O immortal one, what can the indifference the malice, of a mortal man, do to us now?')
This is the only ṛca which makes some see hallucinogenic properties of Soma. John Brough rejected Wasson's theory identifying Soma as a mushroom, Amanita muscaria, and referred to ephedrine (in particular to that extracted from *Ephedra sinica*), and noted that it "is a powerful stimulant, and would thus be a more plausible preparation for warriors about to go into battle than the fly-agaric, which is a depressant." (for use of *parahaoma* by soldiers, see reference to the Ab-Zohr in *Denkard* 8.25.24).[48]
In 1989, David Flattery, with linguistic support from Martin Schwarz, concentrated again on Iranian *haoma*. The two again paid particular attention to the hallucinogenic properties that may be interpreted from the texts, and discounted Ephedra because they could not observe Zoroastrian priests becoming intoxicated. They concluded that it was "therefore neither likely that Ephedra was a substitute for *sauma nor that it was *sauma itself" and that the ephedrine and pseudoephedrine alkaloids extracted from Ephedra had to be mixed with the extract from some other plant to achieve the described effects. Flattery proposed the second plant was *Peganum harmala* (harmal, harmel, Syrian rue, see also harmaline), known in Iranian languages as *esfand*, *sepand* or other similar terms related to Avestan word *spenta* ('sacred', 'holy'). Flattery considered harmel to be the real *haoma*, with ephedra only being the secondary ingredient in the *parahaoma* mixture.[49]

An alternative explanation is that this is exalted liturgy and can only be explained in metaphorical terms.The chief Zoroastrian sacrament is the consecration of haoma. The yazata of plants, Haoma tends to be assimilated to Ameretāt, yazatā of Immortality and protector of plants. Ameretāt (Amurdād), like the White Hōm is: 'the chief of plants; the for the plants of the world belong to her, and she makes plants grow and increase flocks of animals, because all creatures eat and live by her'. (GBd. XXVI 113). 'Gathic' Ameretāt replaced the ancient Haoma.[50]
Haoma is a priest of the sacrifice; his name is derived from the sacred plant. Haoma, the priest, makes the offering of consecrated haoma to the other gods: Haoma 'was the first to offer up the haomas with a star-adorned, spirit-fashioned mortar upon high Haraitī.' (Yt.X.90). Identified as an ephedra, the plant grows on the mountains of Central Asia and Persia. 'In India one species only can be said to occur throughout the Himalaya, viz. Ephedra vulgaris, *Rich.* (= E. Gerardiana, *Wall.*); but this is also distributed to Central and Western Asia and to Europe. The other two Indian species have a more easterly distribution, the one extending from Garhwal to Afghanistan and Persia (E. Pachyclada, *Boiss.*) and the other being met with in the Punjab, Rajputana, Sind, and distributed to Afghanistan and Syria (E. peduncularis, *Boiss.*).'[51]
Mary Boyce notes that E. Pachyclada, *Boiss.* is called *hum, huma, yehma* in the Hari-Rud valley. Haoma is pressed and consecrated in the Yasna sacrifice; the yazata urges Zoroaster: 'Gather me, O Spitama, press me for drink, praise me for strength!' (Y.IX.2 as translated by W.B. Henning). In *Dēnkard* (Dk.VIII.3.29f.--Sanjana, Vol. XIV), Zoroaster consecrates haoma to be drunk by the bull of a righteous man, whereby the animal was cured of sickness. The consecrated haoma which gives spiritual strength on earth is the symbol of the mythological White Hōm, also called the Gōkarn Tree, which grows in the waters, at the source of Aredvī Sūrā. (Vd. XX.r; Zsprm.XXXV.15; GBd.XVI.4; MX.LXII.28-30; she is ana_hito_, that is, immaculate: Yt.X.88). Haoma 'derives its contentment from the

ābzōhr', that is, from the libation of consecrated haoma to the waters. 'The well-grown hōm...is the symbol of that White Hōm of the Gōkarn, from which (will be) manifest the immortality of Fraśegird'. (Dd., Purs. 47.16--PKA.98.17-20). This White Hōm, the 'pain-dispelling Tree', has more power of healing than any other plant; for through it 'the dead will become living, and the living immortal', when they partake of it at the final yasna of Fras'egird.. Haoma is the chief of all plants, urwarān rad. (GBd. VIe,4). There is explicit reference to 'Hōm Yazad who is in the Gōkarn'. (GBd.XXVI.93: Hōm Yazad ī andar gōkarn). Based on these references, Mary Boyce concludes: 'It seems possible, therefore, that the "hōm of three kinds" which is said in the same Bundahis'n chapter belong to Hōm Yazad may consist of the natural hōm, the consecrated hōm, and the mythological White Hōm.'"There appear to have been two separate rites in this connection. In one, called yas't pad zo_hr, the ritual corresponded closely with that which is still performed. The animal was sacrificed before the service took place and its flesh was roasted to provide gōśodāg for the cāśnī during Hā VIII. The zōhr of fat to the sacred Fire was offered at the same time. This oblation was made by the assisting priest called the fraberetar or frabartār, who left the enclosure of the yasna to carry it to the Fire." Y.XI.7 recalls the ancient observance: 'Swiftly may you cut from the flesh an offering (draonah) for the very strong Haoma.'[52]

The points to be noted from these notes of Mary Boyce are:

River Sarasvatī (Aredvī Sūrā Anāhitā) was associated with Haoma.The functions of the priests, Haoma and Frabartār, were delineated during the consecration of Haoma. The names and functions of the priests are comparable to Hotr. and Pratiprasthātā of the Brāhmaṇa period. The Ṛgveda does not identify nor delineate the functions of a set of priests, pointing to the possibility that the processes detailed in the Ṛgveda ante-date the reference to Haoma in the Avestan tradition. "Āpastamba has prescribed the Hotṛ's duties in connection with the New-moon and the Full-moon sacrifices in ĀpŚS. XXIV.11-14, and at the end he says that the remaining duties of the Hotṛ in connection with the New-moon and the Full-moon sacrifices have been prescribed along with the Adhvaryu's duties in that connection, and that his other duties (in connection with the modification-sacrifices) should be taken from the Ṛgveda...The tradition of adopting the Ṛg-hautra throughout by a Taittirīya seems to have been originated probably from the fact that a Taittirīya had to resort to Ṛgveda for the Hautra at the Soma-sacrifice--the most significant part of the Vedic rituals. What was to be taken for the Soma-sacrifice was accepted for other rituals also. According to Baudhāyana (BŚS II.4), all the sixteen officiating priests are to be formally chosen by the sacrificer at the setting up of the sacred fires itself. It was, therefore, natural that the sacrificer chose the Hotṛ belonging to the Ṛgveda in view of his requirements at a Soma-sacrifice."[53]

The Graeco-Russian archeologist Viktor Sarianidi claims to have discovered vessels and mortars used to prepare Soma in 'Zoroastrian temples' in Bactria. He claims that the vessels have revealed residues and seed impressions left behind during the preparation of Soma. This has not been sustained by subsequent investigations.[54] Besides the residue of Ephedra the archeologists discovered the residues of Poppy seeds and Cannabis. The vessels also had impressions created by Cannabis seeds. Cannabis is well known in India as Bhang and sometimes Poppy seeds are used with Bhang to make the ritual drink Bhang Ki Thandai.

In 1994, Viktor I. Sarianidi claimed that ancient ritual objects found at BMAC archeological sites in Central Asia bore traces of Ephedra stalks and Papaver (poppy) seeds. In 1995, Harri Nyberg investigated the specimens provided by Sarianidi but could not confirm the claim (cited in Houben, 2003). Another site provided material which Sarianidi had declared contained traces of Ephedra, Papaver and Hemp (Cannabis) in 1998–1999]. It was analysed in 2002–2003 by three independent teams, but they found no traces of the claimed contents. (Bakels, 2003).[55]

Soma substitutes for the original Peganum harmala: Amanita muscaria, Ephedra vulgaris, Sarcostemma brevistigma

"Indian Brahmans know the plant now used as soma in south Indian rituals, Sarcostemma brevistigma, to be a substitute for an earlier 'soma'. The 'soma' which Sarcostemma has directly replaced, however, seems not to have been the original plant but an Ephedra, a nonintoxicating plant which was itself a secondary constituent of rituals.'[56]

Ephedra is called soma, som, sumanai, asmania, amsania, asminabuti_ and somalatā in Dardic and Indic languages. Avestan barezis., baresman (Zoroastrian barsom; Persian ba_lis. meaning 'cushion') are strewn than held in the hand; this is cognate with Vedic barhis. An important part of some Zoroastrian rituals is the tying of the barsom twigs into a bundle. The lexemes may simply refer to woody twigs.RV 4.18.13: *apaśyam jāyām amahīyamānām adhā me śyeno madhv ā jabhāra*, 'I saw the woman in distress; then the eagle brought me the Madhu,' (says Indra).

Gernot L. Windfuhr[57] has pointed out that Soma was neither hallucinogenic nor intoxicant and proceeds to identify Soma as ginseng, a root used as a stimulant. The identification of Soma as a root is questionable because ginseng has no component to connote amśu/asu. Falk interprets, from Vedic and Avestan contexts, Soma as a plant and concludes that it was ephedra, used as a stimulant. The Avestan references to Haoma as a plant can be explained as a ritualistic representation of the Soma refining process of the earlier days on the banks of the Sarasvati river. Yasna refers to the scent of the plant (Yasna, 10,4) but RV does not. There is, however, reference to the intense smell of the type common in the workshop of a metalsmith who uses k kṣāra (plant-based alkalis) to oxidise the impurities or baser metals in an ore block. Griswold notes that there are only two references to haoma in the Gāthās of Zoroaster, one mentioning dūraośa ' the averter of death' (Yasna, XXXII.14), the standing epithet of haoma in the later Avesta, and the other alluding to 'the filthiness f this intoxicant'(Yasna, XLVIII.10).These allusions are sufficient to prove that the intoxicating haoma was under the ban of the great reformer.[58]
The entire edifice of identification of soma as an 'intoxicant' is built up on the assumption that the Vedic texts do refer to the 'ectasy' generated by drinking soma juice. The 'ecstasy' may be an exaggeration by the Vedic poets; in the Atharvaveda even the remains of the sacrifice (4.34.35; 11.1.25), the odana (porridge) can produce 'ecstasy' (Keith 1925: I,275). Since the Soma was prepared freshly three times a day, in three savanas, there could have been hardly enough time for the

fermentation to occur to make it an intoxicant. "...the use of Ephedra in present day Iranian haoma rituals was probably paralled by the use of Ephedra in the soma rites of the north Indian Vedic schools, which endured until the tenth centry Islamic invasions of north India. Today soma rites are rare and are found only in south India, where schools of Vedic priests were to some extent reestablished by refugees from these invasions. The plant which reports uniformly indicate to be used as soma in these south Indian rites is an asclepiadacious, leafless climber, Sarcostemma brevistigma Wight & Arn. (Synonyms include: Asclepias acida Roxb., Sarcostemma acidum Voigt., and Sarcostemma viminale Wall. ex Decne. A.C. Burnell (1878: viii n.), states that, while Sarcostemma was used for soma on the east coast of India, on the west coast two species of Ceropegia, 'C. Decaisneana' and 'C. Elegans' were used, but he does not say how he knew of the ritual use of these species. The two Ceropegias are also asclepiadacious vines and probably merely substitute for Sarcostemma brevistigma in local rites). The twigs of Sarcostemma brevistigma contain a milky sap, but when dry they may be difficult to distinguish from Ephedra stems. Sarcostemma are tropical species and could not have been available for use as soma in Vedic times because they are absent from the flora of north India, and must therefore have been adopted only when, long after the Vedic period, Brahman priests emigrated to south India. These priests must have then selected Sarcostemma to substitute for the plant traditionally used as soma in north India. Ephedra species do not seem to occur in south India, nor in fact near the ritual centers of the northern plains themselves, so, to have been used there during the many centuries of Vedic practices, they would have to have been imported from adjacent uplands to the north and northwest. (Note: The importance of soma plants is reflected in the ritual enactment of the purchase of a cart of soma plants described in Śathapathabrāhmaṇa 3.3.1.1. f (see Hillebrandt 1891: 160-167; Dandekar 1973: II, 112-144; Kashikar 1964: 270-277; and Staal 1979). That it was Ephedra which Sarcostemma replaced as soma is evidenced by the fact that in Nepal today Ephedra is called by the Sanskrit name somalatā 'soma creeper' (Singh 1979; Shreshtha 1979; Manandhar 1980). The Islamic invasions resulted in the flight of Hindu refugees both to south India and to Nepal. Although these refugees do not appear to have established Vedic rites in Nepal, they introduced the Sanskrit language there. Sanskrit names for plants in Nepal date from the arrival of these refugees (J.F. Staal)...Some of the Ephedra species known by names reflecting haoma/soma contain, in quantities conditioned by rainfall and season, ephedrine, a sympathomimetic alkaloid somewhat similar in physiological action to adrenaline...Ephedra is unknown in traditional Indic or Iranian folk medicine, while in China, where it has been recognized for many centuries as a medicine, it is not regarded as intoxicating and its consumption lacks ceremonial or religious associations. The clearest demonstration that Ephedra cannot have been sauma exists in the very fact that Ephedra extracts are today drunk as haoma by Zoroastrian priests who do not become intoxicated from them...Peganum harmala is a commonplace weed without significant economic value, as compared with other Iranian plants, and in general unremarkable, except in the one respect that it alone among Iranian plants contains the visionary drugs harmaline and harmine. This property is not exploited today, but because it is th sole significant distinctive feature of harmel, the only way the plant could have acquired sanctity among all Iranian peoples was for these drugs to have been used and for their effects to have been widely experienced and esteemed." [Flattery & Schwartz (1989)].

"In Margiana, Sarianidi has discovered vessels which chemical analysis has shown to contain organic remains of Ephedra. They came from temple-like buildings at Togolok-21 and Gonur-1, with white-plastered rooms having platforms along walls with sunk-in vessels, and adjoining rooms having ceramic stands ans sieves...At Gonur-1 the ritualistic vessels also contained remains of poppy and cannabis, at Togolok-21 traces of poppy were found on stone mortars and pestles (Sarianidi 1987; Sarianidi 1990: 102 ff.; Sarianidi 1993, 8; Sarianidi 1993; Kussove 1993)...if the Margiana temples and their vessels date to the BMAC period (ca. 1900-1700 BC) and if the vessels cfontain remains of Ephedra, we may assume that the Dāsas of Margiana did in fact press Soma, and that they had introduced the cult from the early phases of the Andronovo (i.e. Petrovka) culture."[59] Haug[60] notes: 'The Soma plant is not a mere plant, but a creeping and somewhat twisting semi-shrub with a series of leafless shoots which contain an acidulous milky juice. Its present botanical name is Sarcostemma intermedium (de Candolle, Prodromus, p. 538). It grows everywhere in India. Sarcostemma brevistigma and S. brunonianum are closest to it (ibid). R. Wight[61] gives an illustration of it which should be compared with the text on p. 17."These arguments to identify anyone of the plant varieties as soma are based on the supposition that some type of ecstasy has to be induced the juice of the plant, assuming that the R.gveda does indicate that the imbibing the juice results in intoxication, hallucination or ecstasy. The term mada (root mad-) with cognate words in Indic, is a reference to the effects of haom and the context of 'intoxication' is restricted to the Yasna 9-11 (i.e. the Hōm Yasht): Y 10.8: ā athō yō haomahe madō (the intoxication of Haoma is accompanied by bliss-bringing Rightness); Y 10.14: fras.a frayantau tē madō (May thy intodicants come forth clearly); Y 10.19: raoxs.na frayantu tē madō (they intoxications come forth to me (clearly); Y 11.10: twaxṣāi haomahe madāi (for the active intoxication of Haoma for well being, for Rightness)-- these references seem to refer to 'intoxication' conjointly with references to 'Rightness' -- aṣa. Yasna 10.14 Avestan madō is translated mēniṣn 'thinking'; and in Yasna 11.10 Avestan madāi is not translated at all in the Middle Persian (Pahlavi) translations of the Avestan passages.arthavantah śabdasāmānyāt, 'vedic stanzas are significant because (their) words identical (with those of the spoken language)'. (Niruktam 1.16) gobhih śrīṇīti matsaram (Niruktam 2.4): 'The word gauh is a synonym of 'earth'...Matsarah means soma; it is derived from (the root) mand meaning to satisfy. Matsarah is a synonym of greed also; it makes man mad after wealth. Payas (milk) is derived from (the root) pā (to drink), or from pyāy (to swell)... -- matsara iti lobhanāma, abhimatta enena dhanam bhavati, payah pivatervā pyāyatervā'.[62]

Jan E. M. Houben[63] writes: "despite strong attempts to do away with Ephedra by those who are eager to see *sauma as a hallucinogen, its status as a serious candidate for the Rigvedic Soma and Avestan Haoma still stands". This supports Falk, who in his summary noted that "there is no need to look for a plant other than Ephedra, the one plant used to this day by the Parsis." (Falk, 1989)
Maybe, Houben's endorsement of ephedra as an identification of soma is also questionable since in the Indian tradition, soma substitutes were used. The substitutes were plants. What was the original soma described in the ancient document, *Ṛgveda*?[64]
According to Durga, synonyms of gold follow those of the earth, because gold, being found in earth, is intimately associated with it. 'The following fifteen (words) are synonyms of gold. From what (root) is hiran.yam derived? It is circulated (hriyate) in a stretched form, or it is circulated from man to man (tena hi vyavahārah kriyate), or it is useful and delightful, (or it is the delight of the heart),or it may be derived from (the root) hary, meaning to yearn after.' (Niruktam 2.10). Adrih (thunderbolt) is (so called because) with it he splits (mountains), or it may be derived from (the root) ad (to eat). It is well known: they are eaters of soma. The word rādhas is a synonym of wealth: with it, they conciliate. Bring that wealth to us, O Lord to whom treasures are known, with both thy hands. Let both thy hands be full...may we, with an active mind,partake of thy pressed soma,as if it were paternal property' (Nir. 4.4, 6): adrivan adrirādṛṇāyenena api vātteh syāt te somādo itiha vijnāyate; rādha iti dhananāma; rāghnuvantyanena; tannastvam vittadhanobhāgyām hastābhyāma_hara;ubhau samubdhau bhavatah...te manasā sutasya bhakṣīmahi pitr.yasyeva dhanasya).

The essential part of the ātaṣ-zōhr (the zaotra to the Waters) is the fat of a sacrificial animal. (Boyce 1966). The use of ghr.ta or animal fat can be explained as necessary to attain the temperature required to achieve oxidation of baser metals from a compound quartz such as electrum."In the translations of Vīsperad 8.1 and apparently Nērangistān 30, the Pahlavi glosses in m'd- are interpreted as forms from meh 'greater' (mehēnīdan 'to increase' etc.). In the translation of Hōm Yasht (Yasna 9-11), this m'd- is elaborated by glosses which show it was taken as referring to knowledge. Thus madō (Yasna 10.14; 10.19) is glossed vidyā by Neriosengh, and madem mruye (Yasna 9.17) is glossed m'dṣn gōw tis-ē-m pad frahang gōw ku-m dānāgīh bawād 'speak *māyiṣn, i.e. say something to me in instruction: that I may have knowledge'...The Middle persian word for 'intoxicated' is mast, whence mastīh 'intoxication'...Avestan masti- 'knowledge' (from the root mand-)...in Yasna 9.20 it is stated that haoma grants, to those who avidly study the sacred text, holiness (spānah-) and masti...wisdom.[65]

It is extraordinary that despite these Pahlavi interpretations of the term madō, it is supposed to represent 'intoxication'. mada (Skt. lexicon) m. hilarity , rapture , excitement , inspiration , intoxication RV. &c. &c. ; (du. {madasya}N. of 2 Sāmans ĀrshBr.) ; ardent passion for (comp.) MBh. ; (ifc. f. %{A}) sexual desire or enjoyment , wantonness , lust , ruttishness , rut (esp. of an elephant) MBh. Kāv. &c. ; (ifc. f. %{A}) , pride , arrogance , presumption , conceit of or about (gen. or comp.) ib. ; any exhilarating or intoxicating drink , spirituous liquor , wine , Soma RV. &c. &c , ; honey Ragh. ; the fluid or juice that exudes from a rutting elephant's temples MBh. Kāv. &c. ; semen virile L. ; musk L. ; any beautiful object L. ; a river L. ; N. of the 7th astrol. mansion Var. ; Intoxication or Insanity personified (as a monster created by Cyavana) MBh. ; N. of a son of Brahma1 VP. ; of a Da1nava Hariv. ; of a servant of S'iva BhP. ; (%{I}) f. any agricultural implement (as a plough &c.) L. ; n. N. of 2 Sāmans ĀrshBr.[66] matam (Tamil lexicon) has a wide array of meanings: esteeming highly any favour received; exhilaration, exultation, joy; strength; pride, arrogance, presumption; 4. animal or vegetable gluten; essence, juice; honey; madness, frenzy; wantonness, lasciviousness; venereal heat; richness of land, fertility;. inebriety, intoxication; semen; abundance; greatness.[67] It is notable that among the 'meanings' adduced to the lexeme, 'matam' in Old Tamil are included: 1. exhilaration, exultation, joy; 8. richness of land, fertility.The early semant. of the lexeme, mada, seems to be related to the exudation from a rutting elephant's temples; this metaphor and the adjective evolved could as well represent the semant. 'pride' or 'esteem'; like the awe evoked by an elephant in rut. As the Soma processing gets completed and is offered to the gods, to Indra in particular, there is a sense of 'exhilaration' at having achieved an 'exudation' which makes the sacrificer 'haughty' having produced something which has value and can lead to 'riches'; riches are the recurrent theme in the R.gveda referred to in the context of soma pavamāna, the processed soma. Zand ī Wahman Yasht III, 6-22 reads: (6) Ohrmazd the Sacred (abzōnīg = Avestan spenta-) Spirit, creator of the righeous corporeal existence, took the hand of Zoroaster and put liquid omniscient wisdom into it, and said 'drink it'. (7) And Zoroaster drank it and omniscient wisdom was mixed into Zoroaster...(19) I saw a tree with seven branches on it, one gold, one silver, one copper, one brass, one lead, one steel and one mixed iron. (20) Ohrmazd said to Zoroaster Spita_ma: 'This is what I prophesy: (21) The archetypal tree which you saw is the material existence which I, Ohrmazd, created. (22) Those seven branches which you saw are the seven ages which have come.[68] spenta- occurs in the Avesta (Vīsperad 9.3) as an epithet of haoma in the phrase haoma sūra spenta 'the haomas, powerful, sacred', and is the only adjective associating sauma with the name of any Iranian plant. This reference is again, as in Yasht III, 6-22, to the sacredness of the haoma and does not necessarily establish that it was a 'plant'. The Hōm Yasht (Yasna 10.13) states: Thou (Haoma) makest rich in men, more spenta-, and more insightful whomever apportions thee combined with gav- ('flesh/cattle-product); it is in Bundahiṣn (17.20) that (Haoma) is called the chief of medicinal herbs.Yasna 9.1: At the mortar time (the first period of the day), Haoma came upon Zarathushtra, purifying the fire and intoning the Gathas. Zarathushtra asked him: (2) 'Who, man, art thou, whom I see as the most beautiful in all the material world, luminous with thine own life?' Then the righteous du_raos.a Haoma answered: 'I am, O Zarathushtra, the righteous du_raos.a Haoma. Take me, Spitāma, extract me that I may be drunk, praise me with might, as the other saos.yants (saviors) have pressed me'. (3) Thus spake Zarathushtra: 'Praise be to Haoma! Which mortal in the material world first extracted thee? What reward was granted him? What benefit came to him?' [This passage became the basis for Gernot Windfuhr (1986) to argue that haoma was the (geographically remote and psychomorphologically irrelevant) ginseng plant because (the most highly valued) ginseng roots have a homunculus

shape (with one eye)]. The beginning of Hōm Yasht results in the birth of illustrious sons and this benefit was realized by the first four mortals who extracted haoma. Haoma says (Yasna 9.13-15) that the fourth to have extracted him was Pourushāspa: 'To him were you born, you, righteous Zarathushtra, in the house of Pourushāspa, opposed to daēvas, following the law of the ahuras. (14) Famed in Aryana Vaējah, you were the first to sing out the Ahuna Vairya prayer; four times, each (time) sung out louder. (15) You who made all the demons disappear beneath the earth, those who had earlier rushed against this earth in the form of men. You who are the strongest, who are the bravest, who are the most active, who are the swiftest, who are the most victorious of the creatures of the Two Spirits.'
Ṛṣi Praskaṇva kāṇva, devatā pavamāna Soma:
tam mamrayījānam mahisham na sānav amśum duhanty ukshaṇam giriṣṭhām
tam vaavaśānam matayah sacante trito bibharti varuṇam samudre
RV 9.095.04 (The priests) milk forth the Soma cleansed (dwelling) on a high place like a buffalo, the sprinkler, places between the grinding-stones; praises attend upon the longing Soma; (Indra) who dwells in three abodes supports him, the defeater of enemies, in the firmament. [The priests milk forth: grāvaṇo vatsāṛtvijo duhanti (Taittirīya Samhitā: 6.2.11.4); who dwells in three abodes: or, tritah may be an epithet of somah; varuṇam may be an epithet of indram]. Alternative trans.: They drain the ams'u, this steer who dwells on mountains…
tā vā dhenum na vāsarīm amśum duhanty adribhih soma duhyanty adribhih
asmannā gantam upa no rvāśincā soma pītaye
ayam vām mitrāvarun. ā nrbhih sutah soma ā pītaye sutah

RV 1.137.03 They milk for you two with stones, that succulent creeper, like a productive cow; they milk the Soma with stones; come to us as our protectors; be present with us to drink the Soma; thos Soma has been effused, Mitra and Varun.a, for you both; effused for your drinking. (Alternative trans.: The priests rnilk this ams'u for you both [Varuna and Mitra, two gods], like the auroral milk cow, with the aid of stones they milk the Soma, with the aid of stones.)

Lubotsky[69] noted the phonological and morphological similarity between Proto-Indo-Iranian and Sanskrit in 55 loan words. Apparently, substratum Indo-Iranian (spoken in BMAC) and substratum Indo-Aryan (spoken in Punjab) denoted the same language or dialects of the same language. Some examples of loanwords were:

- Skt. amsu- `Soma plant'; Av. asu- 'Haoma plant'
- Skt. atharvan- : Av. aerauuan-/araurun- `priest'
- Skt. bhisaj- m. `physician'; Av. bi- `medicine', LAv. biaziia- 'to cure'
- Skt. chaga- : Oss. saeg / saegae `billy-goat'
- Skt. dursa- `coarse garment' : Wakhi dərs `wool of a goat or a yak'
- Skt. gandha- `smell' : LAv. gainti- `bad smell'
- Skt. gandharva- : LAv. ganedərəva- `a mythical being'
- Skt. Indra- name of a god; LAv. Indra- name of a daeva
- Skt. istaka- f. (VS+); LAv. istiia- n., OP isti- f., MiP xist 'brick'
- Skt. jahaka- : LAv. duzuka-, Bal. jajuk, duzux, MoP zuza `hedgehog'
- Skt. kesa- `hair' : LAv. gaesa- `curly hair'
- Skt. nagnahu- (AVP+) m. `yeast, ferment'; PIr. *nagna- `bread'
- Skt. phala- : MoP supar `ploughshare'
- Skt. seppa-, but Prkrit cheppa- : LAv. xsuuaepa- `tail'
- Skt. sikata- : OP sika- `sand'
- Skt. suco- : LAv. suka- `needle'
- Skt. ustra-; Av. ustra-, 'camel'
- Skt. yavya- /yaviya/ `stream, canal'; OP yauviya- `canal'.

The loan word *amśu* (Skt.)/*asu* (Av.) has been preserved in Tocharian as *ancu*, as noted by Georges-Jean Pinault.

A Tamil word is: அஞ்சுவர்ணத்தோன் añcu-varṇattōṉ , *n.* < id. +. Zinc; துத்தநாகம். (R.) This phrase lit. means 'of the colour of *amśu.*' In Bronze-age, it was known that copper and zinc create a brass alloy which has the colour of gold. "A 'copper' coin is dipped into a solution of sodium zincate in contact with zinc metal. The coin is plated with zinc and appears silver in colour. The plated coin is held in a Bunsen flame for a few seconds and the zinc and copper form an alloy of brass. The coin now appears gold."[70] అంసగుడ్డ [aṃsaguḍḍa] *amsa-guḍḍa*. [Tel.] n. Polishing cloth (used by carpenters.) కొయ్యకు మెరుగువచ్చేటట్టు తోమే గుడ్డ. (Telugu)

Tocharian is acknowledged to be a satem group IE language. If Tocharian was spoken in Mt. Mujavant (Muztagh Ata), the mleccha-speakers were dasyu, mleccha-vācas, who like ārya vācas were also dasyu. They brought *soma* impregnated within *añcu* 'iron'for Rigvedic people to process it. This *añcu* is metaphorically referred to by Valmiki in the context of *suryāmśu* and *ayah-jālāni*'net of iron' which was smashed by the falcon. Gayatri was the falcon who fetched *soma.*

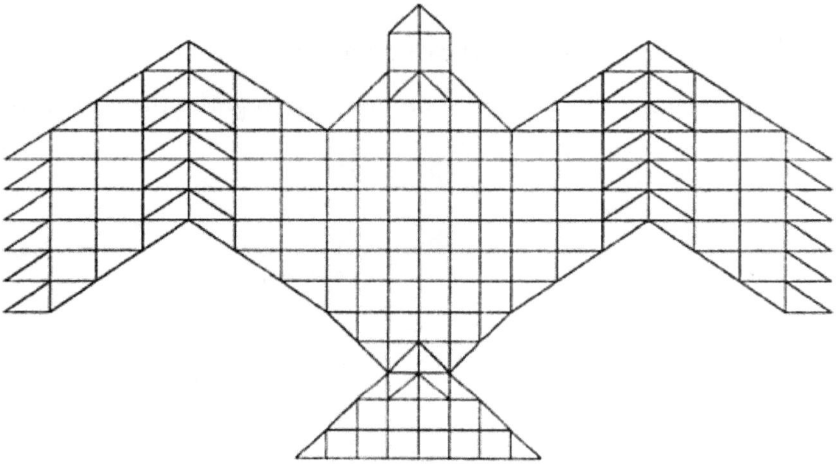

In Agnicayana, the vedi (fire-altar) is in the shape of śyena 'eagle', hence called śyenacit.

Here is the quote from Valmiki Ramayana and English translation related to the Rgvedic narrative of eagle fetching the soma.

See how Valmiki refers to Garuda smashing the iron-grid guard (ayo jālāni).

This matches with the update I have made to the blog entry about Tocharian ancu- 'iron' which is cognate with Rigvedic amśu- which describes soma.

From Valmiki Rāmāyaṇa, araṇya kāṇḍa refers to Garuḍa:

ayo jālāni nirmathya bhittvā ratna gṛham varam |
mahendra bhavanāt guptam ājahāra amṛtam tatah || 3-35-35

Trans. Smashing the guard of iron-grid completely and crashing the unbreakable diamond -like strongroom in which the ambrosia is safeguarded, then Garuda carried off ambrosia from the palace of Indra.[71]

अंशुजाल [aṃśujāla] n S A collection of (sun-) beams, a pencil of rays. (Marathi)

The semantic component of 'clothing or cover' and Marathi compound: अंशुजाल [aṃśujāla] is consistent with the garuḍa narrative of breaking the ayah jālāni 'iron-grid or iron-net' shield of a metamorphic mineral compound, to get to the ambrosia, amṛtam -- soma.

Meaning of the word, *amśu* used by Valmiki

Valmiki's description of how sun's rays heat the icy water of Himalaya, results in an extraordinary metaphor – related to minerals -- of 'a great mountain of sorrow, with its deep gorge of brooding, its minerals of heaving sighs, thickets of desolation, numberless creatures of delirium, plants and rushes of misery, and peaks of grief, care and woe."

aṁśú m. ' filament esp. of soma -- plant ' RV., ' thread, minute particle, ray '.Pa. *aṁsu* -- m. ' thread '; Pk. *aṁsu* -- m. ' sunbeam '; A. *ā̃h* ' fibre of a plant ', OB. *ā̃su*; B. *ā̃s* ' fibre of tree or stringy fruit, nap of cloth '; Or. *ā̃su* ' fibrous layer at root of coconut branches, edge or prickles of leaves ', *ā̃s* f. ' fibre, pith '; -- with -- *i* -- in place of -- *u* -- : B. *ā̃iś* ' fibre '; M. *ā̃sī˜* n. ' fine particles of flattened rice in winnowing fan '; A. *ãhiyā* ' fibrous '. (CDIAL 4). aṁśuka ' *fibrous ', n. ' cloth, garment ' lex. [aṁśú --] अंशु [Monier-Williams lexicon, p. 1,1] [L=47] m. a

filament (especially of the सोम plant), a kind of सोम libation S3Br., thread, end of a thread , a minute particle, a point , end, a ray , sunbeam. Cf. अग्रांशु [agrāṃśu] m S The extremity of a ray of light; the focal point. अंशुजाल [aṃśujāla] n S A collection of (sun-) beams, a pencil of rays. (Marathi)

अंश means partial incarnation, अंश, आवेश, and अवतार are the three kinds of Supreme Divine's manifestations. अंशकम् A solar day. अंशिन् a. Having parts or members (अवयविन्); अंशिनः स्वांशगात्यन्ताभावं प्रति मृषात्मतां -Ved. Paribhāṣā. अंश्य a. [अंश्-कर्मणि यत्] Divisible. अंशुः [अंश्-मृग° कु.] 1 A ray, beam of light;

चण्ड°, घर्म° hot-rayed the sun; सूर्यांशुभिर्भिन्नमिवारविन्दम् Ku.1.32; Iustre, brilliance चण्डांशुकिरणाभाश्च हाराः Rām.5.9.48; Śi.1.9. रत्न°, नख° &c. -2 A point or end. -3 A small or minute particle. - 4 End of a thread. -5 A filament, especially of the Soma plant (Ved.) -6 Garment; decoration. -7 N. of a sage or of a prince. -8 Speed, velocity (वेग). -9 Fine thread -Comp. -उदकम् dew-water. -जालम् a collection of rays, a blaze or halo of light

Ta. ācu hilt. *Ka.* āyuga handle of a sword. (DEDR 342). áṁsya of *Ṛgveda* may refer to a metallic scythe (sickle), cognate with Ku. ā̃sī ' scythe '. Aŋsa [see next] point, corner, edge; freq. in combn with numerals, e. g. catur° four -- cornered, chaḷ°, aṭṭh°, soḷas° etc. (q. v.) all at Dhs 617 (cp. DhsA 317). Aŋsu [cp. Sk. aŋśu (Halāyudha) a ray of light] a thread Vin iii.224. -- mālin, sun Sāsv 1. (Pali) அம்சபூதன் amca-pūtaṉ, n. < aṃša- bhūta. One who forms part, as of a deity; அமிசமாயிருப்பவன். நம்முடைய அம்சபூத ரொருவரை (குருபரம். 166).(Tamil) அமிசை amicai, n. < aṃša. Lot; தலை யெழுத்து (destiny). ஆசை யிருக்கிறது தாசில்பண்ண, அமிசை யிருக்கிறது கழுதை மேய்க்க. Semantics of अंशुकं help identify अंशु which is a 'clothing or cover' to 'soma'. When the rṣi-s employ the poetic metaphors in the vedic allegory related to soma, the reference to अंशु is an enveloping mineral compound - 'iron' element called अंशु covering the core dhātu – soma, 'electrum'. Radiance of the 'sun' in the phrase used by Valmiki, suryāmśu samtaptah can be explained as the heating by radiant mineral अंशु In a poetic exposition, Valmiki uses the term amśu to describe the sun's heat: suryāmśu samtaptah ('heated by sunbeam') and vinihśvasita dhātunā ('minerals in the shape of groans and sighs'). In the context of the poet's metaphor, the word amśu cannot be explained as related to part of a plant (e.g. 'stalk').

The semantics of 'clothing' are found on Tocharian-Sanskrit lexical isogloss:

aṃśuk (n.masc.) 'garment'
L JWP 'garment'.
F Obl.Sg. *aṃśuk.*
T ◆Obl.Sg. YQ II.9 b4.
D From Skt. *aṃśuka-* 'cloth, fine or whi
cloth, muslin' (MW:1b).

अंशुकम् [अंशवः सूत्राणि बिषयो यस्य; अंशु ऋश्यादि° क] 1 A cloth, garment in general; सितांशुका मङ्गलमात्रभूषणा V.3.12; यत्रांशुकाक्षेपविलज्जितानां Ku.1.14; चीनांशुकमिव केतोः Ś.1.33; स्तन° a breast-cloth. -2 A fine or white cloth; धुन्वन् कल्पद्रुमकिसलयान्यंशुकानीव वातैः Me.64; usually silen or muslin. -3 An upper garment; a mantle. -4 An under garment; कररुद्धनीविगलदंशुकाः स्त्रियः Śi.13.31. -5 A leaf. -6 Mild or gentle blaze of light (नातिदीप्ति) (कः also; स्वार्थे कन्.) -7 The string of a churning stick. cf अंशुकं नेत्रवस्त्रयोः । cf. also अंशुकं सूक्ष्मवस्त्रे स्यात् परिधानोत्तरीययोः । किरणानां समूहे च मुखवस्त्रे तदिष्यते ॥ Nm. (Apte, p.2) *Ta.* a̲nsu selvage, edge of a cloth (< Te.). *To.* oc edge, bank of river, border of thicket. *Ka.* añcu edge, brim, boundary, bank, shore, selvage, border, skirt. *Te.* ancu skirt, border or selvage of cloth, edge (of sword, etc.), shore, brim. /Cf. Skt. añcala- edge or border of a garment. (CDIAl 168) (DEDR 57).అంచు [añcu] *antsu*. [Tel.] n. Selvage, skirt, border. ఏటి అంచుస on the edge of the river. గిన్నెదొఝుక్క అంచుదాకా brimful. అఊరి అంచుస hard by the town.

These lexical entries provide a semantic lead to the *amśu/asu* used to describe Soma/Haoma; the term in early Rgveda connotes the streaks of metal, seen like fibres of a stringy fruit or nap of cloth [ās (B.)]. In the Avesta, "the term *asu* is only used in conjunction with a description of *haoma*, and does not have an established translation."

The kavi sees soma is clothed in sunbeams *aṁsu* (Pkt.) Pkt. *aṁsu* -- m. ' sunbeam '(CDIAL 4).

The amśu was ruddy like a gaura mṛga (RV. 7.98,1). Av. Zairi 'yellow, golden-hued, green'; Skt. Hari; tenderness/pliant asu (Av. Na…myasu Y.9.16.30); the colour of Soma filaments contained in the ore block are 'reddish' or 'yellow' (aruṇa/aruṣa or hari/zāiri A characterization of Soma in RV 9.97.9: colour of Soma is babhru (grayish brown); by night it appears silvery white and by day it is hari (colour of fire).

Regarding the ritual purchase of the Soma, TS.6,1,6,7 states that one buys the Soma with a ruddy, yellow-eyed cow; 'this, one should know, is the form of Soma: then one buys it with its own deity. That became gold… Those who discourse on brahman say, 'how is it that offspring are produced through that which is boneless, and yet are born with bones?' Because one offers the gold, placing it in the ghee, therefore offspring are born… with bones."

In the tradition of the Black Yajurveda, ĀpŚ. 10,25,11 states that the adhvaryu should buy the Soma with gold saying: " I buy the bright (s'ukra, Soma) withbright (gold), the glittering (candra) with glittering, the amṛtam with amṛtam to match thy cow" (TS. 1,2,7,1); the Soma-dealer answers: "King Soma deserves more than that". Adhvaryu washes king Soma with water and unfolds him (ĀpŚ.11,1,11). "Every shoot of thee, O Soma, must swell for Indra…" (TS. 1,2,11,1).The purpose of the yajña is: ' by means of ghee as the vajra and two sacrificial ladles as their arms the gods slew Vṛtra. Vṛtra is the Soma. One should know that they slay Soma, when they sacrifice with ghee in his presence. By means of these mantras one makes Soma swell again." (TS. 6,2,2,4)

Metaphors of soma pressing

'Mātariśvan fetched one of you (Agni and Soma) from heaven; the eagle twirled the other from the cloud-rock'.(RV. I.93,6). cf. "it is plucked from the rock by the falcon (RV. 1.93.6); soma comes from the mountains, giriṣṭhām: RV V.43.4; soma seated on the mountain top: RV IX.18.1 [Notes: why the reference to adrau, in dual, two stones? maybe, silver ore and gold ore co-mingled in electrum?] The RV reference to Soma 'growing' on the mountains (giriṣṭhā) is explained in the context of the ores obtained from the mines in NW India. (giriṣṭha: RV. III.48,2; V.43.4; IX.18.1, 62,4; parvatāvṛdh: RV. IX.46.1) Hence, the reference to Somam adrau (RV. 5.85.2) plucked in two rocks. RV. 10.97.18, 19 refer to the group of herbs having Soma as their king (Somarājñih); the growth of herbs on the mountains is the obvious reference here.

The links of Soma with rocks are vivid. (adri: RV. V.85,2; I.93,6).[72] Soma flourished during the rainy season, swelling with milk (RV. II.13,1), strengthened by the rain-cloud, parjanya (RV. IX.82,3; 113,3). Yasna (X.3): 'I praise the cloud and the waters that made thy body to grow upon the mountains.' Later rituals state that Soma had to be purchased from a śūdra, who was a trader in Soma who was like the gandharva who held back the celestial Soma. (cf. kṣudraka = maker of minute beads or minor work in gold (Arthaśāstra: 2.13.37and 40).
There is a pun on the semantics of 'thunderbolt/stone' and 'eagle': aśáni f. ' thunderbolt ' RV., °*nī* -- f. ŚBr. [Cf. *áśan* -- m. ' sling -- stone ' RV.] Pa. *asanī* -- f. ' thunderbolt, lightning ', *asana* -- n. ' stone '; Pk. *asaṇi* -- m.f. ' thunderbolt '; Ash. *ašī́* ' hail ', Wg. *ašē̃́*, Pr. *īšī*, Bashg. "*azhir*", Dm. *ašin*, Paš. *ášen*, Shum. *ä'šin*, Gaw. *išín*, Bshk. *ašun*, Savi *išin*, Phal. *ā̃šun*, L. (Jukes) *ahin*, awāṇ. &circmacrepsilon;*n* (both with *n*, not *ṇ*), P. *āhiṇ*, f., *āhaṇ*, *aihaṇ* m.f., WPah. bhad. *ā̃ṇ*, bhal. 'tildemacrepsilon;*hiṇi* f., N. *asino*, pl. °*nā*; Si. *sena*, *heṇa* ' thunderbolt (CDIAL 910). śyēná m. ' hawk, falcon, eagle ' RV.Pa. *sēna* -- , °*aka* -- m. ' hawk ', Pk. *sēṇa* -- m.; WPah.bhad. *śeṇ* ' kite '; A. *xen* ' falcon, hawk ', Or. *seṇā*, H. *sen*, *sẽ* m., M. *śen* m.,*śenī* f. (< MIA. **senna* --); Si. *sen* ' falcon, eagle, kite '. (CDIAL 12674).

Harappa seal impression. h-161a. Eagle glyph.

Incised eagle from Tepe Yahya (Kohl in Potts 2011: 218, fig. 9.7). Eagle glhyph comparable to the glyph on Harappa seal impression.

Tocharian language as an Indo-European language has revealed a word anzu in Tocharian which meant 'iron'. It is likely that this is the word used for soma in *Ṛgveda*. In the context of identification of Muztagh Ata of Kyrgystan as Mt. Mujavat (mentioned as a source of soma in *Ṛgveda*), it is notable that in Mesopotamian legend of Ninurta, god of war and agricultural fertility hunts on the mountains, Anzu which is the lion-headed Eagle with the power of the stolen Tablet

of Destinies. The 'eagle' is identified as śyena in *Ṛgveda* and Avesta (saena meregh) as the falcon which brought the nectar, Soma. It is likely that soma as electrum (silver-gold ore) was bought from the traders who brought ancu from Mt. Mujavat. Soma is said to have come from heaven (RV 9,63.27) and to have been brought by the eagle. It was brought by the eagle – śyenābhṛt (RV1.80.2). The bird (śyena) brought Soma from that highest heaven (RV 4,26.6). "The straight-flying hawk, conveying the Soma from afar; the bird, attended by the gods, brought, resolute of purpose, the adorable exhilarating Soma, having taken it from that lofty heaven." Thunderbolt is also a significant component of Mesopotamian mythology. Marduk, sun god of Babylon, with his thunderbolts pursues Anzu after Anzu stole the Tablets of Destiny.

Zu, also known as Anzu and Imdugud, in Sumerian, (from *An* "heaven" and *Zu* "to know", in the Sumerian language) is a lesser divinity of Akkadian mythology, and the son of the bird goddess Siris. He was conceived by the pure waters of the Apsu and the wide Earth. Both Zu and Siris are seen as massive birds who can breathe fire and water, although Zu is alternately seen as a lion-headed eagle.

Zu as a lion-headed eagle, ca. 2550–2500 BC, Louvre.

Anzu was a servant of the chief sky god Enlil, guard of the throne in Enlil's sanctuary, (possibly previously a symbol of Anu), from whom Anzu stole the Tablet of Destinies, so hoping to determine the fate of all things. In one version of the legend, the gods sent Lugalbanda to retrieve the tablets, who in turn, killed Anzu. In another, Ea and Belet-Ili conceived Ninurta for the purpose of retrieving the tablets. In a third legend, found in *The Hymn of Ashurbanipal*, Marduk is said to have killed Anzu.

Lydia, king Croesus (561-46 BC), [pure] gold stater: foreparts of Lion and bull (obv.), incuse (rev.) Fitzwilliam Museum.[73]

Etruscan *ar* = fire, Latin *āra* = altar., hearth; ārdēre 'to burn, be on fire'.[74] Ash. *arū´*, *úrə*, 'silver', Wg. *urẽ́i*, Kt. *ŕǖ*, *arǖ*, Pr. *urúdotdot;*, Gmb. *wurṓ*, Kal. (LSI) *ṛāwa*, rumb. *rūa*: more prob. < **rūpiya* -- s.v. rū´pya -- ? rajatá ' silvery ' RV., n. ' silver ' AV. Pa. *rajata* -- n. ' silver ', Pk. *rayada* -- , *rayaya* -- n., Si. *ridī*, Md. *rihi.* -- (CDIAL 10576). ARU 'copper' (*AKKADIAN*) ara, era 'copper' (Pali.Pkt.) āra 'brass' as in ārakūṭa (Skt.) era = copper; erako = molten cast (G.)

Hieroglyph/ homonym: arū = lion (As god of devastation, Nergal is called A-ri-a)(Akkadian).[75] Ari (Numbers 24:9) or Aryeh (2 Samuel 17:10) is the Hebrew for "lion", cognate to Akkadian aria, Aramaic arya. The word is in use as a male first name. Gur-aryeh "lion cub" is attested in Jacob's blessing on Judah (Genesis 49:9), "Judah is a lion's whelp; on prey, my son, have you grown". The Hebrew name Ari-el translates to "lion of God". aru = eagle (Akkadian/Assyrian) *ara* 'spokes' (Skt.) ará m. ' spoke of a wheel ' RV. 2. āra -- 2 MBh. v.l. [√r̥] 1. Pa. *ara* -- m., Pk. *ara* -- , °*ga* -- , °*ya* -- m.; S. *aro* m. ' spoke, cog '; P. *ar*m. ' one of the crosspieces in a cartwheel '; Or. *ara* ' felloe of a wheel '; Si. *ara* ' spoke '. 2. Or. *āra* ' spoke '; Bi. *ārā* ' first pair of spokes in a cartwheel '; H. *ārā* m. ' spoke ', G. *ārɔ* m.(CDIAL 594).

abāru = lead; antimony (annaku is most unlikely to be lead rather than tin).(cf. CAD A (II): 126; AHw 49) (Akkadian/Assyrian). abaru = enclose, surround; aburru = enclosure (Akkadian/Assyrian) abaru = be strong, powerful; strength, power (Akkadian/Assyrian) Hieroglyph/homonym: abru = wing (Akkadian/Assyrian) koṭe 'forge'.(Mundarica) खोदणें [khōdaṇēṃ] v c & i To dig. 2 To engrave. (Marathi) कोंदण [kōndaṇa] n (कोंदणें) Setting or infixing of gems.(Marathi) koḍ 'artisan's workshop' (Kuwi) kõdā 'to turn in a lathe'(Bengali)(CDIAL 3295) Hieroglyph/homonym: koḍe 'young bull' (Telugu)

These lexical isoglosses point to lion and bull as hieroglyphic representations of hearth and forge: *āra* and *koṭe*

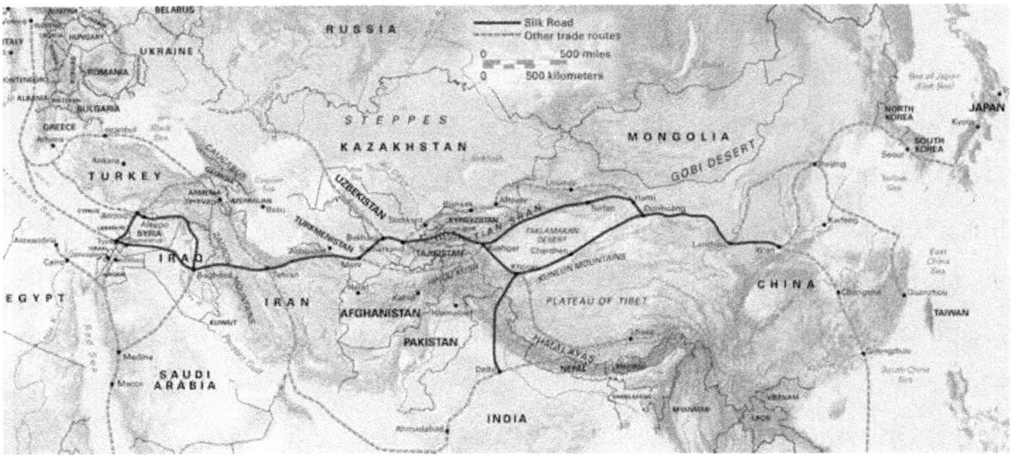

mākṣikā, 'pyrites, *madhu dhātu*'

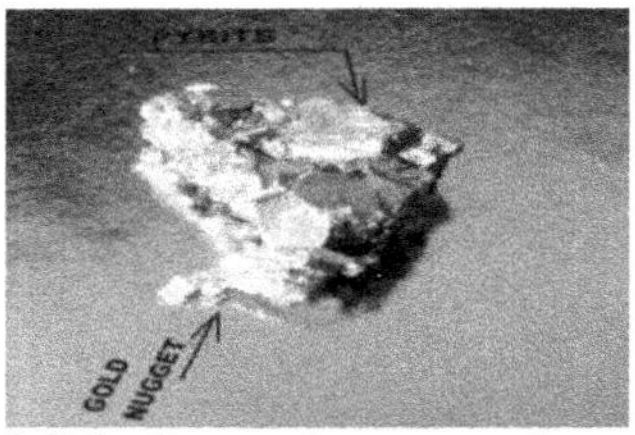

Mākṣikā refer to pyrites. Pyrite. Named in antiquity from the Greek "pyros" for "fire" because sparks flew from it when hit with another mineral or a metal. Pyrites are referred to *akkinikkal* 'flint, pyrites' in Tamil. Mākṣika has also the meaning of 'madhu' in Suśruta. It is also a honey-like mineral substance of pyrites in *Mahābhārata*. A synonym for pyrites is: madhu dhātu (Skt.)

Pyrite on a gold nugget. Pyrite is referred to as "Fools' Gold", since many a prospector brought home the shiny Iron Sulfate, and staked claims on their "gold " deposit, which turned out to be pyrite. All that glitters is not gold. Pale brass-yellow hue might have earned it the nickname fool's gold because of its resemblance to gold.

Chalcopyrite (kælke'paɪraɪt/ *KAL-ko-PY-ryt*) is the most important copper ore, a copper iron sulfide mineral that crystallizes in the tetragonal system. Trace amounts of Ag (gold) are reported. $CuFeS_2$[76]

"Oxidised ore from Macraes area. The brown colour indicates that the pyrite has decomposed to iron oxide (rust), liberating the tiny lumps of gold. The gold may remain in the iron oxide or move away in groundwater… Gold in the quartz veins occurs as very small grains, generally totally enclosed in hard quartz. In addition, most of the gold is contained in sulphide minerals: pyrite (FeS_2, fools gold) or arsenopyrite (FeAsS) which are in turn totally enclosed in quartz. The gold content of quartz veins was 10-50 grams per tonne of ore. Mining hard-rock gold requires considerabley more technological input than alluvial gold. Historically, hard-rock mining was a minor part of the gold mining industry in Otago because it is a very capital-intensive process."[77]

ṛṣi Kakṣīvān Dairghatamasa (Auśija), devatā aśvinīkumāra:

uta syā vām madhuman makṣikārapan made somasyauśijo huvanyati

yvam dadhīco mana aa vivaasatho thaa śirah prati vām aśvya vadat

RV 1.119.09 That honey-seeking bee also murmured your praise; the son of Usij invokes you to the exhilarating of Soma; you conciliated the mind of Dadhyañc, so that, provided with the head of a horse, he taught you (the mystic science).

Alternative trans.: To you, O Aswins, that fly betrayed the soma… mākṣikā = pyrite ores; fly. cf. "mākṣikam (pyrites), digested hundred times with juice of plantain leaves, and then steeped for three days in oil, clarified butter and honey, and then heated strongly in a crucible yields its essence."[78]

Note the pun on the word, mākṣikā meaning both 'bee' and 'pyrites or quartz'. Mākṣikā are pyrites; hema Mākṣikā and tāmra Mākṣikā denote gold and copper pyrites. RASARATNA SAMUCCAYA 77,81, 89-90: Mākṣikam is born of mountains yielding gold...

Almost all epithets attributed to Soma (such as amśu [śukram or bright, pure metallic ore protrusions analagous to shoots of a plant], golden, yellow, shining, resplendent, flowing, filtering: pavitram; crushing on stones; provenance of soma in mountainous terrain) can be explained by this metallurgical-allegorical identification. Even the reference to the seller from Mt. Mujavant who is paid and chased away after taking delivery of the ore product can be explained in the

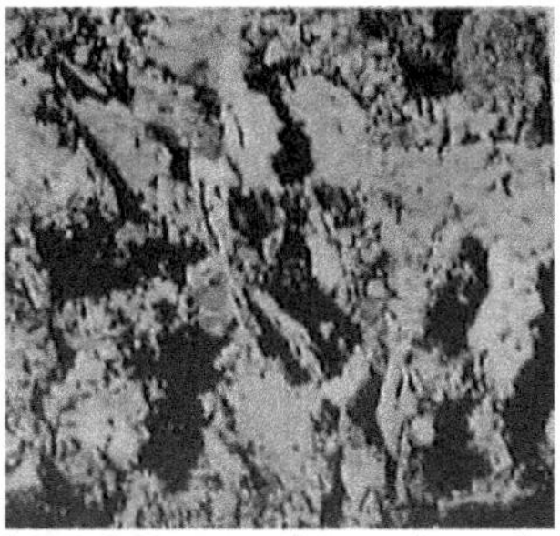

braahmaṇa days involving the secretive alchemical processes (agni-rahasya; somanala yantra); these practices continue into the Arthaśāstra days with an extraordinary role played by the Adhvaryu in a political nexus within the king's domain. It is not a mere coincidence that śulba sūtra also have sūtras shrouded in geometrical-allegorical terms: śulba = copper! Kātyāyana in his śulbasūtra says that his sūtras have their meaning concealed. So too can the reference to Mākṣikā in RV. 1.119.9 (fly, pyrite ores!) be explained.

Leaf formation on gold from the Mother Lode, Nevada country, California.[79] "Gold in rocks usually occurs in invisible disseminated grains, more rarely as flakes large enough to be seen and even more rarely as masses or veinlets. Crystals about 2.5 cm. (1 inch) or more across have been found in California."[80] Ball also refers to an old record of the discovery of a gold mine in Afghan Seistan and also notes Bannu, Peshawar, Hazara, Rawalpindi, Jhelam, Ambala and certain Punjab Himalayan princely states such as Kangra as gold-panning centres. Even today, gold panning is licensed by the District Collector of Yamunanagar (Haryana) for gold-panners to work on the river bed of River Sarasvati at a place called Lohgarh. north of Siwalik mountain ranges (Nahan), consistent with the tradition of referring to River Sarasvati as hiraṇyavartan ī (river carrying gold).

Ṛṣi Jamadagni Bhargava refers to ams'u as Soma in the following rca addressed to pavamāna soma:

asāvy amśur madāyāpsu dakṣo giriṣṭhāh
śyeno na yonim āsadat
RV 9.062.04 The mountain-born Soma flows for exhilaration, mighty in the (vasatīvarī) waters; he alights like a falcon on his own place. [amśu may also be interpreted as metal-streaks in an ore block].
Ams'u! Ams'u is a beam of bright mineral streaks on mineral ore blocks.
RV 9.86.46: *asarji skambho diva udyato madah pari tridhātur bhuvanāni arṣati amśum rihanti matayah panipnatam girā yadi nirṇijam ṛgmiṇo yayuh* (Er ward ausgegossen, der Pfeiler des Himmels, der emporgehaltene Rauschtrank; er fliesst mit drei Bestandteilen um die Welten. Die Dichtungen lecken an dem schreienden Stengel, wenn die Versdichter mit ihrer Rede Staat machen – Geldner (1951-7: 3,84) ('He was poured out, the pillars of heaven, which held up strong drink, it flows with three components to the world. The seals lick the screaming stalk if the State Versdichter do with her speech.') (Il vient-de-se-deverser, etai du ciel, breuvage offert, il coule autour des mondes, (ce dieu) triparti. Les pensées-poétiques lèchent la tige miraculeuse, quand *les (poètes) pourvus de strophes* sont allés avec le chant vers la robe-d'apparat (qu'a revêtue le *soma*).' Renou (1955-69: 9.36) ['He comes-to-be-discharged, prop the sky, drink offered, it flows around the worlds, (the god) tripartite. Thoughts-poetic lick miraculous rod, when (poets) provided stanzas with the song went to the dress-d'apparat (recently concluded the soma).']
A significant attribute of amśu is śukram as noted by Ṛṣi Atri Bhauma, devatā viśvedeva:
daśa kṣipo yunjate bāhū adrim somasya yā śamitārā suhastā
madhvor sugabhastir giriṣṭhām canis'cadad duduhe śukram amśuh

RV 5.043.04 The ten express of the juice, (the fingers), and the two arms of the priests, which are the dexterous immolators of the Soma, take hold of the stone; the exulting, skilful-fingered (priest) milks the mountain-born juice of the sweet Soma, and that Soma (yields its) pure juice. [The text has only śukram amśuh = sa ca amśuh śukram nirmalam rasam dugdhe, and that Soma has milked the pure juice; or amśu may be an epithet of adhvaryu, the extensively present priest, amśur vyāpto adhvaryuh].

Alternative trans.: The ten fingers, the two arms, harness the pressing stone; they are the preparers of the Soma, with active hands. The one with good hands has milked the mountain-grown sap . . . the amśu has yielded the dazzling.

The lexeme śukram is interpreted as 'pure'. In the alternative translation, śukram is interpreted as 'dazzling'. This latter semantics related to 'brightness' is attested in RV 5.045.10 Sūrya has ascended above the glistening water, as soon as he has put to his bright-backed steeds; sage (worshippers) have drawn him, like a ship, across the sea; the waters hearing his commands, have come down. [Sūrya has ascended: sūryo aruhat śukram arṇas = sūrya has mounted the bright water, that is, he has become everywhere visible, but it may be an allusion to the sun's rising apparently out of the sea].

Amśu is personified in the context of bestowing wealth, in RV 8.5.26 by Ṛṣi Brahmātithi kāṇva, devatā aśvinī kumāra:

yathota kṛtvye dhane latamśum goshv agastyam
yathā vājeṣu sobharim

RV 8.005.26 And in like manner as (you protected) Ams'u when wealth was to be bestowed, and Agastya when his cattle (were to be recovered), and Sobhari when food (was to be supplied to him).

Maharshi Bharadwaja's text on Vaimānika Śāstra refers to a Rājaloha: Bodhānanda Vritti: (Commentary by Bodhānanda) Prāna-kṣāra or ammonium chloride 4 parts,

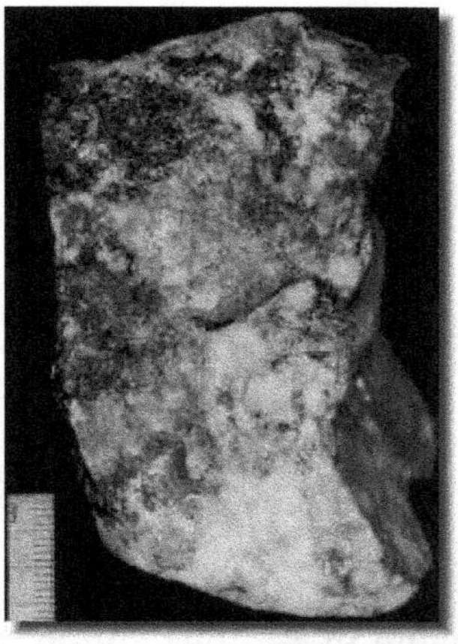

wild Bengal gram 32 parts, śaśakaṇḍa (or lodhra?) benzoin? 18 parts, nāga or lead 20 parts, sea-foam 16 parts, mākṣika or iron pyrites 6 parts, panchānana or iron 20 parts, pāra or mercury 15 parts, kṣāra-traya or 3 kinds of salt: natron, salt-petre, borax, 28 parts, pancānana or mica 20 parts, hamsa or silver 17 parts, garada or aconite 8 parts, and pancāmrita or 5 sweets--curds, milk, ghee, sugar, honey, these should be filled in the melter, and after boiling, and drawing the liquid through two outlets, fill in the crucible and place in furnace, and blow to 800 degrees' heat, and then transfer it to the cooler. That will be Rājaloha, pure, golden-coloured, tensile, and mild. The vimāna, made out of this loha or alloy, will be very beautiful and delightful.[81]

In the second chapter of Vaimanika śāstra, Maharshi Bharadwaaja:notes: "ūṣmapāstriloha Mayāha." Sūtra 1. "ūṣmapā metals are made up of 3 metals." Bodhānanda Vritti: The heat-proof metals are made out of the three, Souma, Soundāla, and Morthwīka mentioned in the previous chapter. It is said in "Loha Ratnākara" that each of the three yields varieties of seed metals. Their names are, in souma group,--souma, soumyaka, sundaāya, soma, panchānana, ūṣmapa, śaktigarbha, jāngalika, prānana, śankha, and lāghava; The names of the metals of soundīra origin, are viranci, souryapa, śanku, uṣna, sūrana, śinjikā, kanku, ranjika, soundīra, mugdha, and ghundāraka. In the mourthwīka group, the 11 are anuka, dvyanuka, kanka, tryanuka, shvetāmbara, mridambara, bālagarbha, kuvarcha, kantaka, kṣvinka and laghvika."[82] The reference to a category called Souma metal is remarkable. Souma, haoma as metal !

For e.g., Soma is described as parvatāvṛdhah in a verse, that the pyrites are from the mountain slopes: 9.046.01 Begotten by the stones the flowing (Soma-juices) are effused for the banquet of the gods' active horses. [Begotten by the stones: or, growing on the mountain slopes]. The part of Soma which is pressed by Adhvaryu (RV. 8,4) is the amśu (lit. shoot or stalk). Soma is described as maujavata (RV. 10,34; lit. produced on Mount Mūjavat); also as dwelling in the mountains (giriṣṭhā) or growing in the mountains parvatāvṛdhah: RV. 9,46). In one figure of speech, Varuṇa is stated to have placed soma on the rock (RV. 5,85) and in another, the eagle carries off soma from the rock (RV. 1,93). Terrestrial mountains are the abode of soma (RV. 9,2).Soma is the branch of a ruddy tree (RV. 10,94). It is the ruddy or tawny shoot which is pressed into the strainer (RV. 9,92). During pressing with ten reins (i.e.fingers: RV. 6,44), soma is figuratively placed in the heaven, the highest place of the cows (RV. 5,45); other figures of speech are purification with the hands (RV.9,86), with ten fingers (RV. 9,8.15), by ten maiden sisters (RV. 9.1.6) . Stone (adri; also, aśna, bharitra, parvata, parvataā adrayah: RV. 8,2; 3,36; 3,35; 10,94).) isused to crush Soma (RV. 9,67; 9,107); pounding is the verb (RV. 10,85). The stones are on a skin ['chewed on the hide of the cow' (RV. 9,79]. The stones are placed on the vedi or altar (RV. 5,31). Ten reins guide the crushing stones (RV.10,94); ten fingers yoke the stone (RV. 5,43) and hence compared with horses (RV.10,94). [Ṛgveda uses the general technique of pressing using stones, though the processusing mortar and pestle is known (RV. 1.28); this latter practice is used by Parsis. Avesta also states that Haoma grows on the mountains].As a juice, Soma is called the rasa, fluid; and in one hymn it is pītu (lit. beverage).[Rasavāda = alchemy].

When Soma purifies itself, Soma wins cattle, chariots, gold, the light of heaven, and water for them (RV. 9,78,4).

RV. 9,8,39; 38 implore Soma to clarify itself while procuring gold.RV. 9,75,3: ava dyutānah kalaśam acikradan nṛbhir yemānah kośa āhiraṇyaye = Soma rushed down in the jars with loud cries, held (in hands) by themen in the golden vessel (kośe). Sarasvati is hiraṇyavartanī (RV. 6,61,7) or one endowed with a goldencourse. Jaiminīya Upanis.ad Brāhmaṇa notes that Vāk is transcendental and is the great, mystic principle of creation and universal existence. (Jaim. Up. Br. 1.28.1-10). Vāk is suparṇī māyā. (ŚB 3.6.2.2; cf.suparṇa garutmān, the well-winged eagle associated with the asura sun: RV1.163.6; savitā: RV 10.149.3). The term, 'suparṇa' seems to be releated a variegated stone in RV 5.047.3-4) and may explain the nature of creation that is sought to be linked with Vāk.

RV 5.047.03 The showerer (of rain), the shedder of dew, the radiant and quick-going (car) has entered the region of the paternal east; the many-tinted andpervading (luminary) proceeds to both extremities of the firmament, (and so) preserves (the world). [Many-tinted and pervading luminary: p ṛṣṇir as'māvicakrame rajaspatyantau: aśma = vyāpaka or sarvatra vyāpta, pervading; also, it means, a stone, an allusion to a pāṣāṇa, or stone, which in some ceremonies is placed in the āhavanīya fire; aśma may also imply a simile, the term of comparison being dropped, luptopamāvāśmā sādṛśah].The bull, the ocean, the ruddy suparṇa went into the womb of the primeval father.He comes out set as variegated stone in the middle of the heaven. He watches overthe two limits of space. (Geldner).5.047.04 The four (chief priests) sustain him (with oblation and praises), seeking their own welfare; the ten (regions of space) invigorate him, their embryo, to travel (his daily course); his three elementary rays swiftly traverse the boundaries of the sky. [The four chief priests: the text has only catvārah,'four'; ṛtvijah are implied; his three elementary rays: tridhātavo gāvah, supposed to be the causes of cold, heat and rain. Or, simply three ore elements, tridhātu 'three minerals': copper, silver, gold].

References to electrum may be noticed in RV. 8,45,22 where the metal silver is called 'whitish hiraṇya'; rajata is used as an adjective to mean 'whitish, silver-coloured'. [See ĀpS. 5,29,2 which states that rajatam hiraṇyam should not begiven as a dakṣiṇā.]

Soma is pitā devānām (RV. IX.109,4) or father of the gods. Hiraṇyagarbha, the golden germ was evolved in the beginning (RV. 10,121,1`). Hiraṇyagarbha is the title of Prajāpati, who is declared as the only divinity who encompasses all the created things (jātah patir). "(he) who by his might has ever been (babhūva) the sole divinity of the world that breathes and blinks, who rules over these two-footed and four-footed (beings), to what divinity shall we pay homage with oblation?" (RV. 10,121,3).

Aitareya Brāhmaṇa verses 10.12.1-3 continue the soma sacrifice (the aponaptrīya) with the statement: The waters are the sacrifice; in that they come to the waters, verily they come to the sacrifice. Moreover the waters are strength and sap...Moreover the waters are immortality...'The waters' is the first form of the thunderbolt; 'Sarasvatī' is the second form of the thunderbolt (RV 10.30.12); this is a hymn of 15 verses (RV 10.30), that is the third form of the thunderbolt. The gods with the thrice-forged thunderbolt pushed away the asuras from these worlds...The Mādhyamas (the mādhyama ṛṣis are listed in Āśvalāyana Gr.S.3.4) performed a session on the Sarasvatī. Then Kavaṣa sat down in the midst, they said to him,'Thou art the son of a female slave; we will not eat with you'. He rushing on in anger praised the Sarasvatī with this hymn; she followed after him; thereupon they felt themselves free from passion; they went after him and said 'O seer, homage be to thee; harm us not; thou art of us the best, seeing that she follows after thee.' Thus they informed him; they removed his anger. This is the greatness of Kavaṣa and the founder of the hymn (is he). In that they go with their wives (it is because)_ the Gandharvas as commissioners (prayāhitāh) in the waters guard the Soma of Indra...He recites twenty (verses); they make up the Virāj; the waters are connected with the Virāj, the Virāj is food, the waters are food... So much for the Aponaptrīya.

The rasa of the Soma is emphasized (RV. 8,3,20; 9,67,8; 15; 9,76,1 describes the rasa as kṛtvya or efficacious, as dakṣa or ability. Somya rasa (RV. 9,67,8) is the 'sap, which constitutes the essence, best, beneficial element of Soma'. The colour of the rasa is hari (yellow, tawny)(RV. 9,19,3; 9,25,1; 9,103,4; 9,78,2; 10,96,6 and7.) RV. 8,29,1 refers to Soma as babhru (reddish-brown) and a youth who is applying a golden ointment (añji... hiraṇyayam) to himself. RV. 9,107,4 refers to Soma as utsah hiraṇyayah: a spring of gold.[83] RV.9,86,43: *sindhor ucchvāse patayantam ukṣaṇam hiraṇyapāvāh paśum āsugṛbhṇate*: "purifiers of gold seize in them (i.e. the vasatīvarī water left standing overnight) the animal (paśū), i.e. the bull (Soma) that flies in the upheaving of the river." Thus in this hymn, the gold which is purified refers to the rasa 'juice' of Soma which is golden.

Atharva veda (AV.IX.6) can be interpreted as providing the clearest statement on the smelting process of the Soma yajña which is echoed in later-day alchemical texts:"...the shed for housing the Soma cars...green sticks that surround the sacrificial altars (as a fence to restrict the range of fire)...The grains of rice and barley that are selected are just filaments of the Soma plant. The pestle and mortar are really thestones of the Soma press. The winnowing-basket is the filter, the chaff the Somadregs, the water the pressing-gear. Spoon, ladle, fork, stirring prong are the wooden Soma tubs; the earthen cooking pots are the mortar-shaped Soma vessels; this earth is just the black-antelope's skin...The man who supplies food hath alwayspressing stones adjusted, a wet Soma filter, well-prepared religious rites...he who hath this knowledge wins the luminous spheres."

asem, asemon (Egyptian), 'electrum'

Electrum is a naturally occurring alloy of gold and silver, with trace amounts of copper and other metals (which are referred to as quartz or pyrites). Electrum is mentioned in an expedition sent by Pharaoh Sahure (2487 to 2477 BCE) of the Fifth dynasty of Egypt.

Electrum is a natural alloy of gold with at least 20 percent silver and contains also copper, iron, palladium, bismuth and perhaps other metals. 'The colour varies from white-gold to brassy, depending on the percentages of the major constituents and copper.'[84]

Greek word ἤλεκτρον (elektron) mentioned in the Odyssey meaning a metallic substance consisting of gold alloyed with silver. The same word was also used for the substance amber, probably because of the pale yellow color of certain varieties, and it is from the electrostatic properties of amber that the modern English words "electron" and "electricity" derive. Electrum was often referred to as white gold in ancient times but could be more accurately described as "pale gold".

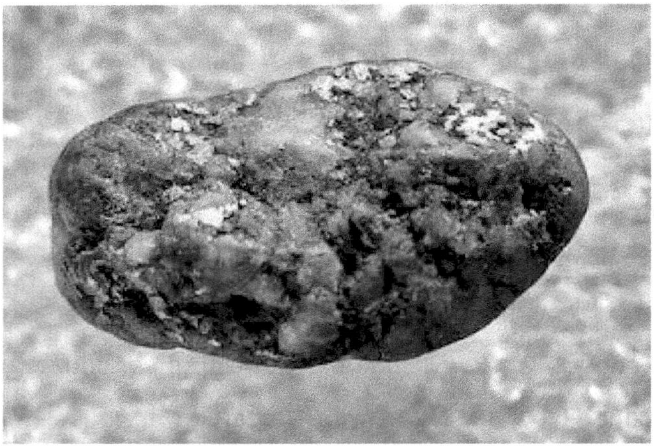

Manhattan, Manhattan District, Nye Co., Nevada, USA. 1.8 x 0.7 x 0.6 cm. Electrum is a rare natural amalgam of gold and silver (sometimes with trace amounts of copper and other minerals as well). This smooth, water-worn nugget is from Nevada. It weighs about 7.5 cts. Ex. Carl Davis Coll.Locality: Round Mountain Mine, Round Mountain District, Nye Co., Nevada, USA

A piece of crystalline aborescent electrum is exposed on a dense reddish electrum rich matrix.Specific locality details: High Grade Vein, Phase 5, 6005 Bench, Round Mountain Mine.Analysis shows the make up of the electrum to be 66.7% Gold, 33.3% Silver.

Variety of Gold containing Silver, usually with >20% Ag [85]

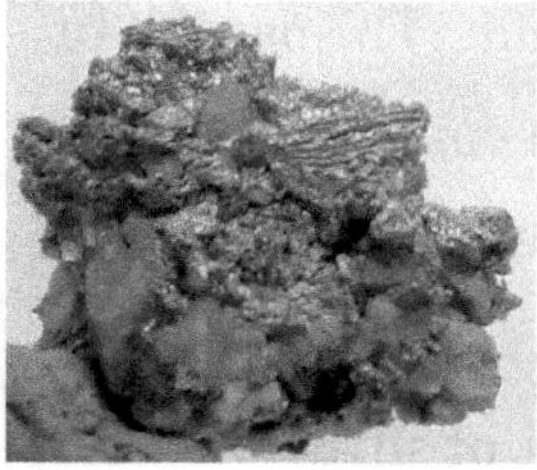

Provided by Thames Valley Minerals[86] - Locality: Round Mountain Mine, Round Mountain District, Nye Co., Nevada, USA A rich mass of finely defined octahedrally grown electrum over milky white crystalline quartz.Specific locality details: High Grade Vein, Phase 5, 6005 Bench, Round Mountain Mine.Analysis shows the make up of the electrum to be 66.7% Gold, 33.3% Silver.[87]
A Tamil lexicon of Winslow (1862) provides a philological trace: Soma maṇal, is interpreted as meaning veḷḷimaṇal, sand containing silver ore! Soma, Soma maṇal, asemon, asem, electrum may perhaps denote the same substance that dazzled and drew travellers of antiquity in search of indus gold. It may perhaps be the same substance [which required the purificatory 'mineral waters'] contained in the kamaṇḍalu symbols in the icons of the yakṣa legacy. It may perhaps be the same substance said to be amṛtam which was considered to be the elixir of life, of immortality. It may perhaps be the same substance referred to, in sheer poetry, as amritam āyur hiraṇyam. Gold is immortality.Soma! The very justification for the vedic hymns; the quintessence of the only technological process elaborated in magnificent poetry and philological excursus in the grand allegory, the Rigveda.[88]

Electrum was used as early as the third millennium BC in Old Kingdom Egypt. In the Babylonian Talmud (+2nd cent.), asemon is a commonly used word referring to bullion (gold, silver mixed). Leiden X papyrus (c. +3rd cent.) says: "no.8. It will be asem, (i.e. electrum, an alloy of gold and silver) which will deceive even the artisans (a tin-copper-gold-silver alloy); no. 1. Falsification of gold (a zinc-copper-lead-gold alloy)…"[89] . Hopkins states: "The existence of this alloy (asse*m) may have been the original cause for the suggestion of transmutation since by adding silver to it, one would get a metal nearly identical with the crude silver from the mine; and by adding gold, something indistinguishable from gold. [The paucity of the Egyptian language may perhaps have been responsible for a confusion. Gold was 'the yellow metal', and the alloy produced was also a 'yellow metal'.]"[90] Metals were not fully distinguished from their alloys; all carried names such as aes, electrum etc. Ayas meant metal. Asem denoted the natural alloy of silver and gold; it also meant any bright metal made with copper, tin, lead, zinc, arsenic and mercury. Twelve or thirteen different alloys were called asem…[91]

"At Gungeria, in districtBalaghat, 102 pieces of silver plates were discovered along with 424 copper implements. The silver was found to be admixed with 3.7% gold (...1100 B.C. -800 B.C.). The presence of 3.7% gold in these silver pieces indicates the extractionof silver from electrum..."[92]

The parallels with the Indian alchemical tradition are apparent: tankam gold in dravidian-Chinese becomes ṭankaṇa 'borax' (a reagent!) in indo-aryan, ṭanka 'gold coin'; the terms hiraṇyam, hema-bìjam, connote the yellow metal. The word, thong, means 'copper' in Thai language.

Egyptian Asem was Rigvedic soma.

Gold was the flesh of the sun god, [Petrie Museum of Egyptian Archaeology][93] by association it assured immortality. Ptah-Tatenen promised Ramses II happiness, wisdom, wealth and eternal power which was based on the strength of metals: "I have set thee as everlasting king, ruler established forever. I have wrought thy limbs of electrum, thy bones of copper, thy organs of iron."

The blessing of Ptah, Ramses II

James Henry Breasted, Ancient Records of Egypt, Part Three, § 403

Electrum was mostly imported from countries south of Egypt: Punt, Emu, the south countries :

Punt, 80,000 measures of myrrh, [6,000] ... of electrum, 2,600 [...] staves, [... ...]

King Sahure, Palermo Stone

James Henry Breasted, Ancient Records of Egypt, Part One, § 161

Every [statue] is overlaid on its body with electrum of Emu

Thutmose III, inscription of the speos of Artemidos

James Henry Breasted, Ancient Records of Egypt, Part Two, § 298

..... necklaces, amulets, and pendants of real electrum, brought to his majesty from the south countries as their yearly impost

Thutmose III

James Henry Breasted, Ancient Records of Egypt, Part Two, § 654

Electrum was worked and used similarly to gold: chariots, thrones and offering-tables were wrought with it, ceilings, roofs, columns and pyramidions covered with it, amulets, statues and jewellery fashioned from it.

Soma, locus is Mūjavant

Mujavat people are identified with the Gandharis. (Atharvaveda V-XXII-5, 7, 8, 14).

RV 10.34.1 states: *somasyeva maujavatasya bhakṣo vibhīdako jāgṛvir mahyam acchān* (an alerting eatable or food from mount Mūjavat). As draught of Maujavata soma, so doth, the enlivening vibhīdaka delight me.

Griswold[94] notes: 'The mountain Mūjavant (if it was a mountain and not simply the name of a people),being closely connected with the Gandhāris (AV. V.22,5,7,8,14)…

In the Tait. Samh. I. 8,6,2 and the AV. Passages referred to above the Mūjavants are taken as a type of distant folk, to which Rudra with his fever-bearing bow is entreated to depart. In fact Mūjavant is as far off and mysterious as the river rasā. Possibly both embody dim reminiscences of the undivided Indo-Iranian days." Macdonell[95] identifies association with Gandharva: "Gandharva is, moreover, in the RV often associated (chiefly in the ninth book) with Soma. He guards the place of Soma and protects the races of the gods (9.83.4; cp. 1.22.14). Observing all the forms of Soma, he stands on the vault of heaven (9.85.12). Together with Parjanya and the daughters of the sun, the Gandharvas cherish Soma (9.113.3). Through Gandharva's mouth the gods drink their drought (AV.7.73.3). The MS (3.8.10) states that the Gandharvas kept the Soma for the gods… It is probably as a jealous guardian of Soma that Gandharva in the RV appears as a hostile being, who is pierced by Indra in the regions of air (8.66.5) or whom Indra is invoked to overcome (8.1.11). … Soma is further said to have dwelt among the Gandharvas…" After reviewing many scholarly attempts at identification of soma, Frits Staal[96] notes: "We have seen in the ritual dialogue that the chief Nambudiri priest asks the Soma merchant: "Is it from Mount Mujavat?" and the merchant replies: "It is from Mount Mujavat." Mujavat is the name of the mountain from which, according to *Ṛgveda* 10.34.1 and other early sources, the best Soma came. Where was it located? All we know is that Mujavat is the name of a mountain. The -vat suffix is a common possessive and the name means: "having muja-" or perhaps: "inhabited by the Muja tribe." The element muja is not Indo-European. Michael Witzelconsidered several possible etymologies in 1980 (104-5 nn.16-7). According to one, muj- or its relative munj- may be preserved in the name of the Munjan people who live north of the Hindu Kush in the Kotcha Valley. There are also possible cognates in Burushaski, the language of Hunza. More recently, Witzel (1999: 345, 363) has suggested Muztagh Ata, a colossal mountain (24,386 ft.) close to the sources of the Oxus and Yarkand-Tarim Rivers. Tagh and ata are common Uighur words for "mountain" and "father" and the name means "Muz Mount Father." There are at least two other mountains carrying the name Muztagh and of which Muztagh Ata may be called the father because it is higher. The important point of Witzel's linguistic equation is that muz- is easily related to Vedic muj-. Mount Muztagh Ata, now on the border of Tajikistan and China's Xinjiang, is beyond the northeast frontier of northeast Afghanistan, the area through which Indo-Aryan speakers trekked...Tarim Basin. That basin has recently come into the news because of the discovery of numerous so-called mummies (really dessicated corpses), with tattooed skins and clothes surviving in excellent condition and often accompanied by little bags containing Ephedra...The newsworthy feature of these corpses is that their physical appearance and DNA analysis demonstrate that they belonged to people who have been called by various terms: European, Europoid, or Caucasian. Corpses found after the third century A.D. are increasingly Mongoloid and Chinese. It has been widely assumed that the language spoken by these mummies before they were mummies was Indo-European. If that is so, their language must have been Indo-Iranian or an early form of Tocharian--the easternmost Indo-European language family...It is true that the evidence for Tocharian is Buddhist and of a later date, but it is also true that it was spoken in the very same area of Xinjiang. All Tocharian documents have been discovered along the northern Silk Road. The Tarim mummies have been found along the northern and southern branches both, but in the north they are mostly concentrated near Lop Nor, far to the east and close to China proper. Along the southern branch, a series of finds leads close to the source of the Yarkand-Tarim River, the colossal mountain complex towered over by Muztagh Ata, favorite candidate for the best Soma...To sum up. The Tarim is the river of the mummies who probably spoke an Indo-European language, perhaps Indo-Iranian, Iranian, or Indo-Aryan. The Oxus is the river of the Indo-Iranian speakers who trekked south on the eastern side of the Caspian Sea. If Muztagh Ata is the same as Mujavat, Soma is the personification of the Indo-Aryan or Vedic contribution to the formation of Indian culture. No wonder that Soma developed into the most characteristic Vedic ritual, perhaps the oldest surviving ritual of humanity and certainly the most prolific. "

If Tocharian speakers were aware of the Mujavant mountain and if Soma came from this mountain, what did Tocharian's call Soma? Ancu ! 'iron'. This word 'ancu' is cognate with ams'u which is used in the Rgveda to describe Soma. Soma was a metallic ore, a compound of silver and gold called by metallurgists as: electrum. Thus, for Rgvedic kavi, description of soma in metaphoric terms comparing it to a plant should not be treated literally as a reference to a 'plant'. The reference could as well have been to a metallic ore subjected to refining process of smelting in fire which could raise upto 1500 degrees C in a yajña -- agniṣṭoma, for example -- which lasted continuously for 5 days and 5 nights.

Tushāra, Tocharian

It is likely that Mujavat were Tushara.Tushara, Tocharians were mleccha (meluhha) speakers. Mujavat are a people mentioned in *Ṛgveda*. Mujavant was the source of soma. Mujavat is Muztagh Ata Himalayan mountain range in Kyrgystan. Mujavat spoke Tocharian a satem branch of Indo-European.
தூசர்[1] tūcar , n. < தூசு[3]. Troops; படைஞர். இந்திரன் முதலோர் தூசர் (குற்றா. தல. தக்கன் வேள்விச். 125).(Tamil)

तुष -ग्रहः, -सारः fire. [túṣa m. ' chaff of grain ' AV. 2. *thuṣa -- . 3. *dhuṣa -- . [Variation t ~ th ~ dh suggests non -- Aryan origin: cf. also MIA. bhusa -- ~ busa -- 1](CDIAL 5892)]

ʦitra-thŏsi । हिममहाबिन्दवः m.pl. large lumps of snow or hail falling (like those that usually fall in this month). -wôñu -वोञु&below; । चैत्रजलम् m. the snow-water that comes down in the mountain torrents in this month (looked upon as very pure, cool and, owing to its origin among the mountain plant wholesome). (Kashmiri)

తుషారము [tuṣāramu] tushāramu. [Skt.] n. Dew, snow, mist. మంచు. Small drops, a sprinkling. తుంపర. adj. Cool. చల్లని. (Telugu)तुषार [tuṣāra] m (S) Thin rain, mizzle, drizzle: also spray. 2 Dew.(Marathi) The Vayu Purana (47, 44) and the Matsya Purana, (121, 45) mention that:

सान्ध्रान् स्तुखारान् लम्पकान् पह्लवान् दरदान् छकान्

अताञ्जनापदाञ्चक्षु प्लावयन्ती गतोदधिम्

तुषार tuṣāra a. [तुष्-आरन् किञ्च Uṇ.3.139.] Cold; frigid, frosty or dewy; अपां हि तृप्ताय न वारिधारा स्वादुः सुगन्धिः स्वदते तुषारा N.3.93; Śi.9.7. -रः 1 Frost, cold; तुषार- वृष्टिक्षतपद्मसम्पदाम् Ku.5.27. -2 Ice, snow; पदं तुषारस्रुति- धौतरक्तम् Ku.1.6; प्रपतत्तुषारो हेमन्तकालः Ṛs.4.1. -3 Dew; R.14.84; Ś.5.19. -4 Mist, thin rain, spray, espe- cially of cold water; पृक्तस्तुषारैर्गिरिनिर्झराणाम् R.2.13;9.68; U.5.3. -5 A kind of camphor. -6 A kind of horse; ताजिताः खुरशालाश्च तुषाराश्चोत्तमा हयाः Aśvachikitsā. -Comp. -अद्रिः, -गिरिः, -पर्वतः the Himālaya mountain; ते तुषाराद्रिवाताः Me.19. -करः 1 the moon. -2 camphor. -कणः a dew-drop, an icicle, hoar-frost; इतरा तु जलापात- तुषारकणनश्वरी Ks.19.5. -कालः winter. -किरणः, रश्मिः the moon; Amaru.49; कलया तुषारकिरणस्य पुरः Śi.9.27. -गौर a. 1 white as snow. -2 white with snow. (-रः) camphor. (Apte lexicon) túṣāra m. sg. and pl. ' frost, snow, mist, dew, thin rain ' MBh., adj. ' cold ' Kālid.Pk. tusāra -- n. ' hoarfrost, snow '; Ku. tusyāro, tos ' frost ' (y?); N. tusāro ' snow, hoarfrost, dew '; B. tusār ' cold, dew, drizzle '; H. tusār ' cold ', m. ' cold, frost, snow, ice, hail, dew, mist, thin rain, blight, crop ripening in cold season ', tusārā, °rū ' cold, frosty '; M. tusār, °rā m. ' drizzle '; Si.

tusara ' dew, mist ', adj. ' cold '. -- K. tṻrun ' to freeze ' < *tuhār -- ?(CDIAL 5894)[97]

This further augments mleccha of Indian linguistic area since Tocharians (Tusharas) of Mujavant who supplied soma were mleccha speakers (MBh.)

शूद्राभीराद दरदाः काश्मीराः पशुभिः सह । खशिकाश च तुखाराश च पल्लवा गिरिगह्वराः

(VI.10.66)

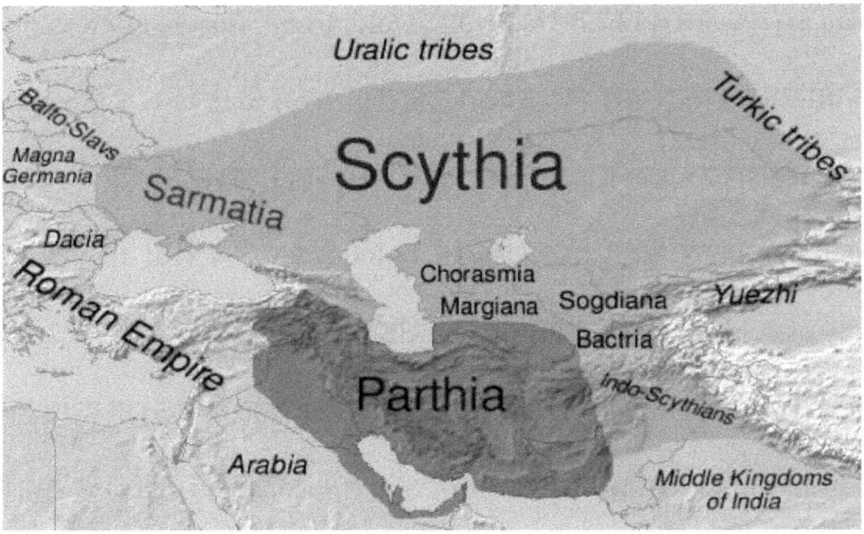

Saka.

Gold artifacts of the Saka in Bactria, at the site of Tillia tepe.Tilliaa Tepe is located in the Western portion of the region of ancient Bactria.
Valmiki Rāmāyaṇa includes Janapadas of Andhras, Pundras, Cholas, Pandyas, Keralas, Mekhalas, Utkalas, Dasharnas, Abravantis, Avantis, Vidarbhas, Mlecchas, Pulindas, Surasenas, Prasthalas, Bharatas, Kurus, Madrakas, Kambojas, Daradas, Yavanas, Sakas (from Saka-dvipa), Rishikas, Tukharas, Chinas, Maha-Chinas, Kiratas, Barbaras, Tanganas, Niharas, Pasupalas etc (Ramayana 4.43).

Rāmāyaṇa (I.54.17; I.55.2 seq), refers to people called the Sakas, Kambojas, Yavanas, Pahlavas, Kiratas, Haritas/Tukharas, Barbaras and Mlechchas who joined the army of sage Vasishtha during the battle of Kamdhenu against Aryan king Viswamitra of Kanauj.
References to groups of people in Mahābhārata

Sabha Parava of Mahābhārata enumerates numerous kings from the north-west paying gifts to Pandava king Yudhistra at the occasion of Rajasuya amongs whom it mentions the Kambojas, Vairamas, Paradas, Pulindas, Tungas, Kiratas, Pragjyotisha, Yavanas, Aushmikas, Nishadas, Romikas, Vrishnis, Harahunas, Chinas, Sakas, Sudras, Abhiras, Nipas, Valhikas, Tukharas, Kankas etc (Mahabharata 2.50.1.seq).

In the context of Krsna digvijaya, the Mahabharata furnishes a key list of twenty-five ancient Janapadas viz: Anga, Vanga, Kalinga, Magadha, Kasi, Kosala, Vatsa, Garga, Karusha, Pundra, Avanti, Dakshinatya, Parvartaka, Dasherka, Kashmira, Ursa, Pishacha, Mudgala, Kamboja, Vatadhana, Chola, Pandya, Trigarta, Malava, and Darada (MBH 7/11/15-17). Mahabharata (XIII, 33.20?23; XIII, 35, 17-18), lists the Sakas, Yavanas, Kambojas, Dravidas, Kalingas, Pulindas, Usinaras, Kolisarpas, Mekalas, Sudras, Mahishakas, Latas, Kiratas, Paundrakas, Daradas etc as the Vrishalas/degraded Kshatriyas.

Tushara kingdom is mentioned in the travels of Pandavas in the northern regions beyond the Himalayas:- Crossing the difficult Himalayan regions, and the countries of China, Tukhara, Darada and all the climes of Kulinda, rich in heaps of jewels, those warlike men reached the capital of Suvahu (3:176). The Udyogaparava of the Mahabharata (MBH 5/19/21-23) tells us that the composite army of the Kambojas, Yavanas and Sakas had participated in the Mahabharata war under the supreme command of Sudakshina Kamboja. The epic repeatedly applauds this composite army as being very fierce and wrathful. Some verses of Mahābhārata also attest that the Tusharas or Tukharas were also included in the Kamboja division (for example, MBH 6.66.17-21; MBH 8.88.17).

Then a hundred cars, a hundred elephants, and a number of Saka and Tukhara and Yavana horsemen, accompanied by some of the foremost combatants among the Kambojas, quickly rushed against Arjuna from desire of slaying him.

(Mbh.8.88.5410)

Mbh.12.64:- Here we have the following interesting passage mentioned as told by Vishnu in the form of Indra (!) to king Mandhatri:- What duties should be performed by the Yavanas, the Kiratas, the Gandharvas, the Chinas, the Savaras, the Barbaras, the Sakas, the Tusharas, the Kankas, the Pathavas, the Andhras, the Madrakas, the Paundras, the Pulindas, the Ramathas, the Kamvojas, the several castes that have sprung up from Brahmanas and Kshatriyas, the Vaisyas, and the Sudras, that reside in the dominions of Arya kings? What are those duties again to the observance of which kings like ourselves should force those tribes that subsist by robbery? I desire to hear all this.

O illustrious god, instruct me. O chief of all the deities, thou art the friend of us Kshatriyas' Indra said, All the robber tribes should serve their mothers and fathers, their preceptors and other seniors, and recluses living in the woods. All the robber tribes should also serve their kings. The duties and rites inculcated in the Vedas should also be followed by them. They should perform sacrifices in honour of the Pitris, dig wells, and dedicate them to universal service, give water to thirsty travellers, give away beds and make other seasonable presents unto Brahmanas.

Tusharas (alias Tukharas) were a Mlechcha people, with their kingdom located in the north west of India as per the epic Mahabharata. An account in Mahabharata

añcwāṣi (adj.) 'iron-'
L POU 'ferreus'.
F Nom.Sg.Masc. *añcwāṣi*, Obl.Sg.Masc. *añcwāṣiṃ*, Obl.Sg.Fem. *añcwāṣṣāṃ*, Nom.Pl.Masc. *añcwāṣiñi*, Nom.Pl.Fem. *añcwāṣṣāñ*, Obl.Pl.Fem. *añcwāṣṣās*.
T ◆Nom.Sg.Masc. 295 a1 *sälpmāṃ añcwāṣi lyalypu(r)y(eṣ)*; ◆Obl.Sg.Masc. 166 b4 *slam nāntsunt pälkont añcwāṣiṃ pat* , 225 b6; ◆Obl.Sg.Fem. 340 a7 *prutkoṣ riyaṃ añcwāṣṣāṃ* 'imprisoned in the iron city'; ◆Nom.Pl.Masc. 204 a1, YQ N.3 a4; ◆Nom.Pl.Fem. 295 a3 *sälpmāṃ añcwāṣṣāñ päñ-känt śolymeñ*, YQ N.3 a7!; ◆Obl.Pl.Fem. THT 3369 b1; ◆fgm. THT1583.2 a1 *añcwāṣi///*.
D Derived from *añcu** 'iron' [B *eñcuwo*].

(Mbh 1:85) depicts Mlechchas as the decendands of Anu, one of the cursed sons of king Yayati. Yayati's eldest son Yadu, gave rise to the Yadavas and youngest son Puru to the Pauravas that includes the Kurus and Panchalas. Only the fifth son Puru's line was considered to be the successors of Yayati's throne, as he cursed the other four sons and denied them kingship. Pauravas inherited the Yayati's original empire and stayed in the Gangatic plain who later created the Kuru and Panchala Kingdoms. They were the followers of proper Vedic culture. Yadavas made central and western India their stronghold. The descnedands of Anu, also called Anavas migrated to Iran, of which the Tusharas settled in Turkmenistan, Turkistan (in Afghanistan) and Turkey. The Tushara country mentioned in the epic could be Turkmenistan, a Central Asian Republic or the Turkistan of Afghanistan.
Tocharian thesaurus entries.

Pinault[98] discusses, in a brilliant linguistic excursus: "*ancu- is admitted by Lubotsky (2001: 304, 310) as meaning 'Soma plant', being the substratum source of Ved. ams'u- 'Soma plant' and Late Av. asu- 'Haoma plant'...This claim presupposes that the Soma/Haoma cult had been borrowed from the BMAC culture together with the name of the plant...A very useful discussion of the whole problem, with abundant bibliography, has been provided by Houben (2003), in his report of the conference held at Leiden University in July 1999..." (ibid., p.184)

"...The contrast between Soma as god and ams'u- as material unit is clear from the following mantra (TS 1.2.11a, etc. quoted in SB 3.4.3.19) *amśur-amśus te deva somāpyāatām indrāyaikadhanavide* 'Let stalk after stalk of thine swell strong, O divine Soma, for Indra, the winner of one part of the booty!'. It is true that in Vedic literature *amśu-* refers only to the twigs of the Soma plant and not of any other plant, but it is only to be expected, given the prestige of the hymns, where the word was used in hieratic language for the whole Soma plant: in this poetic usage, it can be explained by a commonplace metonymy, and by the pressure to give many names to Soma. Therefore, I shall assume that **ancu-* originally referred to the 'twig' or 'stalk', as a special term given to the 'body' of the holy plant, which was the most important part for ritual purposes. There exists in Tocharian no word of similar form referring to a plant or part of a plant. From the Tocharian vocabularies,we have Toch. A. **ancu* 'iron', the basis of the derived adjective *ancwaashi* 'made of iron', to which corresponds Toch. B *encuwo*, with the parallel derived adjective encuwanne 'made of iron'...The two forms go back to CToch. *oencuwoen-* non.sg. **oencuwo*, the final part of which is a regular product of IE *-on. Nasal enlargement (from: IE *-on-) of nominal stems is very common in Tocharian. This noun is deprived of any convincing IE etymology (cf. Adams 1999:80), which is not surprising, since IE did not have a common word for 'iron'. The connection with an Iranian form *as'wanya- according to Bailey (1957: 55-56), which does not fit in with the first cluster, was later abandoned (Bailey, Harold W., 1979, Dictionary of Khotan Saka. Cambridge: Cambridge University Press, pp. 32,

487). The CToch. form may reflect a term proper to the Central Asiatic region, cf. Chorasmian hnc'w 'iron' ('iron tip', see Benzing 1983: 319) < Iranian *anśuwan- Schwartz[99]: the formal shape is extremely close to the CToch. transposition, so that the Iranian and Tocharian words may have been borrowed from a common substratum language. The problem now becomes: if the original meaning of *ancu had been 'sacred plant', or the like, it would become impossible to explain the meaning of the CToch. loan-word. A simple solution to this dilemma is near at hand. Metals are not named from designations of plants, but they are often named after the colour, see for instance Ved. hiraNya- and suvarNa- 'gold', rajata- 'silver', lohita- or loha- 'copper', etc.[100] A secondary differentiation (from AV onwards) was also provided by colour adjectives, cf. lohitam ayah 'reddish metal' (for 'copper') vs. s'yaamam ayah 'dark metal' (for 'iron'). The primitive system opposed Ved. ayas- (Av. aiiah-) 'metal of utility' to hiraNya- 'noble metal': the former term originally referred to 'copper', later to 'iron'. I recall that the prominent colour of iron ore is rusty red, reddish-brown. Besides Toch. B eñcuwo (A *añcu), we know several names of metals in Tocharian: B yasa (A was) 'gold', B ñakante (A nkiñc) 'silver', B pilke 'copper', B lant* (adj. lantaṣṣe) 'lead'. Interestingly enough, the name of copper is obviously derived from the root palk- 'to shine': it originally meant 'shining like fire, gleaming', as corresponding to loha-, lohita-, which referred to copper for its red colour. It would be likely that the name of iron be derived from another colour, that is 'rusty (brown)'. Compare the designations of the colours in Tocharian: B ratre A rtar 'red', B tute 'yellow', AB tsem 'blue', B motartstse 'green', B erkent- A arkant- 'black', B kwele 'grey'. Going back to Vedic, we may assume that the borrowed word *ancu- referred to the characteristic colour of the twig or stalk of the sacred plant. The soma plant is qualified and also designated by various colour adjectives: hari-, aruṣa-, aruṇa-, babhru-. The terms hari- (cf. Av. zairi-) 'yellow, fawn' to 'green'...(p.187) "...It is all the more interesting to find an isolated reference to foreign (non-Aryan) people who also practise the Soma cult, while using amśu-: RV VIII.53.4c (Vālakhilya hymn) śiṣṭeṣu cit te madirāso amśavah 'Among the ś. also the exciting (Soma) plants belong to you (Indra)'. The form śiṣṭa- with variants śīṣṭra-, śīrṣṭra- testifies to a non-Aryan name with 'intrusive -r-' (Kuiper 1991: 7,70). It would be one of the last echoes of the widespread practice of the cult of the sacred plant in Central Asia. To summarize my present contribution to the Soma/Haoma problem, I should like to point out the most important provisory results: (i) The term Ved. amśu-, Av. asu- goes back to a noun borrowed from some donor language of Central Asia, as confirmed by CToch. *oeñcuwoen-. (ii) Since the original meaning referred to the colour of the marrow, that is the internal part of the twigs of the plant, one may wonder whether the designation of the heart of the plant as 'the rusty red one' had already been coined by the ritualists of the donor language, or whether this denomination was conceived by the speakers of Indo-Iranian, in order to possess a supplementary secret term to designate this holy substance. The last interpretation is admittedly tentative, because it concerns one of the most discussed issues of Indo-Iranian studies, and it will certainly be refined and tested according to other parameters. I should point out that this example is not fundamentally different from others which have been discussed previously. Once it is admitted that Ved. amśu-, Av. asu- are of foreign origin, it is legitimate to look for the most similar form in other languages of Central Asia. Since one finds a corresponding noun of very close, almost identical, formal shape, but with a very different meaning, referring to 'iron', there are two possible strategies..."(p.189).

"...we have Toch. A. *ancu 'iron', the basis of the derived adjective ancwaashi 'made of iron', to which corresponds Toch. B encuwo, with the parallel derived adjective encuwanne 'made of iron'...The two forms go back to CToch. oencuwoen- non.sg. *oencuwo, the final part of which is a regular product of IE *-on...This noun is deprived of any convincing IE etymology...The term Ved. *ams'u-*, Av . *asu-* goes back to a noun borrowed from some donor language of Central Asia, as confirmed by CToch. **oencuwoen-*...the BMAC language would not belong to the Indo-European family; it does not seem to be related to Dravidian either...New identifications and reconstructions will certainly help to define more precisely the contours of the BMAC vocabulary in Indo-Iranian, as well as in Tocharian."(ibid., p.192)]."

Noting that Pinault underscores the provisory nature of the explanation, the following alternative explanation may be offered for the lexical isogloss: Tocharian adjective *ancwaashi* 'made of iron', can also be explained as a reduplication of ancu 'metal', that is *ancu + was* 'metal, iron' (Proto-Ugric). *Ancwaashi* is consistent with semantics: 'mineral-metal', if *-waashi* in *ancwaashi* (Tocharian) is cognate with: áyas n. ' metal, iron ' ayil iron (Tamil). ayir, ayiram any ore (Malayalam). aduru native metal (Kannada) ajirda karba very hard iron (Tulu) (DEDR 192) RV.

Pa. *ayō* nom. sg. n. and m., *aya* -- n. ' iron ', Pk. *aya* -- n., Si. *ya.*(CDIAL 590). The exact metal denoted by ayas is uncertain. Agni is called ayodamṣṭra, 'with teeth of Ayas,' (RV 1.88.5, 10.87.2); Agni is called ayodamṣṭra, 'with teeth of Ayas,' (RV 1.88.5, 10.87.2). In the Vājasneyi Samhitā (18.13), Ayas is enumerated in a list of six metals: gold (hiraṇya), Ayas, śyāma, loha, lead (sīsa), tin (trapu). Here śyāma ('swarthy') and loha ('red') must mean 'iron' and 'copper' respectively; ayas would therefore seem to mean 'bronze'. In many passages in the Atharvaveda (11.3.1.7 and Maitrāyaṇi Samhitā) and other books, the Ayas is divided into two species – the syāma ('iron') and the lohita ('copper' or 'bronze'). In the śatapatha brāhmaṇa (5.4.1.2), a distinction is drawn between Ayas and lohayāsa, which may either be a distinction between iron and copper as understood by Eggeling (Sacred Books of the East, 41, 90), or between copper and bronze as held by Schrader (Prehistoric Antiquities, 189). In one passage of the Atharvaveda (5.28.1), the sense of iron seems certain. Possibly, too, the arrow of the Rigveda (6.75.15), which had a tip of Ayas (yasyā ayo mukham), was pointed with iron. Copper, however, is conceivable, and bronze quite likely. Iron is called śyāma ayas or śyāma alone (AV 9.5.4). See also kārṣṇāyasa. Copper is lohāyasa or lohitāyasa. A heater of Ayas is mentioned in the Vājasneyi Samhitā (30.14; Taittirīya brāhmaṇa 3.4.10.1) and bowls of Ayas are also spoken of (7.10.22; Maitrāyaṇi Samhitā 4.2.13). Lat. aes copper, bronze; aurichalcum brthe; Rumanian. arama copper.aios- (Pokorny entry), IE aisk- 'ore, metal (copper, bronze, iron).'(Pokorny Master PIE etyma). *was* 'metal, iron' (Proto-Ugric). Hieroglyphs/homonyms: ayo, aya 'fish' (G.Mu.)

There are two words in Indian linguistic area which connote economics as a separate department or subject: artha, kāṇḍa ayo 'fish' (Mu.) + kaṇḍa 'arrow' (Skt.) ayaskāṇḍa 'a quantity of iron, excellent iron' (Pāṇ.gaṇ) The semantics have been explained; it is likely that the phrase connoted metal of stone ore. aya = iron (G.);

ayah, ayas = metal (Skt.) khũṭ Brahmani bull (Kathiawar G.); khũṭro entire bull used for

agriculture, not for breeding (G.)(CDIAL 3899). Rebus: khũṭ a community, sect, society, division, clique, schism, stock (Santali). Decoded rebus: khũṭ 'community' (perhaps, a guild). khũṭro = entire bull; khũṭ= brāhman.i bull (G.) khuṇṭiyo = an uncastrated bull (Kathiawad. G.lex.) khũ̃ṭaḍum a bullock (used in Jhālwāḍ)(G.) kuṇṭai = bull (Ta.lex.) cf. khũ̃dhi hump on the back; khuī̃dhũ hump-backed (G.)(CDIAL 3902).

The inscriptions on seals m1118 and K032 (with zebu or bos Taurus indicus pictorial motif) have been decoded: aḍar ḍhangar khuṭ 'native-metal-blacksmith community (guild)(making) excellent metal'. kuṭi, 'smelting furnace' (Mundari.lex.).kuṭhi, kuṭi (Or.; Sad. koṭhi) (1) the smelting furnace of the blacksmith; kuṭire bica duljaḍko talkena, they were feeding the furnace with ore; (2) the name of ēkuṭi has been given to the fire which, in lac factories, warms the water bath for softening the lac so that it can be spread into sheets; to make a smelting furnace; kut.hi-o of a smelting furnace, to be made; the smelting furnace of the blacksmith is made of mud, cone-shaped, 2' 6" dia. At the base and 1' 6" at the top. The hole in the center, into which the mixture of charcoal and iron ore is poured, is about 6" to 7" in dia. At the base it has two holes, a smaller one into which the nozzle of the bellow is inserted, as seen in fig. 1, and a larger one on the opposite side through which the molten iron flows out into a cavity (Mundari.lex.)

Following Benno Landsberger, it is agreed that there are words from the fields of agriculture, artisanry, etc. which are from a language or languages used in the upper Mesopotmian area before the arrival of Sumerians. Examples often cited are: engar > ikkaru 'farmer'; apin 'plough'; absin 'furrow'; agab 'leather worker'; nangar > naggaru 'carpenter'; damgar > danger> taggaru 'merchant-agent'; simug 'smith (metal-sculptor)'; ibira, tibira 'coppersmith'; sanga 'priest'.

Many conflict motifs depicted on early Sumerian cylinder seals and artifacts may relate to the gloss: tamhāru damhara [BATTLE] wr. dam-ha-ra "battle"

Akk. *tamhāru* because the word is phonetically close to *tamkāru* 'merchant'. The Sumerian gloss is: damgar [MERCHANT] wr. dam-gar_3 "merchant, trader". As a substrate word, the likely cognate glosses occur in Indian *sprachbund* with the semantics not of a 'merchant' but of a blacksmith as evidenced by the following etyma from Indian *sprachbund.*

Salonen associates the term tamkāru with the earliest stratum of professional designations characterized by two syllables and ending in –ar, as in nagar (nangar), bahar, engar, kapar, arar and usbar (esbar). (Salonen, Armas, 1969, 'Die altesten Berufe und Erzeugnisse des Vorderen Orients,' in *Die Fussbekleidung der alten Mesopotamia* (=AASF 157), pp. 97-119, esp. p. 109). Substrate nouns in –ar (including dam-gar) date from what Salonen calls the late Neolithic or early Chalcolithic period (ca. 5500 to 5000 BCE).(Salonen 1969, esp. p. 118). A substrate origin for both Sumerian dam-gar and Akkadian tamkāru is also suggested by FR Kraus. (Kraus 1973, *Vom mesopotamischen Menschen…* (=MKNAWL n.r. 36/6): 111). תגרn.m. merchant (< Akk *tamkaru* Kaufman, Influences 107; CPA ܬܓܪ LSp 218, SA תגארHam 536:60+) sg. אזל גבי תגרא באתינס he went to a merchant in Athens *EchR* 48:18; pl. תג[ר]ין*FPT* Gen 37:28[04; H סחרים]; *TN* ib.; *FTV* ib. 25:3 [H אשורים]; *TN* ib.; *BR* 663:6 [w. ref. to Gen ib.][101] Insight of the late Benno Landsberger (*Undena Publications, Sources and Monographs*, vol. 1, fascicle 2 (1974), pp. 8-12) resulted in a recognition that many cultural words were neither Sumerian nor Semitic but were substrate. Such words included engar (farmer), apin (plow), apsin (furrow), nimbar (palm), tibir (metal worker), simug (smith), damkar (merchant).[102]

Sargon's trade was managed by private merchants called *damgar* in Sumer and Akkad and tamkārum (pl. tamkāru) in Babylonia and Assyria. This related to the early Bronze Age ca. 2250 BCE. During the 3rd millennium BCE, damgar were professional merchants as agents of temples and palaces. Tamkār sarri was a royal merchant responsible for the sale of commodities of the palace and for acquisition of goods for the royal household. (cf. L. Shiff, The Nur-Sin Archive: Private entrepreneurship in Babylon, 603-507 BCE, Ph.D. diss., University of Pennsylvania, 1987, p. 53-54.) Chief of merchants (LU rab Tamkārū of Nebuchadnezzar II was Hanunu (Hanno), of Phoenician origin.[103]

Inscribed seals of Tamkārū from Thebes in Boeotia provide evidence of international trade by Tamkārū. (E. Porada, The cylinder seals found at Thebes in Boeotia, in *AfO* 38 1981-82, pp. 1-70 (with contributions of HG Guterbock, pp. 71-72, and JA Brinkman, pp. 73-78). Tamkārū from Ugarit had also visited Crete. (HG Guterbock, Hittites and Akhaeans: A new look, in *PAPhS*, 128 (1984), pp. 114-122). A text RS 17.130, a rescript of Hattusilis III sent to Niqmepa notes: when the Tamkārū of Ura, a seaport of the Hittite kingdom, trade in Ugarit and Ugaritians are their debtors,the latter forfeit their immovables, houses and landed property to the king of Ugarit.[104]

ḍā̃gar 'horned cattle' (K.); rebus: *ḍāṅgar* 'blacksmith' (H.) 1. K. *ḍangur* m. 'bullock', L. *ḍaṅgur*, (Ju.) *ḏā̃gar* m. 'horned cattle'; P. *ḍaṅgar* m. 'cattle', Or. *ḍaṅgara*; Bi. *ḍā̃gar* 'old worn-out beast, dead cattle', *dhūr ḍā̃gar* 'cattle in general'; Bhoj. *ḍāṅgar* 'cattle'; H. *ḍā̃gar*, *ḍā̃grā* m. 'horned cattle'. 2. H. *dā̃gar* m. = prec.(CDIAL 5526).

The rollout of Shu-ilishu's cylinder seal.[105] Courtesy of the Département des Antiquités Orientales, Musée du Louvre, Paris.[106] This is a personal cylinder seal of the Meluhhan language. His name was Shu-ilishu who lived in Mesopotamia. Edith Porada noted that the seal's style was Late Akkadian (ca. 2200–2113 BC), possibly even from the succeeding Ur III period (ca. 2113–2004 BC).

'In a letter dated 16 May 1990, Dr. Dominique Collon comments on the iconography as follows: 'The seal depicts a seated figure, identifiable by her long hair as feminine and by her horned head-dress (chipped) as a deity. The flounced robe is also generally an indication of divinity. The child on her lap could be the owner of the seal but is more likely to be an attributor of the godess. The figures approaching the godess are probably the owner of the seal and his wife although it is possible that these are priestly figures. Several centuries later, in Old Babylonian times, it is the king who almost always carries the animal offering but he is probably seeking favourable omens and the deities he approaches are ther particularly connected with omens (see Collon 1986: III.37). On these later, Old Babylonian seals, the figure carrying a situla or bucket is generally a priest but here it is clearly a woman and there is nothing to indicate that she is a priestess of a queen. Both wear Akkadian dress and nothing distinguishes them as foreigners. The significance of the kneeling male figure and the pots behind is difficult to interpret: they could be an attribute of the godess, and the large pots on stands are used even today for water – perhaps an additional reference to the godess' fertility aspect. Among the seals illustrated by R.M. Boehmer (1965) seals 549 and 555 make clear that some sort of drink is involved. Boehmer's plate 47 shows that the scene belongs to a well-established iconographical group and was not specifically created for the Meluhha interpreter – indeed it was probably chosen from a range of ready-cut seals in a seal-cutter's workshop and the inscription was added. This would account for the fact that the figures overlap the inscription frame on both sides. Boehmer attributes the seal to Akkadisch III period – i.e. from Naramsin onwards." [cf. Parpola, 1994, fig. 8.4]

The merchant carrying the antelope may be a *damgar* 'merchant' from Meluhha., Inscription on the cylinder seal records that it belongs to 'Shu-ilishu, Meluhha interpreter', i.e., translator of the Meluhhan language (EME.BAL.ME.LUH.HA.KI) The Meluhhan being introduced carries an goat on his arm. The Meluhhan is accompanied by a lady carrying a kamaṇḍalu. Since he needed an interpreter, it is inferred that Meluhhan did not speak Akkadian.

Antelope carried by the Meluhhan is a hieroglyph: mlekh 'goat' (Br.); mṟeka (Te.); mēṭam (Ta.); meṣam (Skt.) Thus, the goat conveys the message that the carrier is a Meluhha speaker. A phonetic determinant.mrṟeka, mlekh 'goat'; Rebus: melukkha Br. mē<u>lh</u> 'goat'. Te. mṟeka (DEDR 5087) meluhha !

This use of lexemes from Indian *sprachbund*, to explain the rebus readings of hieroglyphs/ homonyms, clearly assumes the presence of artisans/traders who are speakers of Meluhha (cognate mleccha) in Susa/Sumer/Elam.

If mleccha of Rigvedic times were recognized as a group of people, the term which could be a synonym was: asura. The term asura is used in RV 1.108.6: *yad abravam prathamam vāmvṛṇāno ayam somo asurair no vihavyah* 'As I said when choosing you at first, you must fight the Asuras for this soma'. Śathapathabrāhmaṇa 3.2.1.23 ff. explain the nature of speech of the Asura. The Asura cry out during their fight *he'lavo, he'lavo*; this is the same as *he'rayah*, 'Oh, the enemies!'

"Ancient Indian grammarians refer to this as 'ralayor abhedah' (that is, dialectical variations between r and l sounds and noting the difficulty of keeping r and l apart). This is underscored by SS Misra: "The theory is that in earlier portions of the Rigveda Samhitā *r* prevails and gradually *l* prevails more and more in later languages, i.e. in ater Samhitā-s, Āraṇyaka, Upaniṣad, Classical Sanskrit and finally in MIA. But in fact distribution of *r* and *l* is universally dialectical. Some languages show a preference of *r* as the Old Iranian languages and some show a preference of *l* as Chinese. If historically *l* replaced *r* in Indo-Aryan then in New Indo-Aryan languages all should show preference of *r* and others show preference of *l,* which is not the fact. Some show preference of *r* and others show preference of *l.* If we take one IE standard for distribution of *r* and *l*, we find confusion of distribution of *r* and *l* to some extent even in the languages, where it is considered to present the original distribution. Therefore, the Sanskrit Grammarians have accepted '*ralayor abhedah*'. In all other aspects Sanskrit shows archaism and therefore, IE reconstruction is based on Sanskrit mainly. The linguistic changes found in India in the Middle Indo-Aryan stage are found amply, in Greek, Iranian and Hittite which are stamped as very old historical languages of IE."[107]

This means that Asura spoke a dialect of Vedic within Proto-Indian. [hallā 'tumult, noise (P.Ku.N.B.Or.H.); halphal 'shaking, undulation' (CDIAL 14017).] helao 'to move, drive in' (Santali). eraka (adj.) [fr. ereti] driving away, moving J iv.20 (Pali).

Ēla ఏల, ఏలపాట ఏలపదము [ēlapadamu] is a carol or catch used by rowers of boats శృంగారపు పాట. (Telugu) Ēlēlo 'a word which occurs often in the song sung by boatman, the song is called Ēlappāṭṭu (Tamil). The Asura who shout 'helavo, helavo' were sea-farers using tossing boats; they were mleccha. S.C. Roy (The Asuras – ancient and modern, Journal of the Bihar and Orissa Research Society, 12, 1926, 147) notes a Munda tradition that India was previously occupied by a metal-using people called Asuras. The asuric or creative capabilities of the people leads to a description of the River Sarasvati as āsurī Sarasvati.

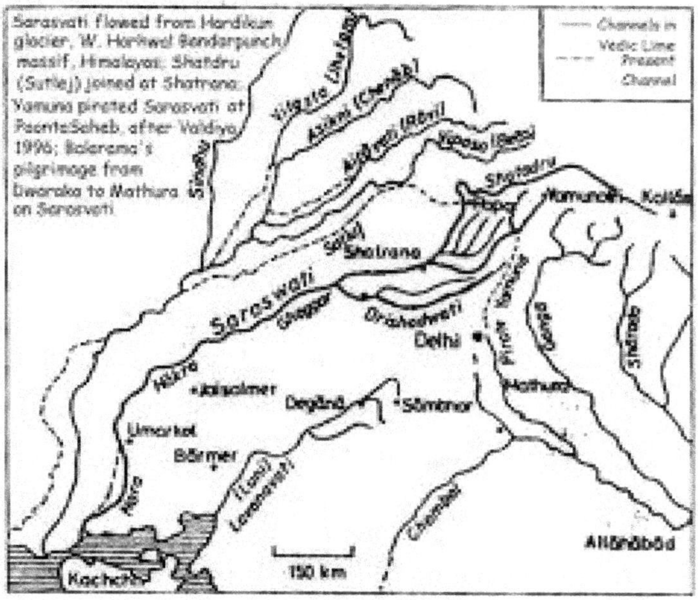

A Pali glosss helps relate the lexeme Proto-Indian ēla- as the locus of sea-farers, to the lexeme: ela (nt.) [?] salt(?) or water(?) in elambiya (= el°ambu -- ja) born in (salt) water Sn 845 (= ela -- saññaka ambumhi jāta); Nd1 202 (elaŋ vuccati udakaŋ)(Pali).

Sarasvati people resided in Sarasvati river basin. Map after KS Valdiya[108].

The acculturation of Meluhhans (probably, the sea-faring Indus-Sarasvati people) residing in Mesopotamia in the late third and early second millennium BC, is noted by their adoption of Sumerian names.[109] "The adaptation of Harappan motifs and script to the Dilmun seal form may be a further indication of the acculturative phenomenon, one indicated in Mesopotamia by the adaptation of Harappan traits to the cylinder seal."[110]

Antelopes, bulls, lions, eagles (wings) are examples of hieroglyphs/homonyms deployed in the interaction area of Ancient Near East and a region of language-speakers who created/used Indus script corpora, now evidenced by about 6000 inscriptions, in the process of trade in Bronze Age products of artisan guilds. Some of these hieroglyphs are read rebus. Ancient texts which include the script corpora provide valuable clues to the languages of the region and advances in metallurgy during the Bronze Age. Further researches on the 1) evolution of technologies and identification of mines and sources of minerals and 2) formation and evolution of languages in Indian *sprachbund*, will advance the studies related to a civilization with the largest expanse of its times in Eurasia from Haifa (Israel) to Daimabad (India) described in biblical terms as *harosheth hagoyim*, 'smithy of nations'.

In the context of the bronze age, the comments of James D. Muhly are apposite to further evaluate the role played by Indus artisans (and the possible diffusion of Indus script glyphs) in the interaction areas of Eurasia, in general and of Elam (BMAC), Persian gulf region, and Mesopotamia, in particular: "The Early Bronze Age of the 3rd millennium BCE saw the first development of a truly international age of metallurgy... The question is, of course, why all this took place in the 3rd millennium BCE... It seems to me that any attempt to explain why things suddenly took off about 3000 BCE has to explain the most important development, the birth of the art of writing... As for the concept of a Bronze Age one of the most significant events in the 3rd millennium was the development of true tin-bronze alongside an arsenical alloy of copper..."[111]

Muhly notes:"A long-distance tin trade is not only feasible and possible, it was an absolute necessity. Sources of tin stone or cassiterite were few and far between, and a common source must have served many widely scattered matallurgical centers. This means that the tin would have been brought to a metallurgical center utilizing a nearby source of copper. That is, copper is likely to be a local product; the tin was almost always an import...The ingots are made of a very pure tin, but what could they have to do with Cyprus? There is certainly no tin on Cyprus, so at best the ingots could have been transhipped from that island... What the ingots do demonstrate is that metallic tin was in use during the Late Bronze Age...rather extensive use of metallic tin in the ancient eastern Mediterranean, which will probably come as a surprise to many people." (p.47)

Tin from Meluhha: Proto-Indian *harosheth hagoyim* 'smithy of nations'

Import of “tin from Meluhha” is known from a Sumerian text from the reign of Gudea of Lagash (c. 2150-2111 B.C.E.) A cylinder seal of Gudea of Lagash (2143-2124 BCE) -- Cylinder B: XIV -- read: "copper, tin, blocks of lapiz lazuli and ku ne (meaning unknown), bright carnelian from the land of Meluhha."[112]

"...tin may well often have travelled by sea up the Gulf from distribution centres in the Indus Valley. In the Old Babylonian period tin was shipped through Dilmun... It is now known that Afghanistan has two zones of tin mineralization. One embraces much of eastern Afghanistan from south of Kandahar to Badakshan in the north-east corner of the country... the other lies to the west and extends from Seistan north towards Herat , the valley of the Sarkar river, where the hills are granitic. Here tin appears commonly as cassiterite, frequently associated with copper, gold, and lead, and in quantities sufficient to attract attention in antiquity... A number of scholars have pointed out the possibility that tin arrived with gold and lapis lazuli in Sumer through the same trade network, linking Afghanistan with the head of the Gulf, both by land and sea."[113]

Cuneiform texts from Mari on the Euphrates record the storage of 500 kilograms of tin, and shipment to cities such as Ugarit on the Syrian coast, to Dan and Hazor in Palestine, and even to Captara, i.e. Crete.[114]

"The Bronze Age exploitation of the Omani copper deposits seems to have coincided with what are most likely two related phenomena: (1) references in Mesopotamian texts to copper from Magan and to obtaining that copper either directly from Magan or through the intermediate agency of Dilmun (the island of Bahrain)-- the copper did not come FROM Dilmun but THROUGH Dilmun; and (2) the period of the Mature Harappan phase of the Indus Valley Civilization.

"This second correlation suggests that contact and trade with Mesopotamia were factors contributing to the development of the Indus Valley civilization, established in an area known to the Sumerians as the land of Melukkha. So close was the relationship that the traders of Dilmun used the same system of weights and measures as that found in the Indus Valley. From the figures given in Sumerian texts it would appear that the Dilmun shekel was about three times heavier than the standard Sumerian one. It has been thought by some scholars that transactions at Ebla (modern Tell Mardikh) were also conducted on the basis of the Dilmun shekel, but this reading of the sign in question in the Ebla texts cannot be substantiated, and all theories regarding references to Dilmun at Ebla remain conjectural...

Tin and the Development of Bronze Metallurgy. Early Use of Bronze.

The most important metallurgical development during the Early Bronze Age was the discovery that adding tin to copper produced a far superior metal, eventually known as bronze. In its classic form, bronze has 10 percent tin and 90 percent copper. The addition of even 2 percent tin has noticeable effects upon the hardness and working properties of copper, but anything over 16 percent tin is undesirable, for a very high tin content makes copper brittle and difficult to work. Objects such as the ax head from the A cemetery at Kish (modern Tell al-Uhaimir; Early Dynastic, or ED, IIIB), with 15.5 percent tin, are probably to be assessed as being of early, experimental alloys.

"The historical development of bronze metallurgy has been difficult to document, and locating ancient sources of tin has proved to be an even more intractable problem...the cache of human figurines from Tell Judeidah (northern Syria), the excavators' date of about 3000 (transition Amuq G-H) still seems the most probable...A pin from Tepe Gawra VIII (early third millennium) siad to have 5.6 percent tin unfortunately can no longer be located, but four artifacts from the Y cemetary at Kish, of ED I date, proved to have more than 2 percent tin. These are the earliest examples of bronze from Mesopotamia. One of these objects, a spouted jar, has 6.24 percent tin..."Sources of Tin and the Tin Trade...The tin was brought to Asshur from some point further east, most likely Afghanistan. The Assyrian merchants purchased the tin for reshipment, by donkey caravan, and sale (at a 100 percent markup) in Anatloia...The Old Assyrian tin trade was on a large scale and enriched three generations of Old Assyrian merchant families...

"Tin exists in nature in the form of cassiterite, an oxide of tin. The cassiterite most likely utilized by Bronze Age metal workers was alluvial or placer cassiterite, popularly known as tin-stone and present as nuggets or pebbles in the beds of streams...Alluvial cassiterite was collected by panning the bed of a stream, much like the recovery of alluvial gold...Gold and tin often occur within the same general area as, for example, in the Eastern (Arabian) Desert of Egypt. Ancient Sardis, the region of the Tmolus (modern Boz Dag) mountain range and the Pactolus River, was famous as an ancient source of alluvial gold, the source of wealth for Croesus, king of Lydia, but no placer cassiterite has been documented from Anatolia...
"Mari and the Tin Trade...the texts from Mari (Tell Hariri), dating mainly to the first half ot the eighteenth century BCE...(tin) came to Mari through Elam, from Susa and Anshan (now identified with the Central Iranian site of Tepe Malyan), and Elamites played a major role in the trade, especially a man named Kuyaya. Certain merchants from Mari were also heavily involved in the tin trade with Elam, among them a merchant named Ishkhi-Dagan (the two appear together in ARM 23 555). The tin came to Mari in the form of ingots (Akkadian lē'u) that weighed about ten pounds each. It is possible to obtain some idea of the relative value of this tin, for a number of the Mari texts provide a tin:silver ratio of 10:1 (the most common ratio; a few texts give ratios from 8:1 to 15:1). This is to be compared with isolated referenced to a tin:gold ratio (48:1), a confusing silver:gold ratio of 4:1 as well as 2:1, and a lead:silver ratio (1200:1). The usual copper:silver ratio at Mari was 180:1 for unrefined 'mountain' copper, with refined (litarally 'washed') copper being valued at 150:1. This means that tin was usually from fifteen to eighteen times more valuable than copper...In later texts from Nuzi (fifteenth century BCE) goods were priced in amounts of tin. An ox cost thirty-six minas of tin; an ass, twenty-four minas. During the Middle Assyrian period tin seems to have functioned as the monetary standard (temporarily replacing the customary silver). Plots of land were purchased with tin...

"The cuneiform archives contain a number of 'recipe' texts, giving the amounts of coper and tin used to make specified amounts of bronze. One of the earlist such texts, from Palace G at Ebla, records that 3 minas, 20 shekels of tin were alloyed with 30 minas of copper to produce 200 objects of bronze, each weighing 10 shekels. In other words, 200 shekels of tin were mixed with 1,800 shekels of copper to produce 2,000 shekels of a 10 percent tin-bronze. In one Mari text 20 shekels of tin were added to 170 shekels of refined copper from Teima at the rate of 1:8, to produce 190 shekels of bronze for a key (to the lock of a city gate)...This means that smiths at Mari were working with the metals themselves--with copper and tin--not with ores or minerals. That is no smelting was being carried out in the vicinity of the Mari palace...

"At the other end of the Mari trade network, the texts record that tin stored at Mari was transhipped to various cities in the Levant, from Karkamish in the north to Hazor in the south. This we learn from a remarkable tin itinerary that concludes with the recording of '1 (+) minas of tin to the Cretan; 1/3 mina of tin to the translator, chief (merch)ant among the Cretans; (dispensed) at Ugarit...' (ARM 23 556). This striking passage indicates that there were Minoan merchants (the text uses the name Kaptaru, generally taken to designate the island of Crete) doing business (perhaps also residing) at Ugarit (modern Ras Shamra) toward the beginning of the Old Palace period in Crete. Furthermore, the Minoan merchants seem to have had a translator (Akkadian, targamannum; the origin of the common European 'dragoman') who was also the leader of the Minoans doing business at Ugarit. Such translators are known from other periods of Mesopotamian history. We have the cylinder seal of a Sargonic official who served as translator for the Melukkha merchants who came to Agade from the Indus Valley, perhaps bringing with them the tin of Melukkha, a commodity mentioned in one of the statue inscriptions of Gudea, ruler of Lagash. A Mari text, dated to the ninth year of the reign of Zimri-Lim, refers to the construction of a 'small Kaptaru boat', perhaps to be taken as a model ship for ritual purposes or as the designation of a ship built for sailing to Crete. A possible parallel for this would be the Egyptian references to Byblos ships (for sailing to the ancien Syrian port of Byblos (modern Jubayl) and Keftiu ships (built for sailing to Crete)...[115]

Note on tin used to alloy with copper to create bronze. "One ingot fragment, probably of the mid-third millennium BCE, possibly found at Tell al-Ubaid, has been identified as alloyed copper. It is 88.2 per cent copper, 8.91 per cent tin with impurities...Muhly (Muhly, JD, 1973, Copper and Tin: The distribution of mineral resources and the nature of the metals trade in the bronze age, Hamden: Archon Books,220 ff.; Muhly, JD, 1976, Copper and Tin, Hamden, Archon Books, 104 ff.) has thoroughly reviewed the ancient textual sources for the use of copper and its trade in Mesopotmia, with extensive commentary on their relation to known deposits in the area. Archaic texts from Uruk (III) indicate that already by the later fourth millennium BCE Dilmun was engaged in the metals trade ." (Moorey, P.R.S., 1994, Ancient Mesopotamian materials and industries, the archaeological evidence, Oxford University Press, p. 245). Muhly notes: "...copper is likely to be a local product; the tin was almost always an import...There is certainly no tin on Cyprus, so at best the ingots could have been transhipped from that island. How did they find their way to Haifa? "[116]

For the trade with Mesopotamia there is both literary and archaeological evidence. The Harappan seals were evidently used to seal bundles of merchandise, as clay seal impressions with cord or sack marks on the reverse side testify. The presence of a number of Indus seals at Ur and other Mesopotamian cities and the discovery of a "Persian Gulf" type of seal at Lothal--otherwise known from the Persian Gulf ports of Bahrain (ancient Dilmun, or Telmun) and Faylahkah, as well as from Mesopotamia-- provide convincing corroboration of the sea trade suggested by the

Lothal dock. Timber and precious woods, ivory, lapis lazuli, gold, and luxury goods such as carnelian beads, pearls, and shell and bone inlays, including the distinctly Indian kidney shape, were among the goods sent to Mesopotamia in exchange for silver, tin, woolen textiles, and grains and other foods. Copper ingots appear to have been imported to Lothal from Magan (possibly Oman, the Mahran region, or southeastern Iran). Other possible trade items include products originating exclusively in each respective region, such as bitumen, occurring naturally in Mesopotamia; and cotton textiles and chickens, major products of the Indus region not native to Mesopotamia.
A good example of contact between Kish and Meluhha (Indus script corpora area) is provided by two seals with identical texts from (a) Kish (IM 1822); cf. Mackay 1925 and (b) Mohenjodaro (M-228); cf. Parpola, 1994, p. 132.

"A copper blade (Marshall 1931: pl. 136, f.3) found in one of the upper levels, though termed a spear-blade, may conceivably have been a knife (Plate IX, no.1). An exactly similar blade, but with a slightly longer tang, was found in the A mound at Kish (Mackay 1929a: pl. 39, gp. 3, f.4)... attention should be called to a steatite seal from Kish, now in Baghdad Museum, which bears the svastika symbol.

(a)

(b)

This seal, both in shape and design upon it, exactly resembles the little square seals of steatite and glazed paste that are so frequently found at Mohenjodaro (Marshall 1931: pl. 144, f. 507-15). I do not think that I err in regarding the Kish example, which was found by Watelin, as either of Indian workmanship or made locally for an Indian resident in Sumer... The curious perforated vessels shown (Marshall 1931: pl. 84, f. 3-18) are very closely allied to perforated vessels found at Kish (Mackay 1929a: pl. 54, f. 36), especially in the fact that besides the numerous holes in the sides there is also a large hole in the base, which suggests that by this means they were supported on a rod or something similar... I have suggested, from evidence obtained by Sir Aurel Stein in southern Baluchistan, that these perforated vessels were used as heaters...[117]

"The land of Melukkha shall bring carnelian, desirable and precious, sissoo-wood from Magan, excellent mangroves, on big-ships!" said a statement in the Sumerian myth, Enki and Ninkhursag (cf. lines 1-9, trans. B. Alster). "In the late Early Dynastic period (about 2500), Ur-Nanshe, king of the Sumerian city-state Lagash, "had ships of Dilmun transport timber from foreign lands" to his capital (modern Tell al-Hiba), just as a later governor of Lagash, named Gudea, did in the mid-twenty-first century. In the early twenty-fourth century, Lugalbanda and Urukagina, two kings of Lagash, imported copper from Dilmun and paid for it with wool, silver, fat, and various milk and cereal products... That these (round stamp) seals were used in economic transactions is proven by the discovery of two important tablets bearing their impressions. One of these tablets was found at Susa, and dates to the first half of the second millennium. It is a receipt for goods, including ten minas of copper (about eleven pounds or five kilograms).

The second tablet, in the Yale Babylonian Collection, is dated to the tenth year of Gungunum of Larsa (modern Tell Senkereh), that is, around 1925, and records a consignment of goods (wool, wheat, and sesame) prior to a trading voyage that almost certainly had Dilmun as its goal. Dilmun seals characteristically depict two men drinking what could be beer through straws, or two or three prancing gazelles...a merchant named Ea-nasir, who is identified as one of the a_lik Tilmun, or "Dilmun traders"...

Ea-nasir paid for Dilmun copper with the textiles and silver that he received from the great Nanna-Ningal temple complex at Ur...The Mari texts contain several references to Dilmunite caravans...Melukkha was a source of wood (including a black wood thought to have been ebony), gold, ivory, and carnelian... Melukkha was accessible by sea...Sargon of Akkad...boasts that ships from Dilmun, Magan and Melukkha docked at the quay of his capital Akkad...While points of contact with other regions are attested, they can hardly have accounted for the strength and individuality of civilization in the subcontinent..

.Unmistakably Harappan cubical weights of banded chert (based on a unit of 13.63 grams) are known from a number of sites located around the perimeter of the Arabian GUlf, including Susa, Qalat al-Bahrain, Shimal (Ras al-Khaimah), and Tell Abraq (Umm al-Qaiwain)...an inscribed Harappan shard has been found at Ras al Junayz... Harappan pottery has been found at several sites throughout Oman and the United Arab Emirates...

A "Melukkhan village" in the territory of the ancient city-state of Lagash, attested in the thirty-fourth year of the reign of Shulgi (2060), may have been a settlement of Harappans, if the identification with the civilization of the Indus Valley is correct...But...there is little evidence of a Sumerian, Akkadian, or Babylonian presence in the Indus Valley... That the language of Melukkha was unintelligble to an Akkadian or Sumerian speaker is clearly shown by the fact that, on his cylinder seal, the Akkadian functionary Shu-ilishu is identified as a "Melukkhan translator"...the word "Melukkha" appears occasionally as a personal name in cuneiform texts of the Old Akkadian and Ur III periods."[118]

Harappan control over the Oman Sea

"Oman peninsula/Makkan lies half way between the two main civilization centres of the third millennium Middle East: Mesopotamia and the Indus valley... an increasing influence of Harappan civilization on Eastern Arabia during the last two centuries of the third millennium. This influence seems to strengthen during the early second millennium where proper Harappan objects are found all over the Oman peninsula: a cubic stone weight at Shimal, sherds of Harappan storage jars on several sites including Hili 8 (period III). Maysar and Ra's Al-Junayz bears a Harappan inscription and Tosi (forth.) has emphasized the importance of this discovery for knowledge of Harappan control over the Oman Sea."[119]

A reference to itinerant metal-smiths who make arrows of metal, in the Rigveda (9.112.2) will have to be re-evaluated in the context of this evidence.

jaratībhih oṣadhībhih parṇebhih śakunānām

kārmāro aśmabhih dyubhih hiraṇyavantam icchatī (RV. 9.112.2)

This is a description of a smithy, perhaps an allusion to the making of copper reducing the ores. The metalsmiths sold the products (a copper implement or copper-tipped arrow or golden ornament) to moneyed-people.

Arsenical bronze occurs in the archaeological record across the globe, the earliest artefacts so far known have been found on the Iranian plateau in the 5th millennium BCE.[120] Early occurrences of realgar – a reddish-yellow arsenic sulfide mineral -- as a red painting pigment are known for works of art from China, India, Central Asia, and Egypt.

Earliest inscriptions on copper tablets were found at Mohenjo-daro. Indus Writing on Metal was found at Harappa also. Copper tablet (H2000-4498/9889-01) with raised script was found in Trench 43. Harappa. (Source: Slide 351 harappa.com) Eight such duplicates of tablets have been found (HARP, 2005); these were recovered from circular platforms. This example of a uniquely scripted tablet with raised Indus script glyphs shows that copper tablets were also used in Harappa, while hundreds of copper tablets with incised script inscriptions were found in Mohenjo-daro.[121] The copper tablet with raised script contains a 'backbone' glyph; decoding: kaśēru 'the backbone' (Bengali. Skt.); kaśēruka id. (Skt.) Rebus: kasērā' metal worker ' (Lahnda)(CDIAL 2988, 2989) An alternate (vikalpa) reading is: *kaṇḍa* 'backbone'. Rebus: *kaṇḍa* 'stone (ore) metal'. Glyph: 'ingot shape': *mũh* 'ingot'.mũhã̄ = the quantity of iron produced at one time in a native smelting furnace of the Kolhes; iron produced by the Kolhes and formed like a four-cornered piece a little pointed at each end (Santali). *dula* 'pair'. Rebus: *dul* 'cast (metal)'. Thus, the three glyphs are read together sequentially as: *dul mũh kaṇḍa* 'cast ingot stone (ore) metal'.

Recovered from circular platforms? Clearly, the circular platforms functioned as sorting, marketing platforms if, in the center of the circle, a storage pot containing metal artefacts, beads, ivory products etc. were kept for display, marketing, trade. [The center of the circle may also have held a drill-lathe.]

Ta'anach, *ṭaṅka* 'mint'; *damgar* 'mint merchant'

Ta'anach 'cult' stand dated to 10th century BCE has hieroglyphs comparable to Mesopotamian and Indus artifacts which yield a link with *ṭaṅka* 'mint' (Indian *sprachbund*) and in the context of *damgar* 'merchant' (Akkadian).

There is a language group which explains *damgar* as Sumerian substrate. That language group is the Indian *sprachbund* which included glosses from 'Language X + Munda = Meluhha (mleccha)'.

Notes on 'pellet' hieroglyph linked with bull/antelope

Parallels associating a 'pellet' hieroglyph or an ox-hide ingot to a bull or bull's head or an antelope can be seen in the following evidences.

Taxila coin[122].

The attached photo of ta'anach 'cult' stand[123] shows two goats flanking a tree in the middle register. The 'standard' is from Tell ti'innik and dated to 10th cent BCE. Tell t'innik is[124] in West Bank, SE of Megiddo in Israel.[125]

Another view of the ta'anach 'cult' stand.[126]

The dotted-circle (pellet) shown above the bull on the top register of the Tell ti'innik ta'anach 'cult' stand parallels the 'pellet' shown between the horns of a bull's head on Warka vase and the pellet shown on the Taxila coin (below the fish on the obverse and between the horns of bull-head on reverse of the coin). The second register from the top, on the stand shows two goats leaping against a stylized plant with mollusks (comparable to the hieroglyphs on Mesopotamian and an Indus prism tablet). [Strong's concordance[127] notes the word tanak as of 'uncertain derivation'. "The archive at Taanach is described by Sellin. In a small room in the citadel "intended apparently as a governor s resi dence," was found a large quadrangular chest made of clay 4 cm. thick. The chest itself was 60 cm. wide and 65 cm. high and had apparently contained clay tablets of which twelve complete or frag mentary ones were -found."[128]] I do not know if the word can relate to *ṭaṅka* 'mint' (Sanskrit). But, some hieroglyphs on the stand read rebus in metallurgical contexts are indicative that the word is cognate with *ṭaṅka*: תַּעְנָךְ tanak

The 'pellet' between the horns of a bull-head on the Taxila coin yields a rebus reading clue: mũh 'face' (Santali); rebus: mũha 'ingot' (Santali) mleccha-mukha 'copper' (Sanskrit). The 'pellet' is clearly a depiction of a metal ingot.

múkha n. ‘ mouth, face ’ RV., ‘ entrance ’ MBh. Pa. *mukha* -- m.; Aś.shah. man.

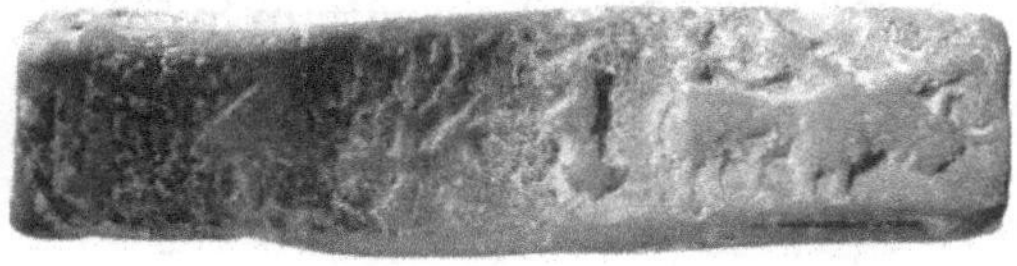

gir. *mukhato*, kāl. dh. jau. °*te* ‘ by word of mouth ’; Pk. *muha* -- n. ‘ mouth, face ’, Gy. gr. hung. *muy* m., boh.*muy*, span. *muí*, wel. *mūī* f., arm. *muç*, pal. *mu'*, *mi'*, pers. *mu*; Tir. *mū* ‘ face ’; Woṭ. *mū* m. ‘ face, sight ’; Kho. *mux* ‘ face ’; Tor. *mū* ‘ mouth ’, Mai. *mũ*; K. in cmpds. *mu* -- *ganḍ* m. ‘ cheek, upper jaw ’, *mū* -- *kāla* ‘ having one's face blackened ’, rām. *mūī˜*, pog. *mūī*, ḍoḍ. *mū̃h* ‘ mouth ’; S. *mũhũ* m. ‘ face, mouth, opening ’; L. *mũh* m. ‘ face ’, awāṇ. *mū̃* with descending tone, mult. *mũhã* m. ‘ head of a canal ’; P. *mū̃h* m. ‘ face, mouth ’, *mū̃hā̃* m. ‘ head of a canal ’; WPah.śeu. *mùtilde;* ‘ mouth, ’ cur. *mū̃h*; A. *muh* ‘ face ’, in cmpds. -- *muwā* ‘ facing ’; B. *mu* ‘ face ’; Or. *muhã* ‘ face, mouth, head, person ’; Bi. *mũh* ‘ opening or hole (in a stove for stoking, in a handmill for filling, in a grainstore for withdrawing) ’; Mth. Bhoj. *mũh* ‘ mouth, face ’, Aw.lakh. *muh*, H. *muh*, *mũh* m.; OG. *muha*, G. *mɔ̃h* n. ‘ mouth ’(CDIAL 10158).

Two goats nibbling on the sacred Tree of Life from a carved ivory relief, Mesopotamia.[129]

Orthography of two goats shown on one side of a prism tablet of Indus script (1431E), is comparable.

Sumerian cylinder seal.[130] Mlekh, mr̤eka 'goat' (Br.Telugu); rebus: milakkhu 'copper'. Leaf on mountain: kamaṛkom 'petiole of leaf'; rebus: kampaṭṭam 'mint'. loa = a species of fig tree, ficus glomerata, the fruit of ficus glomerata (Santali) Rebus: lo 'iron' (Assamese, Bengali); loa 'iron' (Gypsy). Hieroglyph/homonym: डगर [ḍagara]A slope or ascent (as of a river's bank, of a small hill). *tagaru* 'ram' (Tulu). Rebus: ḍāṅgar 'blacksmith' (H.) damgar 'merchant' (Akkadian). The glyphic composition of two goats flanking a ficus leaf is read rebus: meḍ loa kundār 'iron turner mint'.

ṭagara 'antelope'; rebus: *ṭagara* 'tin'. Cf. cognae: *tamkāru, damgar* 'merchant'(Sumerian). *tagaru* 'ram' (Tulu). Read rebus: *tamkāru, dagar, dakar, dam-gar,* '(mint) merchant'. (Sumerian substrate). *The early meaning is likely to be: 'metal-worker, mint-worker'.

The lexeme ta'anach may be cognate with ṭaṅka (Indian *sprachbund*):

டங்கசாலை ṭaṅka-cālai *n.* < *ṭaṅka-śālā*. Mint. See தங்கசாலை. (ஈடு, 1, 9, 8, ஜீ.)(Tamil) ṭaṅkaśālā -- , *ṭaṅkakaś°* f. ' mint ' lex. [ṭaṅka -- 1, śā´lā --]

N. *ṭaksāl*, *°ār*, B. *ṭāksāl*, *ṭā̃k°*, *ṭek°*, Bhoj. *ṭaksār*, H. *ṭaksāl*, *°ār* f., G. *ṭā̃ksāḷ* f., M. *ṭā̃ksāl*, *ṭāk°*, *ṭāk°*, *ṭak°*. -- Deriv. G. *ṭaksāḷī* m. ' mint -- master ', M. *ṭāksāḷyā* m. ṭaṅkaśālā -- : Brj. *ṭaksāḷī*, *°sārī* m. ' mint -- master '.(CDIAL 5434).

Hieroglyph/homonym: தகர் takar, *n.* [Tu. *tagaru*, K. *tagar*.] 1. Sheep; ஆட்டின்பொது. (திவா.) 2. Ram; செம் மறியாட்டுக்கடா. (திவா.) பொருநகர் தாக்கற்குப் பேருந் தகைத்து (குறள், 486).[131]

Hieroglyph/homonym: Ta. takar sheep, ram, goat, male of certain other animals (yāḷi, elephant, shark). Ma. takaran huge, powerful as a man, bear, etc. Ka. tagar, ṭagaru, ṭagara, ṭegaru ram. Tu. tagaru, ṭagarů id. Te. tagaramu, tagaru id. / Cf. Mar. tagar id. (DEDR 3000). Substantive (in the context of a merchant's business): Ta. takaram tin, white lead, metal sheet, coated with tin. Ma. takaram tin, tinned iron

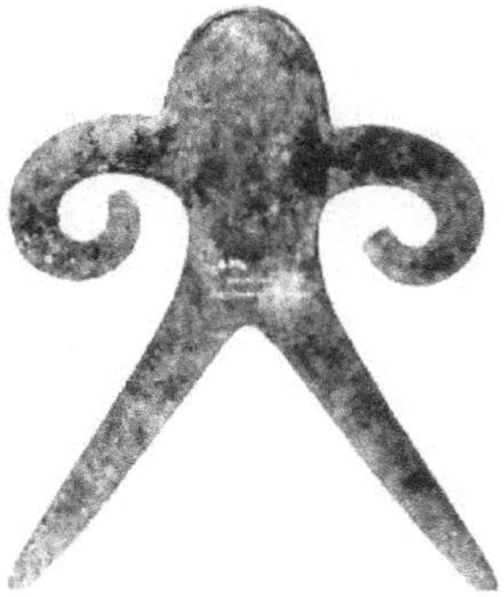

plate. Ko. tagarm (obl. tagart-) tin. Ka. tagara, tamara, tavara id. Tu. tamarů, tamara, tavara id. Te. tagaramu, tamaramu, tavaramu id. Kuwi (Isr.) ṭagromi tin metal, alloy. / Cf. Skt. tamara- id. (DEDR 3001).

Ta'anakh or Taanach is a small village in Israel in Ta'anakh region. Just to the east is a 40-metre-high mound which was the site of the biblical city Taanach. 12 Akkadian cuneiform tablets were found here. The main remains visible today are of an 11th-century Abbasid palace.[132]

Tanakh (Hebrew: תַּנַ"ךְ, pronounced [taˈnaχ] or [təˈnax]; also *Tenakh*, *Tenak*, *Tanach*) is a name used for the canon of the Hebrew Bible.

Phoen., MH and Assyr.; in the latter damgaru or tamkaru, Syr. taggara, {2} = merchant, Del. Ass. HWB, 222.[133] Sumerian damgar, Babylonian tamkarum—usually is translated as "merchant" or, by Babylonian times,"entrepreneur."[134] Cognate with tamkāru, dam-gar '(mint) merchant' Indian *sprachbund* glosses: Mth. ṭhākur ' blacksmith '; ṭhakkura m. ' idol, deity (cf. ḍhakkārī --), ' lex., ' title ' Rājat. [Dis- cussion with lit. by W. Wüst RM 3, 13 ff. Prob. orig. a tribal name EWA i 459, which Wüst considers nonAryan borrowing of śākvará -- : very doubtful]Pk. ṭhakkura -- m. ' Rajput, chief man of a village '; Kho. (Lor.) takur ' barber ' (= ṭ° ← Ind.?), Sh. ṭhăkŭr m.; K. ṭhôkur m. ' idol ' (← Ind.?); S. ṭhakuru m. ' fakir, term of address between fathers of a husband and wife '; P. ṭhākar m. ' landholder ', ludh. ṭhaukar m. ' lord '; Ku. ṭhākur m. ' master, title of a Rajput '; N. ṭhākur ' term of address from slave to master ' (f. ṭhakurāni), ṭhakuri ' a clan of Chetris ' (f. ṭhakurni); A. ṭhākur ' a Brahman ', ṭhākurānī ' goddess '; B. ṭhākurāni, ṭhākrān, °run ' honoured lady, goddess '; Or. ṭhākura ' term of address to a

Brahman, god, idol ', ṭhākurāṇī ' goddess '; Bi. ṭhākur ' barber '; Bhoj. Aw.lakh. ṭhākur ' lord, master '; H. ṭhākur m. ' master, landlord, god, idol ', ṭhākurāin, ṭhăkurānī f. ' mistress, goddess '; G. ṭhākor, °kar m. ' member of a clan of Rajputs ', ṭhakrāṇī f. ' his wife ', ṭhākor ' god, idol '; M. ṭhākur m. ' jungle tribe in North Konkan, family priest, god, idol '; Si. mald. "tacourou" ' title added to names of noblemen ' (HJ 915) prob. ← Ind. Addenda: ṭhakkura -- : Garh. ṭhākur ' master '; A. ṭhākur also ' idol ' AFD 205.(CDIAL 5488)

Homonym/hieroglyph: tagara1 n. 'the shrub Tabernaemontana coronaria and a fragrant powder obtained from it' Kauś., °aka<-> VarBr̥S. [Cf. sthagara -- , sthakara -- n. ' a partic. fragrant powder ' TBr.] (CDIAL 5622).

Copper figurine from Kul Tarike, Iran.[135]

The two glosses, *tagara* 'antelope, ram' and *ayo* 'fish' are depicted in Indian hieroglyphs:

A copper anthropomorph had a 'fish' glyph incised.

Anthropomorph with 'fish' sign incised on the chest and with curved arms like the horns of a markhor. Sheorajpur (Kanpur Dist., UP, India). State Museum, Lucknow (O.37) Typical find of Gangetic Copper Hoards. 47.7 X 39 X 2.1 cm. C. 4 kg. Early 2nd millennium BCE. Tagara 'ram' + ayo 'fish'; rebus: tagara 'tin', ayo 'metal' rebus: damgar 'merchant.' (Assyrian); hence, the compound tagar + ayo has semantics: 'metal mint-merchant'.

Fish on an Indus seal. National Museum 135.

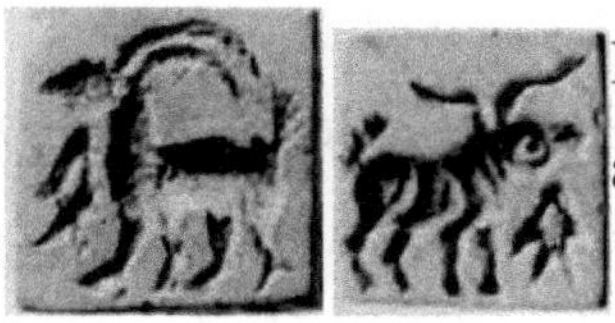

Kalibangan 37, 34 Two Kalibangan seals show an antelope and fish glyphs as the inscription.

Mleccha epigraphs on Warka vase

Warka vase which is a carved alabaster stone vessel (height: ca. 105 cm.; upper diam.: 36 cm.), found in the Sumerian Inanna temple complex. Assyriologists in their sixth excavation season at Uruk in 1933/1934 discovered the vase. The vase is named after the modern village of Warka - known as Uruk to the ancient Sumerians. It is dated to ca. 3200-3000 BCE.[136] Uruk (Akkadian: *Uruk*; Aramaic: *Erech*; Hebrew: *Erech*; Greek: Ὀρχόη *Orchoē*, Ὠρύγεια *Ōrugeia*; Arabic: وركاء, *Warkā.*)was founded in 4500 BCE by Enmerkar.
The vase uses hieroglyphs and is, in effect, a 'Rosetta stone' to help decode early writing systems and to identify language(s) of the creators of this artifact. It can be called the 'Meluhha rosetta stone'. The identification of clear, unambiguous, pictorial motifs carved on the Warka vase, as hieroglyphs is confirmed by parallels on Indus script corpora and select bronze-age artifacts (e.g. Uluburn shipwreck).
Warka vase. Stone alabaster. Museum number: IM19606. Original Source: "The Oriental Institute of The University of Chicago".[137]
Clear, unambiguous, pictorial motifs carved on the Warka vase, are:

Fig.1

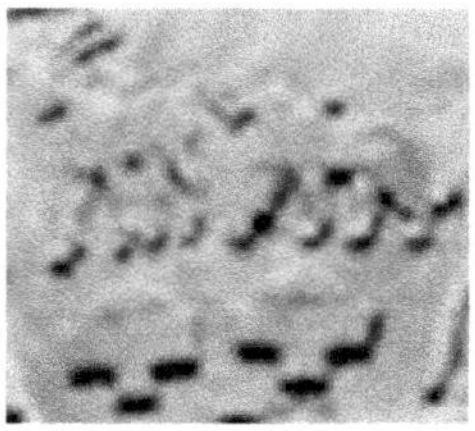

Fig.2

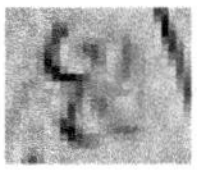

Fig.3

Fig.4

The two 'T-shaped' hieroglyphs (topped by bun-shaped ingots) shown together with an antelope and a tiger may denote 'fire-altars + ingots.'
Hieroglyph/homonym: arū = lion (As god of devastation, Nergal is called A-ri-a)(Akkadian) Etruscan *ar* = fire, Latin *āra* = altar., hearth; ārdēre 'to burn, be on fire'. Ash. *arū´*, *úrə*, 'silver', Wg. *urḗi*, Kt. *ŕū̥*, *arū̥*, Pr. *urú;*, Gmb. *wurṓ*, Kal. (LSI) *rāwa*, rumb. *rūa*: more prob. < **rūpiya* -- s.v. rū´pya -- ? rajatá ' silvery ' RV., n. ' silver ' AV. Pa. *rajata* -- n. ' silver ', Pk. *rayada* -- , *rayaya* -- n., Si. *ridī*, Md. *rihi.* -- (CDIAL 10576). Pushto: ور *wa<u>rr</u>*, s.m. (2nd) The scab of a wound. 2.

Small pieces of gold and silver collected together, a kind of miscellany, a mass. Pl. وړونه *warrūnah*. See خيړ

aru 'copper' (Akkadian) ara, era 'copper' (Pali.Pkt.) āra 'brass' as in ārakūṭa (Skt.) era = copper; erako = molten cast (G.)

1. An antelope and a tiger are shown above two bun ingots atop a fire-altar. (Fig.1) The antelope and tiger hieroglyphs atop two ingots are: (i) ranku 'antelope'. Read rebus: ranku 'tin'. (ii) *kola* 'tiger'. Read rebus: *kol* 'alloy of five metals, *pañcaloha'*.
2. Between two storage jars containing ingots is shown a bull's head with a 'pellet' between the horns. (Fig.2) *mũh* 'face'. Read rebus: *mũh* '(metal) ingot.' *ḍhangar* 'bull'. Read rebus: *ḍhangar* 'blacksmith (metalsmith)'.
3. A ram is shown ahead of the two storage jars. (Fig.3) The ram hieroglyph leading the two storage jars with ingots is *tagaru* 'ram' (Tulu). Read rebus: *tamkāru, dagar, dakar, dam-gar,* '(mint) merchant'. (Sumerian substrate).
4. A procession of bovidae and a set of sprouts are shown on the bottom registers. (Fig.4) (i) *khar-warg* 'herd of sheep, goats'. Read rebus: *khār 'blacksmith'*. Sheep and goats above 3 years of age are termed خر ورګ *k̲h̲ar-warg* and خر ه ورګ *k̲h̲ar-warga'h*. (Pushto). (ii) *warak* 'wool'(Wg.) Read rebus: *wăr̆ek* 'house' (Pr.), *vāra* -- 'door, gate-way' (Sanskrit) (iii) *tagaraka* 'tabernae montana coranaria'(Sanskrit). Read rebus: *tagara* 'tin' (Kannada). The hieroglyph tree: *kuṭi* 'tree'; *kuṭhi* 'smelter/furnace' (Santali).
5. Two reed bundles adorned with scarves. (i) The reed hieroglyph: *khāg, khāgṛā* 'reed for pens'(Bengali), *khagaṛā* 'the reed *Saccharum spontaneum*'(Oriya). Read rebus: *kā̃gar* 'portable brazier' (Kashmiri)] (ii) Scarf is ligatured to the reed post. *dhaṭu* 'scarf' (WPah.). Read rebus: *dhatu* 'mineral' (Santali) The reed bundles adorn the temple-gateway: *wăr̆ek* 'house' (Pr.), *vāra* -- 'door, gate-way' (Sanskrit).

The pictorial motifs narrated on the vase in four registers are not mere decorations. It is not mere coincidence that many pictorial motifs on the Warka vase recur on Indus script corpora.

Fig.5 Fig.6 Fig.7

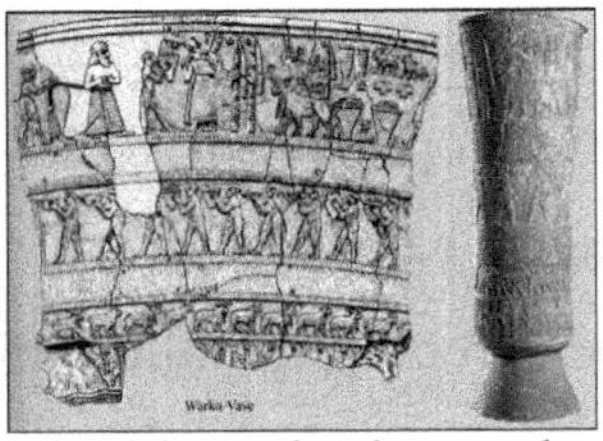

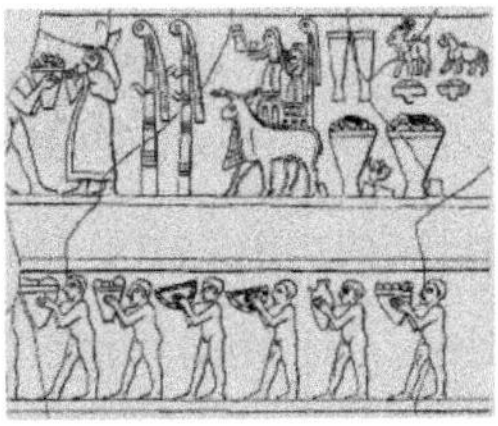

The hieroglyphs on the Warka vase conveyed an economic message in the context of deposits of treasure into the (Inanna temple) treasury (as evidenced by the narrative of the second register which shows large storage jars, liquid containing jar, and baskets being carried in).

It is suggested that the pictorial motifs are hieroglyphs which can be read rebus. Also suggested is that the creators of the pictorial motifs on the Warka vase were speakers of a language which underlies the 6000+ inscriptions of Indus script corpora.

What was the underlying language of the message? One language source is the Indian *sprachbund* (language union), which can also be called '*Meluhha*'.

What was the message (that is, what treasures were carried for depositing in the temple treasury)? Treasure carried into the temple treasury included: tin ingots, ingots of minerals/metals and alloyed metal ingots.

On the hieroglyphs of the top register, a goat or ram walks towards a pair of reeds ligatured with scarfs. Two large storage jars contain ingots. (That these relate to metal is indicated by the phonetic determinant of a bull's head dangar 'bull'; danger 'blacksmith'). The Uruk (Warka) vase with its hieroglyphs comparable to Indian hieroglyphs and the identification of a few substratum Meluhha words in Sumerian

– is a pointer to this possibility of Meluhhan presence and influence. Source of image: "The Warka Vase or the Uruk Vase is a carved alabaster stone vessel found in the temple complex of the Sumerian goddess Inanna in the ruins of the ancient city of Uruk, located in the modern Al Muthanna Governorate, in southern Iraq. Like the Narmer Palette from Egypt, it is one of the earliest surviving works of narrative relief sculpture, dated to c. 3,200–3000 BC. The vase was discovered as a collection of fragments by German modern village of Warka - known as Uruk to the ancient Sumerians."[138]

Explaining 'pellet' as hieroglyph read rebus in Mleccha

Impression of an Indus-style cylinder seal (Fig.30) of unknown Near Eastern origin in the Musee du Louvre, Paris. One of the two anthropomorphic figures carved on this seal wears the horns of water buffalo while sitting on a throne with hoofed legs, surrounded by snakes, fishes and water buffaloes. Copyrighted photo by M. Chuzeville for the Departement des antiquites orientales, Musee du Louvre.

A pair of bisons flank a round spot in the bottom register of the cylinder seal impression.

(Fig.31) urseal15 Gadd, PBA 18 (1932), p. 13, Pl. III, no. 15; Legrain, MJ (1929), p. 306, pl. XLI, no. 119; found at Ur in the cemetery area, in a ruined grave. There is a round spot upon the bull's back.

(Fig.32) Fig. 99; Failaka; no. 174 impression; two bull heads emanating from a chequered square; two persons drinking; altar and sun; bull in the lower register.

Hieroglyph/homonym: homa = bison (Pe.); hama id. (Mand.); soma = a wild buffalo (= bison) (Kui); homma bison (Kuwi); ho_ma sambar (Kuwi)(DEDR 2849). Rebus: hom, hon = gold (Ka.); samanom 'gold' (Santali)
Hieroglyph: P. *ḍabb* m. ' spot '; P. *dhabbā* m. ' spot '; N. *dhabbo* ' stain, spot ', H. *dhabbā* m., G. *dhābũ* n.(CDIAL 5529). Hieroglyph: ḍabe, ḍabea 'large horns, with a sweeping upward curve, applied to buffaloes' (Santali) Rebus: ḍab, ḍhimba, ḍhompo 'lump (ingot?)', clot, make a lump or clot, coagulate, fuse, melt together (Santali) Hieroglyph: *ḍābā* 'large hollow vessel to feed cattle from'(B.) *dhābā* in Indian *sprachbund* can be semantically explained as a workshop storehouse to hold *ḍab* 'melted, fused (ingots)'.

Cylinder seal (Fig.33): man grasping an antelope, bull's head over ingot. Between the horns of the bull, a pellet is shown.[139]

Cylinder seal (Fig.34) shows an ox-hide ingot associated with an antelope:

Cylinder seal: palmette tree flanked by winged griffin and caprid; figure between them with raised hands; an ox-hide ingot combined with four raised dots is shown above the winged griffin.[140]

Hieroglyph: गोदा [gōdā] m A circular brand or mark made by actual cautery

(Marathi) गोटा [gōṭā] m A roundish stone or pebble. 2 A marble (of stone, lac, wood &c.) 2 A marble. 3 A large lifting stone. Used in trials of strength among the Athletæ. 4 A stone in temples described at length underउचला 5 fig. A term for a round, fleshy, well-filled body. गोट्ळा or गोटोळा [gōṭuḷā or gōṭōḷā] a (गोटा) Spherical or spheroidal, pebble-form. (Marathi)

Rebus: गोटा [gōṭā] A lump of silver: as obtained by melting down lace or fringe. (Marathi)

Indus seal (Mohenjodaro, Fig. 35) showing fire-altar, with dotted circles and pellets around the altar. Source: Indus script corpora

Hieroglyphs: Four 'round spot' glyphs around the 'dotted circle' in the center of the composition: gōṭī 'round pebble. *dolo* 'the eye' (deśi. Hemachandra). Rebus: *dul* 'to cast metal in a mould' (Santali) It is possible that 'fish-eyes' or 'eye stones' referred to in ancient Mesopotamian texts as imports from Dilmun (Akkadian IGI-HA, IGI-KU6) mentioned in Mesopotamian texts., refer to the hieroglyph of dotted circle (hieroglyph: fish-eye or antelope-eye). In the centre of the fire-altar is a dotted circle, dul 'cast metal (ingot)'. The four pellets surrounding this dotted circle may denote gōṭā 'lumps of silver'.

Rebus: kōṭhī] f (कोष्ट S) A granary, garner, storehouse, warehouse, treasury, factory, bank.

krvṛi f. 'granary (Wpah.); kuṛī, kuṛo house, building'(Ku.)(CDIAL 3232) कोठी [kōṭhī] f (कोष्ट S) A granary, garner, storehouse, warehouse, treasury, factory, bank. (Marathi) कोठी The grain and provisions (as of an army); the commissariat supplies. Ex. लशकराची कोठी चालली-उतरली- आली-लुटली. कोठ्या [kōṭhyā] कोठा [kōṭhā] m (कोष्ट S) A large granary, store-room, warehouse, water-reservoir &c. 2 The stomach. 3 The chamber of a gun, of water-pipes &c. 4 A bird's nest. 5 A cattle-shed. 6 The chamber or cell of a huṇḍí in which is set down in figures the amount. कोठारें [kōṭhārēṃ] n A storehouse (Marathi)

Diffusion of Metallurgy: Meluhha and western Afghanistan sources of tin
"Investigators in all periods have been faced with one major fact. Because southern Mesopotamia is virtually lacking in mineral resources, the materials used to make the metal artifacts found there must have come from another locale. Thus, our research led to the metallogenic zones in Iran, Afghanistan and Oman, where ores of copper, amont others, are known to occur in substantial quantities...we have also uncovered significant new information on tin deposits which could have been exploited in antiquity...Other metals were also used for this purpose (alloying) by ancient metal workers, most notably arsenic, antimony and lead. Arsenic, in particular, played an important role in the early metallurgy of the Near East...The earliest occurrence of tin-bronze date to the 4th millennium.Though the total number of artifacts analyzed from this period is not large, those of tin-bronze are even fewer: three pins from Necropolis A at Susa (with tin contents of 4%, 8% and 2.3% respectively), and an awl from Sialk III (0.95%). In the later 4th and early 3rd millennia, greater tin values occur--5.3% in a pin from Susa B; and 5% in an axe

from Mundigak III in Afghanistan; but these are still exceptional in a period characterized by the use of arsenical copper...arond 270 BC, during Early Dynastic III in Mesopotamia...eight metal artifacts of forty-eight in the celebrated 'vase a la cachette' of Susa D are bronzes; four of them -- three vases and one axe -- have over 7% tin. The analyses of objects from the Royal Cemetery at UR present an even clearer picture: of twenty-four artifacts in the Iraq Museum subjected to analysis, eight containing significant quantities of tin and five with over 8% tin can be considered true bronzes in the traditional sense...In addition, a contemporary shaft-hole axe from Kish contains 4% tin, and significant amounts were detected in a few artifacts from Tepe Giyan and Tepe Yahya IVB in Iran, and Hili in Oman. Thus, we see an increasing pattern of tin usage...We explored the area south of Herat, where several deposits of tin were said to exist. At Misgaran, tin appears 500 meters north of a copper mine which was worked in ancient times, although the precise dates of exploitation are not known. The copper ores here contain over 600 ppm (0.06) of tin. Tin-bearing sands, which can be easily beneficiated by panning, were worked in the nearby Sarkar Valley. There too the tin was found in association with copper, green traces of which are visible throughout the landscape...Gudea of Lagash (2150-2111BCE)speaks of the tin of Meluhha...the geographer Strabo (XV.2.10) who, in referring to the inhabitants of Drangiana (modern Sistan), says that they have 'only scanty supplies of wine, but they have tin in their country'...this passage..does accord well with the discoveris in the area of Herat...There are two possible routes from Afghanistan to Mesopotamia. One crosses the northern part of the Iranian plateau, along the Elburz mountains, then through the passes in the Zagros descends to Babylonia and Assyria. In the 1st millennium it was one of the principal supply routes of eastern goods to Assyria. In the 2nd millennium the tin that Assur exported to Anatolia might have followed this route. Along it are found such sites as Tepe Sialk (where the use of tin is attested in the 4th millennium), Tepe Giyan and Tepe Hissar, wehre other finds (such as lapis lazuli at Hissar) implicate them in long-distance commerce in the 3rd millennium.

"The second route is by sea, along the Arabian coast of the Gulf, perhaps also going by land through souther n Iran. It was at the time of Gudea of Lagash and earlier in the Early Dynastic III period, the great supply route of eastern commodities to southern Mesopotamia. It is by this route that the copper of Makkan came, copper which analysis has shown to have originated in the peninsula of Oman. It also brought the products of Meluhha, including lapis lazuli, carnelian, copper, ivory and various woods. Nothing, however, suggests the passage of tin through this area. For example, there is little tin in the artifacts recovered at Qala'at al Bahrain, dating between 2300 and 1800 BC. Furthermore, we know from the work of Limet, who studied texts concerned with metalworking in Sumer, that Mesopotamian metalworkers did their own alloying. We suspect, therefore, that the tin moved through this area in an unalloyed state.

"Recently Oman has yielded the first signs of the use of tin in the region. The analysis of a sword from Hili, dated to the mid-3rd millennium, shows a tin content of 6.5%, and a mold of a tap hole (?) associated with the remains of a furnace held metal with a tin content of 5%. The furnace is dated after the tree-ring calibration of a radiocarbon analysis (MC 2261) to circa 2225 BC...it is clear that the tin was added to the copper and it is also clear that it did not come from Oman itself. At Umm an-Nar artifacts with tin contents on the order of 2% were recovered; the tin must have been mixed with the local copper...Meluhha...the use of tin is attested already in the late 4th or early 3rd millennium at Mundigak III in southern Afghanistan. Tin appears only in small quantities in artifacts from Sahr-i-Sokhta in eastern Iran and at Tepe Yahya in southern Iran...In the Indus Valley, the copper-tin alloy is known at Mohenjodaro.

"...Oman's trade with southeastern Iran and Baluchistan is well attested...Among the products attributed to Meluhha, lapis lazuli and carnelian are found in sites and tombs of the 3rd millennium. We can suggest with reasonable certainty that the tin used in Oman was in transit through Meluhha and that the most likely source was western Afghanistan. The discoveries of tin in artifacts at Hili, though singular, are important because the site lies in an area clearly involved in long-distance trade.

However, there is no clear evidence that the site was a way-station on the route which brought tin from Afghanistan to Mesopotamia. Therefore the presence of tin at Hili indicates only that it was transported in the Gulf area, where it was also used to fill local needs.

"The collective indications are that western Afghanistan ws the zone able to provide the tin used in Southwest Asia in the 4th and 3rd millennia...In order to elucidate the questions raised by our findings, a project aimed specifically at tin-- its sources and metallurgy-- should be organized." (Serge Cleuziou and Thierry Berthoud, Early Tin in the Near East, in: *Expedition*, Vol. 25, No. 1, 1982, pp. 14-19).

Consistent with Occam's razor and following this insightful analysis of the Ved. amśu- cognate Toch. añcu- there is a simple strategy to deal with Ved. *soma-* as a material related to the borrowed word: *añcu-*'iron'... A simple explanation is that Vedic *amśu* denoted a metallic mineral, just as Tocharian *ancu* was a metal.

As the following are lexemes from Indian linguistic area attest, Ved. *amśu/soma-* might have referred to a metallic mineral/stone-ore from the Mount Mujavant (Muztagh Ata).

One gloss from Tamil of the Indian linguistic area attests to the semantics of soma as 'metal': சோமமணல், soma maṇal. Sand containing silver, வெள்ளிமணல். (R.) சோமனுப்பு, somanuppu. Rock-salt, as இந்துப்பு, induppu.(Winslow dictionary)

samanom = an obsolete word for gold (Santali. Campbell lexicon) samāṇo = a goldsmith's pincers (G.)

sambṛo bica = stones containing gold (Mundari.lex.)

hom = gold (Kannada)

somnakay, sovnakay, sōnakai = gold (Gypsy)(CDIAL 13519).

somṇa = gold (Pkt.)(CDIAL 13623)

assem, s'm, asemon = electrum (Old Egyptian. cf. Joseph Needham)
soma man.al = sand containing silver ore (Tamil. Winslow lexicon)
Hieroglyph/homonym: homa = bison (Pe.); hama id. (Mand.); soma = a wild buffalo (= bison)(Kui); homma bison (Kuwi); ho_ma sambar (Kuwi)(DEDR 2849). Rebus: hom, hon = gold (Ka.); samanom 'gold' (Santali)

Cylinder Seal of Ibni-Sharrum Agade period, reign of Sharkali-Sharri (c. 2217-2193 BC) Mesopotamia
Mesopotamia Serpentine H. 3.9 cm; Diam. 2.6 cm Formerly in the De Clercq collection; gift of H. de Boisgelin, 1967 AO 22303 "Buffaloes are emblematic animals in glyptic art in the Agade period. They first appear in the reign of Sargon, indicating sustained relations between the Akkadian Empire and the distant country of Meluhha, that is, the present Indus Valley, where these animals come from. These exotic creatures were probably kept in zoos and do not seem to have been acclimatized in Iraq at the end of the 3rd millennium BC. Indeed, it was not until the Sassanid Empire that they reappeared. The engraver has carefully accentuated the animals' powerful muscles and spectacular horns, which are shown as if seen from above, as they appear on the seals of the Indus."http://www.louvre.fr/en/oeuvre-notices/cylinder-seal-ibni-sharrum

Nude Bearded Hero Wrestling with Water Buffalo; Bull Man Fighting Lion

Cylinder seal and impression Mesopotamia, Akkadian period (ca. 2334–2154 B.C.)

Serpentine

36 x 25 mm Seal no. 159

http://www.themorgan.org/collections/collections.asp?id=193

Cylinder seal with contest scene, 2350–2150 B.C. Mesopotamia Albite H. 15/16 in. (3.4 cm), Diam. 7/8 in. (2.3 cm)

"A seal[141] made in Meluhha The language of the inscription on this cylinder seal found in Susa reveals that it was made in Harappa in the Indus Valley. In Antiquity, the valley was known as Meluhha. The seal's chalky white appearance is due to the fired steatite it is made of. Craftsmen in the Indus Valley made most of their seals from this material, although square shapes were usually favored. The animal carving is similar to those found in Harappan works. The animal is a bull with no hump on its shoulders, or possibly a short-horned gaur. Its head is lowered and the body unusually elongated. As was often the case, the animal is depicted eating from a woven wicker manger."

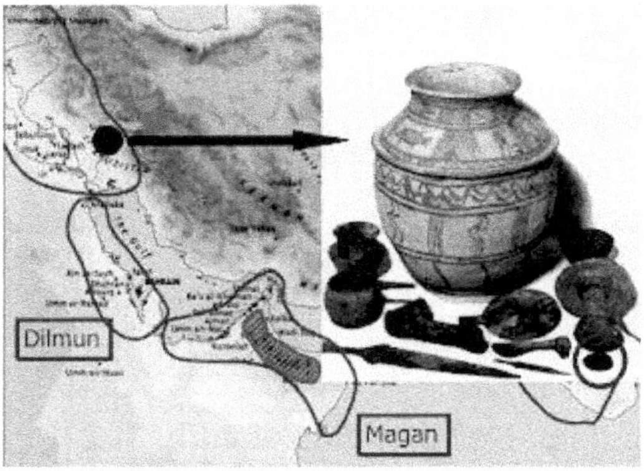

Susa pot, from Meluhha, with metal artifacts. The pot has an inscription, painted with 'fish' hieroglyph.[142]

In addition to Gypsy somnakay which means 'gold', there are also phonetic/semantic concordant references in Indo-European etyma, for e.g. Carl Darling Buck, *A dictionary of selected synonyms in the principal Indo-European Languages,* Univ. of Chicago Press, 1949. Heading 9.64, p.609; "Lat. aurum (> Romance and Celtic words, also Alb. ar), fr. *AUSOM (Sab. AUSUM, Festus); OPruss. AUSIS, OLith. AUSAS, Lith. AUKSAS; here also prob. Toch. WAS 'gold' beside WSI 'yellow'; all prob. as 'reddish' fr. *AUS-(WES-) in words for dawn, Skt. Ushas-etc. The view that the Baltic words were borrowed in very ancient times fr. Lat. *AUSOM is improbable. Walde-P. 1.27. Ernout-M.94.Walde-H.1.86."[143] Of course, *Ṛgveda* refers to ayas prob. as 'bronze'; Lat. aes copper, bronze; aurichalcum brass; Rumanian. arama copper. *AUSOM could be a compounded aes + som? sommu (Telugu) is treasure; Rum. comoara, fr. Slavic, SCr. komora 'chamber, treasury', Slov. komora chamber, etc. fr. Latt. camara, camera vault, arch, in VLat. room, treasure room. Tiktin 396. Berneker 555f. loc. cit. Buck, p. 777.

In the context of yajña, saman = to offer an offering or sacrifice, to place in front of (Santali) homa = the act of making an oblation to the gods by casting clarified butter into the fire, accompanied with reciting mantras; an oblation of clarified butter, an oblation with fire, a burnt-offering; a sacrifice; homāgni = sacrificial fire, the fire for an oblation (Ka.) sāman = song accompanying processing of soma in sāmaveda (Vedic) .

Indo-European and South Asian etyma provide a substantive foundation to confirm the decipherment of Soma as electrum (silver-gold ore/processed product).

Needham observes in his magnum opus, *History of Science and Civilization in China,* the extraordinary linkage between references to soma and gold in hundreds of verses from the Śathapathabrāhmaṇa (an extraordinary text, extremely difficult to interpret); when a reference to soma occurs, reference to gold almost immediately follows. Note the refrains: amrtam āyur hiraṇyam; hiraṇya garbham garbhastham, hemabījam vibhāvasoh. In the Tamil tradition, vedi-iyal refers to alchemy (transmutation of material into gold).

Witzel underscores the importance of Pinault's observations:

" Pinault (2003) connects paṇi /*parna, as a loan word from the BMAC area, with Tocharian B peniyo, A pani 'splendor'...Some four percent of the words in the Rgvedic hymns that are composed in archaic, poetic, hieratic form of Vedic clearly are of non-Indo-European, non-Indo-Aryan origin. In other words, they stem from a pre-Indo-Aryan Panjab substrate...The older Avestan texts (Gathas/Yasna Haptanhaiti) point to a Copper or Bronze Age culture quite similar to that of the RV...Words from substrate languages are defined here as all those words in early

Vedic that do not conform to Indo-European/Indo-Iranian word structure (including sounds, root structure, and word formation) and that have no clear Indo-European/Indo-Iranian etymology…It is important to keep in mind that names taken from a previous language (or from an adstrate) have more often than not lost their (precise) original meaning…It is important to note that Pinault (2003) has now also provided the eastern rim of influence of the BMAC language(s) by identifying some words that have been taken over into early (Common) Tocharian, such as iṣṭ, ancu, carwa, paṇi, āṇi, and athṛ…The most prominent words are those of rituals, deities, and priests: *ancu 'soma plant'; *yātu 'black magic', *atharwan 'priest'…ṛṣi 'seer', *ucig 'sacrificing priest', *carwa 'name of Rudra', *indra, *g(hndharv/b(h)a 'demi-god or demon'…'(Michael Witzel, 2006, Early loan words in western Central Asia, Indicators of substrate populations, migrations and trade relations, in: Victor H. Mair, 2006, *Contact and Exchange in the Ancient World*, University of Hawaii Press, pp.158-190,)

"…some 4% of the words in this sacred text (Rigveda) are clearly of non-IE, nonIndo-Aryan origin, in other words, from a pre-IA substrate." Analysing about 300 non-IE words (related, for e.g. to local flora and fauna, agriculture and artisanship) in Rigveda, Witzel (based on Kuiper) tries to identify a substrate language which may explain the underlying language of Indus script. A significant hypothesis is: "…the possibility of early (Para-)Munda settlements further west than Munda speakers are found now. The Rgvedic substrate words from a prefixing language may be a very early form of Munda (or another variety of Austro-Asiatic) which still used prefixes actively, such as the eastern Austro-As. languages (Mon, Khmer)…if the Rgvedic Para-Munda is a somewhat deviant form of Austro-Asiatic, it represents a very old stage of this language family indeed. In that case, this Rgvedic western Austro-Asiatic would stand next to Munda and eastern Austro-Asiatic (Mon-Khmer)…In other words, the western Austro-Asiatic visible in the RV loans, may have been another type of Austro-As. (therefore, I chose the term Para-Munda, Witzel 1999), -- another sub-family of the great Austro-Asiatic family which stretches from the Greater Punjab to Vietnam and from N. Burma to the outskirts of Singapore…The c.300 words in the RV constitute, after all, the oldest recorded language in the Panjab. It must be underlined that, just like an ancient inscription, these words have not changed since the composition of these hymns c. 1500 BCE, as the RV has been transmitted almost without any change, i.e. we know exactly in which limited cases certain sounds – but not words, tonal accents, sentences – have been changed. The modern oral recitation of the RV is a tape recording of c. 1700-1200 BCE, and as that, of the oldest Austro-Asiatic that we have."[144]

While discounting the reference to c.1500 BCE as a disputable issue, this remarkable statement outlining the structure and form of the language of the 'Panjab' (simply, the Harappan language) is worthy of attention and further deployment to decode the Indus script using this underlying language. This insight by Witzel makes Munda speakers a possible group of speakers of the Indus language underlying the Indus script. An example related to artisanship is cited, while identifying words with ka-, ki-, ku-, ke- prefixes (prominent in Munda) :

"Ved. kuliśa 'axe' which E W A I 374 declares as not securely etymologized, has been connected with Drav. (Tam. kuLir 'battle axe', Kan. kuTTu 'to beat, strike, pound', Kuiper 1955: 163), but also with Munda (in Skt. kuThara, kuddåla 'hoe', Sant., Mundari kutam 'to beat, hammer', Mundari, Ho kutasi 'hammer', Kuiper 1955: 163); Berger 1963: 419 derives *kuDiśa from *k o d e ś , Kharia, Mundari khoNDe'j 'axe', with prefix kon- from Kharia te'j 'break'."

Witzel should be complimented for this remarkable contribution made to theist further researches in unraveling the code of the Indus script (while it is unfortunate that Witzel later changed his position somewhat claiming that Indus script does not code a spoken language at all).

eñcuwo – iñcuwo (n.) 'iron'

[eñcuwo – iñcuwo, -, -//] (255b2, 520b6); –**eñcuwaññe – iñcuwaññe** 'prtng to iron': *laursa eñcwaññe tarne räskre tsopyeṃ-ne* 'with an iron bar they pierced his skull roughly' (22b5), *eñcuwaññe kentse* 'rust' (W-31b1). ■TchA *añcu (id.) (attested in the derived adjective *añcwāṣi*) and B *eñcuwo* (*iñcuwo* is variant on the same order as *inte* is to *ente*, q.v.) reflect PTch *eñcuwo. Further connections are uncertain. Schwarz (1974:409) compares Ossetic *ändon* 'steel' or Chorasmian *hncw* 'id.' and suggests that the Iranian and Tocharian words might be borrowings from some adstratum language in the shape ± *anśuwan. Not with VW (146) the intensive prefix *e(n)-* + some derivative of PIE *ǵʰeu- 'pour.'

encuwo, Tocharian.[145]

It is extraordinary that soma is referred to in dual, or plural (re-inforcing the allegorical nature of the descriptions): "with those two forms" (RV IX.66.2,3,5); "the forms (plural, not dual) that are thine" (RV IX.66.3); "the shining rays spread a filter on the back of the heaven, O soma, with (thy) forms (plural, not dual)" (RV IX.66.5); the dual reference is to the ore-form and the purified/processed form. All the sūkta-s are thus, governed by a framework of four principal metaphors, rendered in scintillating, ecstatic, ādhyātmika poetic resonance : word, prayer, divinities, material well-being. Soma is *vāco agriyah* (RV 9.62.25) 'leader of the Word'. Soma is *kavi* stimulating the poetic creations (*kāvyā*).

Soma is NOT a drink for Brāhmaṇa. RV 7.26.1 states: *na soma indram asuto mamāda nābrahmāṇo maghavṇnam sutāsah* 'Soma unpressed has never intoxicated Indra, nor the pressed juices unaccompanied by sacred hymns.'

Chāndogya Upaniṣad (V.10.4) is emphatic: *eṣa somo rājā tad devānāmannam tam devā bhakṣyanti* ('Soma is king. Soma is food for the divinities. Divinities eat Soma.')

Soma is a Divinity. Soma is a commodity. Soma is a pressed and liquefied rasa; soma is present in the sap of the commodity. RV 9.92.2: *achā nṛcakṣā asarat pavitre nāma dadhānah kavir asya yonau* ('Soma…flowed hither, taking to himself his name on the filter, on his yoni.') In the texts, soma is NEVER named as a plant. That modern Zoroastrians identify a species of Ephedra as Haoma-plant does NOT prove that the original Soma or amśu was a plant or even *amanita muscaria*, a red mushroom.

The physical attributes of haoma, as described in the texts of the Avesta, include:

- the plant has stems, roots and branches (*Yasna* 10.5).

- it has a pliant *asu* (*Yasna* 9.16). The term *asu* is only used in conjunction with a description of *haoma*, and does not have an established translation. It refers to 'twigs' according to Dieter Taillieu, 'fibre' or 'flesh' according to Ilya Gershevitch, 'sprouts' according to Lawrence Heyworth Mills.
- it is tall (*Yasna* 10.21, *Vendidad* 19.19)
- it is fragrant (*Yasna* 10.4)
- it is golden-green (standard appellation, *Yasna* 9.16 et al.)
- it can be pressed (*Yasna* 9.1, 9.2)
- it grows on the mountains, 'swiftly spreading', 'apart on many paths' (*Yasna* 9.26, 10.3-4 et al.) 'to the gorges and abysses' (*Yasna* 10-11) and 'on the ranges' (*Yasna* 10.12)[146]
- Y.9.16
- Thus said Zarathustra:
- Homage to Haoma! Good (is) Haoma,
- well set up (is) Haoma, set up straight,
- good, healing according to the established rules,
- of good shape, giving good invigoration,
- an obstruction-smasher,
- golden-colored with pliable twigs,
- the best when they drink (him)
- and the best flight-maker for the breath-soul. (It makes the breath-soul fly up to heaven).[147]

In the two traditions – Soma/Haoma, why were herbal/alchemical substitutes used for soma?

The simple answer is: I do not know.

One can however conjecture that in Veic sūtra/Avestan haoma period, substitutes were used to continue the prayers which are important components of the yajña, explaining the cosmic/consciousness phenomena observed by the ancient Ṛṣi-s. There were two substitution streams: botanical and metallurgical.

Botanical stream involved choice of oṣadhi, 'herbs'; metallurgical stream involved alchemy, transmutation of base metals into gold. Another explanation, in the metallurgy/alchemy tradition could be that in Soma processing, plants were used as kṣāra to neutralize the oxides in ore-blocks and hence, plants were chosen as soma substitutes.

Expiatory prayers in Indian, vedic tradition apologize to the divinities for the use of a substitute plant (somalatā, e.g. the pūtīka --*Guilandina Bonduc*?) because Soma had become unavailable. Texts provide an extensive list of plants that can be used as substitutes and end the list by saying that any plant is acceptable, provided it is yellow.[148] The original soma was no longer available, only the colour identification remained in the continuum of yajña, offerings as prayers.
Tandya Mahabrahmana 9.5.1-3 suggests the use of pūtika -- *basella cordifolia*? -- as a substitute for Soma. Other substitutes (e.g. Satapatha Brahmana 4.5.10; 5.3.3; 6.6.3) mentioned in many Brahmana texts were praprotha, adara, usana and prsniparni (122). Prsniparni had speckled leaves and its wood was used to protect from the negative effects caused by evil spirits. ApSS 14.24,13 suggests the use of rice and barley as substitutes for Soma.

Jaiminiya Brahmana notes that "if they do not find Soma...they should press out Phalguna plants with tawny panicles. Indra killed Vrtra with the Vajra. The Soma which flowed out of his nose, became these Phalguna plants with tawny panicles. And what was produced on account of the drawing out of the omentum, that became Phalguna plants with red panicles. Therefore they press out Phalguna plants with tawny panicles, since these are more suitable to be used in a sacrifice. They say: 'This (pseudo-Soma) belongs to the Asuras, therefore it should not be pressed out (for a Soma sacrifice)'. (The answer should be:) 'In the beginning all here was with the Asuras. The gods placed this with themselves after their victory. Therefore it should be used for the Soma presing.' If they should not find this (substitute), they should press out Utika plants. Indra having thrown the Vajra at Vrtra but thinking 'I have not slain him' entered the Utika plants. Someone whose Soma they steal loses his help (Uti). They find help for him (in the form of the Utika). When the head of the sacrifice was cut off, the sap which streamed forth out of it became the Utika plants. Therefore also they obviously press out sacrifice itself in the form of these Utika plants. If they should not find this---355. -- they should press out light-coloured grass. When king Soma came to this world, then he stayed in the grasses. This is a trace of him. Thus they press him out (when they press out the grasses). If they should not find this, they should press out the Parna. When Suparna fetched king Soma, then the feather which fell down became the Parna (leaf). That is his trace. Thus they press him out (when they press out the Parna). If they should not find this, they may press out whatever plants there are. When Suparna fetched king Soma and broke him, then the drops which fell down, became these plants. And all plants are related to Soma. That is this trace of him. Him they thereby press out. At the morning pressing one should pour fresh milk, at the midday pressing boiled milk and at the third pressing coagulated milk to (these substitutes of Soma). It is obvious that they also consume this Soma, when they consume milk, for that is the sap of all the plants."[149]

Haoma, in the Avestan tradition, may represent the times when the original soma of *Ṛgveda* was already replaced by substitutes such as pūtīka to achieve soma pavamāna.

Crucible with molten gold.[150]

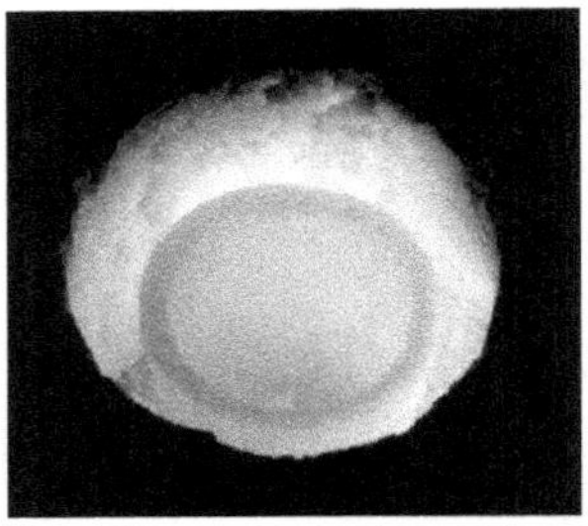

This is an engraving of molten gold being poured into ingot molds.[151]

RV 10.85.3-4 (AV 14.1.3): [*somam manyate papivān yat sampimṣanty oṣadhim somam yam brāhmaṇo vidurna tasyāssnāti kaścana* "one thinks to have drunk soma, when they crush the plant. Of him (soma), which the Brāhmaṇa-s know, no one ever tastes." This text distinguishes between the Soma that the priests know and that which they process. (The same hymn as RV. 10.85.3 in AV XIV.1.3).'O Soma, guarded by that which is meant to cover you, guarded by him who lives in the high (heaven?), you stand listening to the pressing stones. No earthly one eats you.' (RV X.85.4).

Soma is for Indra: "Boldy drink soma from the beaker, Indra!...": soma is not surā; it is divinities' drink; the process is the key: *adribhih sutah pavase pavitra ān indav indrasya jatharesv āvihan* (pressed by the pressing stones, thou clarifiest thyself in the filter, O Soma juice, when penetrating into the entrails of Indra): RV IX.86.23; "thy filter, O Agni, equipped with flames, may it cleanse us, cleanse us with the fruits of sacred songs! with these both, the filter and the fruits (of song), O Divinity Savitr, cleanse me through and through: RV IX.67,22-25; so, Agni is the filter!

Baudhāyana (Taittirīya rescension) provides a list of substances used in the pravargya: skin of black antelope, earth grubbed by a boar, earth from an ant-hill, potsherds from a deserted place, hair from the skin of a black antelope, hair of a

goat, a clump of pūtikā or ādāra plant, milk of goat, lumps of dung of a stallion. RV 9.99.1 *śukrām vayanty asurāya nirṇijam vipām agre* [(the fingers of the priests) weave for the Asura (Soma), at the beginning of the sacred hymns, a white festal garment'.] This *nirṇij* was the woolen filter for filtering pressed Soma.
Ṛṣi Vasiṣṭha Maitrāvaruṇi, devatā Indra:
adhvaryavoruṇam dugdham amśum juhotana vṛṣabhāya kṣitīnām
gaurād vedīyaa avapānam indro viśvāhed yāti sutasomam icchan
RV 7.98.1 Offer, priests, the shining effused Soma o him who is eminent (among) men; knowing better than the Gaura where his distant drinking-place (is to be found). Indra comes daily seeking for the offerer of the libation. [Knowing better: gaurād vedīyān avapānam = avakramya sthitam dūrastham pātavyam somam gauramṛgād api atiśayena = knowing the Soma that is to be drunk, though placed afar off, better than an ox or a deer knows the drinking place of pond].
Soma was pounded with stones or in a mortar, notes Ṛṣi Gotama raahugaṇa, devatā Indra:
barhir vā yat svapatyāya vrjyaterko vā s'lokam āghoṣate divi
grāvāyatra vadati kārur ukthyas tasyed indro abhipitveṣu raṇyati
RV 1.083.06 Whether the holy grass be cut (for the rite) that brings down blessings, whether the priest repeats (the sacred) verse in the brilliant (sacrifice), whether the stone (that expresses the Soma) sound like the priest who repeats the hymn, on all these occasions Indra rejoices. [That brings down blessings: śvapatyāya is resolved into: su and apatya; explained as śobhanapatana hetubhūtāya, for the sake of the descent, or coming down, of what is good].
Soma is associated with the mountains. 'growing' on the mountains (giriṣṭhā) RV. III.48,2; V.43.4; IX.18.1, 62,4; parvatāvṛdh: RV. IX.46.1. Hence, the reference to Somam adrau (RV. 5.85.2) plucked in two rocks. The seller of Soma is asked if Soma comes from the mūjavat mountain. If Soma cannot be so procured, the texts allow for substitutes to be used.

Substrates of mleccha? Vedic, Avestan! soma, haoma

Both Avestan haoma and Sanskrit soma derived from proto-Indo-Iranian *sauma. The linguistic root of the word haoma, hu-, and of soma, su-, suggests 'press' or 'pound'. [Taillieu, Dieter and Boyce, Mary (2002). "Haoma". Encyclopaedia Iranica. New York: Mazda Pub.] The name of the Scythian tribe Hauma-varga is related to the word, and probably connected with the ritual. The word is derived from an Indo-Iranian root *sav- (Sanskrit sav-/su) "to press", i.e. *sau-ma- is the drink prepared by pressing the stalks of a plant.[K.F.Geldner, Der Rig-Veda. Cambridge MA, 1951, Vol. III: 1-9] The root is Proto-Indo-European (*sew(h)-)[M. Mayrhofer, Etymologisches Wörterbuch des Altindoarischen, Heidelberg 1986–2000, vol II: 748]

Beyond the establishment of a common origin of haoma and soma and numerous attempts to give that common origin a botanic identity, little has been done to compare the two. As Indologist Jan Houben also noted in the proceedings of a 1999 workshop on Haoma-Soma, "apart from occasional and dispersed remarks on similarities in structure and detail of Vedic and Zoroastrian rituals, little has been done on the systematic comparison of the two" (Houben, 2003, 9/1a).Houben's observation is also significant in that, as of 2003, no significant comparative review of cultural/sacred Haoma/Soma had extended beyond Alfred Hillebrandt's 1891 comparison of the Vedic deity and the Zoroastrian divinity. [Hillebrandt (1891)]. Payne[152] shows fifty-seven isoglosses shared between Indic and Iranian which link the two, 'a convincingly large number of shared characteristics to justify the Indo-Iranian unity. Indo-Iranian dominates the IE family numerically: of the 144 IE languages listed in Ruhlen (1987: 325), 93 are Indo-Iranian.'[153]

Hundreds of lexical isoglosses of Tocharian-Indo-European have been identified in a thesaurus: "This dictionary describes Tocharian A, one of two Tocharian languages documented in manuscripts of Buddhist texts from the second half of the 1st millennium CE, excavated in the oases of the Tarim basin. The dictionary contains also a thesaurus, based on all the identifi ed texts in Tocharian A, including previously published and unpublished texts from various collections (Paris, Berlin). All forms of words, including variants occurring in the texts, are listed separately with reference to all occurrences and a sample of passages in transcription and

translation. The meaning of a number of words has been better defined and, when necessary, corrected against previous glossaries. Much focus has been laid on phraseology and literary parallels with other Buddhist texts in Sanskrit and Uighur. The description of the verbal forms has been listed according to the stems of the paradigms. The sources of loanwords, e.g., from Tocharian B, Old and Middle Indo-Aryan, Iranian, Old Turkic, and Chinese, as well as the corresponding words in Tocharian B, are also given."[154]

Tocharian thesaurus is indicative of the contacts between Tocharian and Rigvedic in the times when soma was purchased and processed. If so, ancu (Tocharian) can be explained as a phonetic variant of *amśu* (Rigveda). Rigvedic is Proto-Indian. Avestan is Proto-Iranian. It is likely that Proto-Tocharian speakers migrated from PIE Homeland (Urheimat) eastwards and discovered a trade good: *ancu* (Toch.)/*amśu* (Rigvedic). A synonym for the trade good -- *amśu* -- was soma.

The *ancu- amśu* cognates are comparable to another lexical isogloss: *sanga*, 'priest' (Sumerian) and *sanga*, 'body of pilgrims' (Indian *sprachbund*): saṅgá m. ' battle ' RV., 'contact with' TS., ' addiction to ' Mn. [√sañj] Pa. *saṅga* -- m. 'attachment, cleaving to', Dhp. *ṣaǵa*<-> (see sájati: → Khot. *a* -- *ṣaṁga* -- H. W. Bailey BSOAS xi 776), Pk. *saṁga* -- m.; K. *sang* m. 'union'; S. *saṅu* m. 'connexion by

marriage', *saṅgu* m. 'body of pilgrims'; L. *saṅg*, (Ju.) *sãg* m. 'body of pilgrims or travellers'; P. *saṅg* m. 'id., association'; B. *sāṅāt* 'companion';
Or. *sāṅga* 'company, companion'; Phal. *saṅgī´* ' with, to '; P. *saṅg* ' along with ', Ku.gng. *śaṅ*, N. *saṅa*; Or. *sāṅge*, *saṅge* 'near, with'; Bhoj. *saṅ* 'with', H. *saṅg*, G. *sãge*, M. *sãgẽ*. -- In mng. 'company of travellers &c.', though there is no trace of aspirate, poss. < or at least infl. by saṁghá -- WPah.kṭg. (kc.) *sɔ́ṅg* m. 'union, companionship', kṭg. *sɔ́ṅge* 'together (with), simultaneously, with, by' prob. ← H. Him.I 212. (CDIAL 13082). S. L. P. *saṅgī* m. ' comrade ' (P. also ' one of a party of pilgrims '), N. *saṅi*, Or. *sāṅga*, *°gī*, H. *saṅgī*m., M. *sãgyā*, *sāgyā* m.(CDIAL 13084). <saGat>(K) {N} ``^friend''. Cf. <saGga>(P), <saGgO>(M) `brother-in -law'; <saGgo> `company'. *Mu.<saG>, Sa.<saGga>, Kh.<saGgo>(B) `companion', H.<sA~gA> `friendship', Sa.<saGgat> `brother-in-law'. %28511. #28311. <saGgO>(P) {N} ``^company''. Cf. <saGe> `with', <saGga>(P), <saGgO>(M) `brother-in-law', <saiGga>??. *Mu.<saG>, Sa.<saGga>, Kh.<saGgo>(B) `companion', H.<sA~gA> `friendship', Sa.<saGgat> `brother-in-law'; O.<saGgO-re>, ~<sOGgO-re> `with'. %28551. #28351.(Munda etyma).
சங்கம்[1] caṅkam, n. < saṅga. 1. Union, junction, contact; சேர்க்கை. (சூடா.) 2. Friendship, love, attachment; அன்பு. சங்கந் தருமுத்தி (திருக்கோ. 85)
சங்கம்[2] caṅkam, n. < saṅgha. 1. Mustering, gathering; கூட்டம். சங்கமாகி வெங்கணை வீக்க மொடு (பெருங். மகத. 17, 38). 2. Society, assembly, council, senate, academy; சபை. புலம்பரிச் சங்கம் பொருளொடு முழங்க (மணி. 7, 114). 3. Literati, poets; புலவர். (திவா.) 4. Learned assemblies or academies of ancient times patronised by Pāṇḍya kings, three in number, viz., talai-c-caṅkam, iṭai-c-caṅkam, kaṭai-c-caṅkam; பாண்டி யர் ஆதரவுபெற்று விளங்கிய தலைச்சங்கம், இடைச் சங்கம், கடைச்சங்கம் என்ற முச்சங்கங்கள். எம்மைப் பவந்தீர்ப்பவர் சங்கமிருந்தது (பெரியபு. மூர்த்திநா. 7). 5. Fraternity of monks among Buddhists and Jains; சைனபௌத்தர்களின் சங்கம். (Tamil)

Achavaka (Any link with *ancwaashi* 'made of iron' (Tocharian)?

Krishna Yajurveda i. 8. 18:

On the same day they consecrate, on the same day they buy the Soma.
He presents a lotus wreath.
He buys the Soma with calves.
There is a drink for ten.
A hundred Brahmans drink.
The Stotra is the Saptadasa.
The two ornaments he gives to the Adhvaryu, the garland to the Udgatr, the round ornament to the Hotr, a horse to the Prastotr and Pratihartr, twelve heifers to the Brahman, a cow to the Maitravaruna, a bull to the Brahmanacchansin, garments to theNestr and Potr, a wagon drawn by one ox laden with barley to the Achavaka, a draught ox to the Agnidh.
The Hotr is a Bhargava; the Saman of the Brahman is the Srayantiya; the AgnistomaSaman is the Varavantiya.
He takes water of the Sarasvati.

v.4.12 The Achavaka's Saman is the Samkrti; the horse sacrifice is an extensive sacrifice; who knows they say, if all of it is done or not? In that the Achavaka s Saman is the Samkrti, (it serves) to make the horse whole, to win it entirely, to prevent interference. The last day is an Atirātra with all the Stomas, to obtain all, to conquer all; verily he obtains all, he conquers all with it.

vii.1.5 It is the Achavaka who recites this verse.
Now (some say), The thousandth is to be given to the Hotr what is left over, is left over for the Hotr; the Hotr is the receiver of what has not been taken.
Then others say, It is to be given to the Unnetr.
This is left over of the thousand, and the Unnetr is the one of the priests who is left over.

Then some say, It is to be given to all those who have a place in the Sadas.
Then some say, It should be driven away and allowed to wander at will.
Then some say, It is to be given to the Brahman and the Agnidh [6], two shares to theBrahman and the third to the Agnidh.

अच्छावाकः [अच्छं निर्मलं अच्छ आभिमुख्येन वा वक्ति शंसति; वच् कर्तरि संज्ञायां घञ् निपातस्य चेति दीर्घः Tv.] The invoker or inviter, a priest or Ṛitvij who is employed at Soma sacrifices, and is a co-adjutor of होतृ. Each of the four principal priests, होतृ, अध्वर्यु, उद्गातृ and ब्रह्मन् has three assistants, the total number of priests employed at Soma sacrifices being therefore 16; °सामन् *a.* N. of the Sāman to be chanted by an अच्छावाक, also called उद्वंशीय. (Apte lexicon, p. 29)

होतृ M. (fr. √1. हु) an offerer of an oblation or burnt-offering (with fire) , sacrificer , priest , (esp.) a priest who at a sacrifice invokes the gods or recites the ऋग्-वेद , a ऋग्-वेद priest (one of the 4 kinds of officiating priest » ऋत्विज् , p.224; properly the होतृ priest has 3 assistants , sometimes called पुरुषs , viz. the मैत्रा-वरुण , अच्छा-वाक , and ग्रावस्तुत् ; to these are sometimes added three others , the ब्राह्मणाच्छंसिन् , अग्नीध्र or अग्नीध् , and पोतृ , though these last are properly assigned to the Brahman priest ; sometimes the नेष्टृ is substituted for the ग्राव-स्तुत्) (Monier-Williams, p.1306). अच्छः = crystal.

A frequent reference is to amśu- of soma. The gloss is rendered as 'stalk' or 'stem'. Louis Renou calls it 'la tige (de soma)' ('the stem of soma'). Recurrence of the word is indicative of the fact that the word amśu could itself represent the name of the commodity. Grassman's dictionary refers to it as: '*Name der Pflanze, aus welcher der Soma gepresst wurde...Somapflanze, der aus ihr gepresste Somasaft.*' For example, RV 1.46.10 *abhūd u bhā u amśave* is translated by Geldner as 'Licht ist der Somapflanze geworden'. Renou (EVP, xvi,5) renders it: *'...est apparue la lumiere (adaptee) au soma'*. Gelder translates RV 9.15.5 *eṣa śubhrebhir amśubhih* as: '*Dieser (Soma)...mit den...strahlenden Zweigen (Strahlen)*' [This (soma)...with...the bright branches (rays)]. Renou renders this as *a pour acception seconde 'rayon'* (Its second meaning 'ray'). Roth calls amśu the name of the plant or its members: '*Die dem Veda so gelaufige Bezeichnung fur die Somapflanze oder vielmehr ihre Glieder'.*[155]

Renou noted: 'Il est possible que cette nouvelle acception ait ete déjà presente a l'auteur d'AV xiii.2.7 qui nous dit du char solaire qu'il est amśumant-: soit a la fois le soma avec les rameaux ou rejets de sa plante, et la lune avec ses rayons'. ('It is possible that this new meaning has already been presented to the author of AV xiii.2.7 who says he is the sun chariot-amśumant: has both the soma with the release of its branches or plant , and the moon with his rays.')

Bartholomae notes that asu used of Haoma in Avesa may also be the name of the plant itself. (Bartholomae, *Air. W, sv. asav-*: 'schoss, Zweig der haoma-pflanze'.) 'mit biegsamen, zarten Schosslingen'. ('Haoma...whose Asu-plants are tender (?)'. RV 10.17.12 *yas te drapsah...yas te amśuh*. Sāyaṇa's comment: *drapsah rasah...yaś ca te tvadīyah amśuh rasād itarah san* (soma's other part *amśu* as distinct from the juice).

RV 1.137.3: *amśum duhanty adribhih somam duhanty adribhih* (the metaphor of the verb 'to milk' explicitly refers to *amśu* AS *soma.*

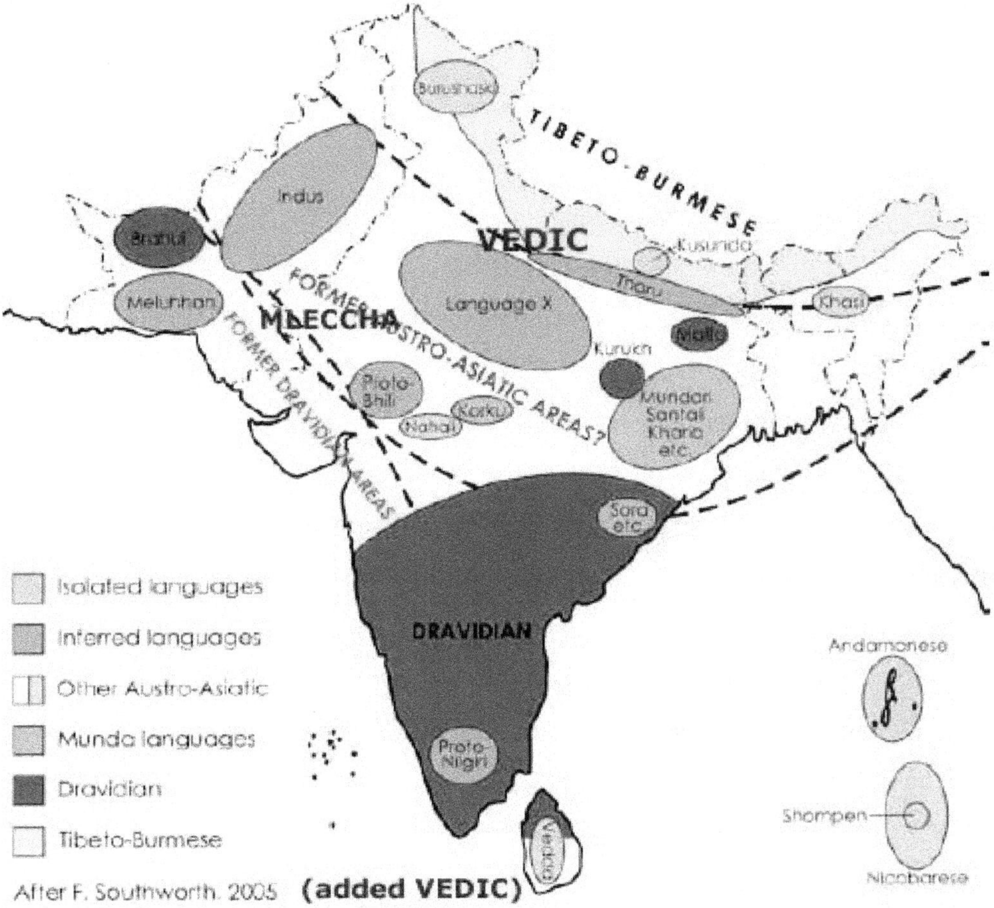

Yasna 10.3: *bareṣnuṣ paiti gairinam*; Yasna 10.17 v*īspe haoma upastaomi yatcit bareṣnuṣva gairinam yatcit jafnuṣva raonam* ('I praise all the haomas whethere those on the heights of the mountains, whethere those in the valleys of the rivers'); RV 8.6.28: [*vipra (Soma)...upahvare girīnām samgathe ca nadīn*ām ('in the hidden place (or on the slope?) of the mountains, and in the confluence of the rivers')] locate Haoma/Soma on mountain heights. RV 8.96.13-15 refers to the river Amśumatī as 'abounding in Soma'. RV 9.66.2 *tābhyām viśvasya rājasi ye pavamāna dhāmanī pratīcī soma tasthatuh* (Renou: Avec ces deux forms, (la pure et la mélange), qui se tiennent face (a nous), o soma, tu regnes sur toutes choses, o Pavam*āna'*). Gonda, however suggests *dhāmanī* are two forms: amśu (the plant) and the pressed juice. (J. Gonda, *The meaning of the Sanskrit term dhāman-*). RV 9.96.17 refers to the first two forms of Soma and RV 9.96.18-19 give the third and

fourth *dhāman*. RV 1.91.4 notes that soma has many *dhāman : yā te dhāmāni divi yā pṛthivyām yā parvatesv oṣadhīsv apsu: tebhir no viśvaih* ('with all these *dhāman* of yours, (O Soma), those in heaven, those on earth, those on the mountains, in the plants, in the waters… ' The two forms may simply be the filtered soma-juice received in two vessels (camū). RV 9.96.20: *vṛṣeva…kanikradac camvor ā vivesa* 'like bull bellowing mightily (the soma-juice) has entered the two vessels'. RV 9.86.47 notes that both vessels had soma mixed with milk: *yad gobhir indo camvoh samajyase* 'when, O soma-juice, you are anointed with milk in the two vessels'. According to Brough, following Gonda, *dhāmanī* may be interpreted as "two places of Soma's divine manifestation."

Mleccha in Indian *sprachbund* (linguistic area or language union)

Meluhha (Mleccha) was the *lingua franca* of the artisans in Indian *sprachbund* of ca. 3500 BCE when writing was invented. The language repertoire of metallurgy attested in Indus writing continued into the historical periods – for example, on thousands of punch-marked coins made in the mints from Gandhara to Anuradhapura -- yielding the *Indian Lexicon* of over 25 ancient languages.

It is significant that Vatsyayana refers to in his lists of 64 arts and calls it mlecchita-vikalpa, lit. 'an alternative representation — in cryptography or cipher — of mleccha words.'

Indian linguistic area map, including mleccha and vedic (After F. Southworth, 2005; VEDIC AND MLECCHA added.)

A language area, mleccha (?language X), is attested in the ancient literature of India. This is the lingua franca, the spoken version of the language of the civilization of about 5000 years ago, distinct from the grammatically correct version called Sanskrit represented in the vedic texts and other ancient literature. Ancient texts of India are replete with insights into formation and evolution of languages. Some examples are: Bharata's Natya Shastra, Patanjali's Mahabhashya, Hemacandra's Deśī nāmamālā, Nighanṭus, Panini's Aṣṭādhyayi, Tolkappiyam– Tamil grammar.

The identification of mleccha as the language of the Indus script writing system is consistent with the following theses which postulate an Indian linguistic area, that is an area of ancient times when various language-speakers interacted and absorbed language features from one another and made them their own: Emeneau, 1956; Kuiper, 1948; Masica, 1971; Przyludski, 1929; Southworth, 2005.

The *Indian Lexicon* (S. Kalyanaraman, 1998) is an exploration in general semantics in over 25 ancient Indian languages, a comparative study of lexemes (which may also be referred to, in a geographical/historical phrase, in the context of lexical isoglosses, as the Indian linguistic area).

This lexicon seeks to establish a semantic concordance, across the languages or *numeraire facile* of the Indian linguistic area: from Brahui to Santali to Bengali, from Kashmiri to Mundarica to Sinhalese, from Marathi to Hindi to Nepali, from Sindhi or Punjabi or Urdu to Tamil. A semantic structure binds the languages of India, which may have diverged morphologically or phonologically as evidenced in the oral tradition of Vedic texts, or epigraphy, literary works or lexicons of the historical periods. This lexicon, therefore, goes beyond, the commonly held belief of an Indo-European language and is anchored on proto-Indian sememes.

The work covers over 1240 groups of semantic clusters which span and bind the Indian languages. The basic finding is that thousands of terms of the Vedas, the Munda languages (e.g., Santali, Mundarica, Sora), the so-called Dravidian languages and the so-called Indo-Aryan languages have common roots. This belies the received wisdom of distinct or separate evolution, for example, the Dravidian or Munda and the Aryan languages.

The lexicon seeks to establish an areal 'Indian' language type, by establishing semantic concordance among the so-called Indo-Aryan, Dravidian and Munda languages. The area spanned is a geographical region bounded by the Indian ocean on the south and the mountain ranges which insulate it from other regions of the Asian continent on the north, east and west.

This lexicon is a tribute to the brilliant work done by etymologists and scholars of Indian linguistics, and to a number of scholars who have contributed to resolving the enigma of the Indus (Sarasvati-Sindhu) Script, of the *lingua franca* of the civilization and to the study of ancient Indian science and technology.

The author believes that the work can contribute to/strengthen the unifying elements of Indian common cultural heritage and the conclusions will counter divisive forces which occasionally hold sway. The author also realizes that language is an extraordinarily emotional issue and is subject to a variety of possible interpretations. Language evolution, itself, is also a philosophical problem *par excellence.*

The justification for this comparative lexicon of languages currently spoken by over a billion people of the world today can be provided at a number of levels:

(1) to bring people closer to the ancient heritage of a Indian language family of which the extant Indian languages (Indo-Aryan, Dravidian and Munda language streams) are but dialectical forms;

(2) to generate further studies in the disciplines of (i) Indian archaeology, (ii) general semantics and comparative linguistics; (iii) design of fifth-generation computer systems; and

(3) to provide a basis for further studies in grammatical philosophy and neurosciences on the formation of semantic patterns or structures in the human brain — neurosciences related to the study of linguistic competence which seems to set apart the humans from other living beings.

The urgent warrant for this work is the difficulty faced by scholars in collating different lexicons and in obtaining classical works such as CDIAL (A Comparative Dictionary of Indo-Aryan Languages) even in eminent libraries.

In tracing the etyma (lit. truth in Greek) of the Indian languages, it is adequate, to start with, to indicate the word forms which can be traced into the mists of history.

Hypotheses on Indian vocabulary

The following hypotheses govern the semantic clustering attempted in this lexicon.

1. It is possible to re-construct a proto-Indian idiom or *lingua franca* of circa the centuries traversed by the Sarasvati-Sindhu doab civilization (c. 2500 to 1700 B.C.E).
2. India is a linguistic area nurtured in the cradle of the Sarasvati-Sindhu doab civilization.

The hypotheses contest two earlier linguistic assertions: (i) Sir William Jones's assertion in 1786 of an Indo-European linguistic family and (ii) Francis Whyte Ellis's assertion in 1816 of a southern Indian family of languages. These two assertions have resulted in two comparative or etymological lexicons of the so-called 'Indo-Aryan' and 'Dravidian' languages. This apparent isolation between the two language families is rejected. The exclusion or isolation of the so-called Austro-Asiatic or Munda (or Kherwāri) languages is also rejected. Instead, it is proposed that there was a proto-Indian linguistic area (c. 2500 B.C.E) which included speakers of these three language groups interacting culturally in the civilizational domain. The underlying assumption is that the so-called Dravidian, Munda and Aryan languages can be traced to an ancient Indian proto-version of Indua language or proto-Indic by establishing the unifying elements, and identifying the substrata in semantic terms. This echoes Pope's observations made in a different context: '… that between the languages of Southern India and those of the Aryan family there are many deeply seated and radical affinities; that the differences between the Dravidian tongues and the Aryan are not so great as between the Celtic (for instance) and the Sanskrit; and that, by consequence, the doctrine that the place of the Dravidian dialects is rather with the Aryan than with the Turanian family of languages is still capable of defence… the resemblances (appeared) most frequently in the more uncultivated Dravidian dialects… the identity (was) most striking in the names of instruments, places, and acts connected with a simple life…'[156]

Methodology and limitations of the work

The methodology to test the hypotheses will be based on the design of a vocabulary super-set (in semantic terms). The governing principle of this lexicon is that phonetic and grammatical laws are subordinate to semantic laws within a language family. Cognates do not have to be concordant in phonetic and morphological forms; cognates have to be concordant in phonetic and semantic forms to suggest linguistic affinity among dialects of a language family. To quote, Tolkāppiyam, "ellāc collum porul. Kuṟittaṉavē" (Tol. Col. Peya. 1), i.e. all words are semantic indicators.

The compounded forms of *sememes* of the *lingua franca* of the Sarasvati-Sindhu doab civilization have been reconstructed from the following sources:

(a) lexical entries of Indian languages found in the comparative, etymological lexicons: CDIAL (A Comparative Dictionary of Indo-Aryan Languages) and DEDR (A Dravidian Etymological Dictionary); etymological groups (as semantic super-sets) culled from lists of ancient verb forms such as those found in the dhātupāṭha, Niruktam, Whitney's lexicon and Vedic lexicon;

(b) lists of ancient noun forms, such as materia medica found in nighaṇṭu's and medical works, annotated with insights from botanical works, pharmacopoeia and works on pharmacognosy ;

(c) epigraphical records of many languages of the region which mainly record economic transactions; and

(d) language lexicons of Indian languages.

This lexicon is organized primarily on a comparative basis and secondarily on a historical basis (and not on a genealogical basis, i.e. not trying to trace the changes in phonetic forms of a sememe). Given the limitations of this organization, it has not been considered essential in this lexicon, to reformulate the old Indian phonetic form with an *. This is an area for further investigations in historical linguistics.

The vocabulary is presented in groups of etyma taken from CDIAL, DEDR, Tamil and other language lexicons of Dravidian, Aryan and Munda languages. The etymological groups are put together as semantic cognates and it will be left for future research work to determine the nature of the interactions (or what linguists call, using a pecuniary term: 'borrowing') between and among the languages which constituted the proto-Indian linguistic area. The results of the research are restricted to the identification, in a comparative lexicon, of comparative *sememes* and morphemes, including many allomorphs (i.e. two or more forms of a morpheme). An attempt to conjecture or decipher the possible *proto-Indian* 'phonetic' forms will require further studies and research work. The results of these studies will help for e.g. (1) to eliminate duplicate semantic clusters included in this lexicon and (2) to re-group the clusters in a true syllabic sequence.

For 'alphabetical` indexing or 'areal` (i.e. by geographical regions) sequencing, Turner's A Comparative Dictionary of Indo-Aryan Languages (CDIAL), Burrow and Emeneau's A Dravidian Etymological Lexicon (DEDR), Pali, Sanskrit, Kannada, Tamil, Munda, Santali and other lexicons of Indian languages are unsurpassed sources. DEDR solves the problem of sequencing by using Tamil morphemes as the reference base for the entire group in Tamil syllabic order. In effect, the vocabulary of this lexicon, include many CDIAL and DEDR entries as sub-sets and constitute a semantic index to both CDIAL and DEDR which will continue to provide the basic references to areal etyma.

The primary justification for choosing a simple sequencing based on a limited number of initial vowels/consonants and consonantal combinations (with intervening vowels or nasals) is that each semantic cluster can be treated as a distinct monograph which may provide material for further study of the Indian language family in which there has apparently been an extraordinary semantic affinity between and among related languages.

One substantive problem in organizing the semantic clusters was the problem of 'alphabetical' or 'syllabic' sequencing. It has been difficult to follow a strict alphabetical ordering in this work. This is due to the author's inability to pin down the ancient 'phonetics' of a sememe or to construct a proto-Indian form. This limitation has resulted in some duplication of terms in more than one semantic cluster. The idiosyncratic sequencing is due to the limits of knowledge of the author; the result has been a number of semantic clusters included in the lexicon containing phonetic forms which may not always correspond with the etymological grouping.

Samuel Johnson refers to a lexicographer as a harmless drudge.[157] What a pleasant and glorious drudge! An etymologist is also a drudge but may provoke, hopefully lively, constructive, linguistic disputes among the proponents of dialects of a language family, on issues such as 'true inheritance' or 'great antiquity'! The disputes (or positive creative tensions), may also draw inspiration and guidance from the past linguistic studies of great scholars who have provided valuable insights into the phonological, grammatical and lexical aspects of a proto-Indian language.

An English semantic index has been included. The index is composed of (i) English meanings, and (ii) flora (names of botanical species in Latin terms), plants and products of plants (in English and vernacular terms which have entered the English lexicon). As in DEDR, no attempt has been made to state the equivalence of Latin flora terms; DEDR entries in a group of etyma record the equivalence found in Hooker at the end of the numbered etymological group.

The index is primarily based on the elegantly designed index of A Dravidian Etymological Dictionary (DEDR). To quote from DEDR: (p.773) "This is an index of the more important meanings recorded for words in the Dravidian languages. No attempt has been made to list all the English meanings given in the entries, since such a procedure would have swollen this index beyond all reason. In fact, in any attempt to keep it within bounds, usually only one of a group of synonyms or near-synonyms has been listed: e.g. *resemble* is listed, but not *similar* and *like*... The derivational system of English words, since it does not coincide with that of Dravidian, has in general been ignored..."

Organization of the work

The dominance of economic activities in the lives of ancient Indians will be apparent from the semantic clusters compiled in this lexicon. Semantic clusters include words expressing cognate 'thoughts'.

The ancient economic court was dominated by plant products such as fragrances, incenses and exudations which were highly valued and in great demand. For example, the ancient Egyptian civilization records trans-continental expeditions to pw'nt (or punt) in search of such plant products which may be designated as Kubera's nava-nidhi or nine treasures of Kubera, in the yakṣa tradition of great antiquity.

The inclusion of names of many plants and plant products in the lexicon, has a strong justification in terms of ancient life-styles. The etyma related to plants have been elaborated with cross-references on therapeutic effects described in works dealing with the subject of pharmacognosy and, in some instances, the references in pharmacopoeia of various countries have also been provided.

Evidence related to proto-Indian or proto-Indic or Indus language

A proto-Indic language is attested in ancient Indian texts. For example, Manusmṛti refers to two languages, both of dasyu (daha): ārya vācas, mleccha vācas. *mukhabāhū rupajjānām yā loke jātayo bahih mlecchavācas'cāryav ācas te sarve dasyuvah smṛtāh* Trans. 'All those people in this world who are excluded from those born from the mouth, the arms, the thighs and the feet (of Brahma) are called Dasyus, whether they speak the language of the mleccha-s or that of the ārya-s.' (Manu 10.45)]. So, there were dasyu who spoke both the dialects: Mleccha vācas and Arya vācas . This distinction between *lingua franca* and literary version of the language, is elaborated by Patañjali as a reference to 1) grammatically correct literary language and 2) ungrammatical, colloquial speech (*deśī*).

"Patañjali added a reference to mlecchas, 'barbarians', to the discussion of the purposes of vyākaraṇa. Kātyāyana's second Vārttikā had given five uses for the study of words, all involving service to, study of and fidelity to Veda. It was Patañjali's Bhāṣyas that then added uses without direct link to Veda, and the first was *mlecchaa mā bhūmety adhyeyam vyākaraṇam*: 'So that we should not become mleccha, grammar is to be studied'. (Joshi & Roodbergen 1986, Bhaasya #23 their enumeration. Cf. Cardona 1988)."[158] Thus, in Patañjali's time, mleccha dialect of Proto-Indian was not a grammatically structured dialect while Sanskrit dialect of Proto-Indian followed the rules of grammar. Mleccha may use apaśabdas 'corrupt speech' unsuitable for ādhyatmika duties. In Jaina records, mleccha are Dasyu. In Jaina geography, karmabhumi has six parts: one khanda was peopled by noble, meritorious good people; the other five were mleccha khandas, peopled by the rest of the inhabitants of the karmabhumi.

An intimation of two dialects of Proto-Indian comes from *Rāmāyaṇa*: when Hanuman approaches Sita devi in Aśokavana, he deliberates if he should speak in Sanskrit or in mānuṣam vāk because Sita should not get frightened that Hanuman was an agent spy of Rāvaṇa, if he addresses her in Sanskrit. He decides to converse in mānuṣam vāk, the lingua franca, as distinct from the literary version.

The term *mlecchavācas* (S'Br. VI.3.1.34) is explained by Sayana that the speech of deva (*devasambandhi*) is Samskritam and the speech of men (*manuṣyasambandhi*) is bhāṣa. [*daivam devasambandhi vākyam samskṛtam mānusham ca manushyasambandhi bhāṣāmayan ca vākyam*] This is temed as milakkhu in Pali and Ardhamāgadhi (Sam. N., V. 466: milakkha in Pali; Ac.S., II.3.8: milakkhu in Ardhamāgadhi). The use of *mleccha vāc* may refer to a Prakrit dialect.[159] *Asurāya* refers to 'Prakritic dialectical differences, assimilation of groups of consonants and similar changes peculiar to Prakrit vernaculars'. It is no mere coincidence that the early inscriptions, those of Aśoka for example, are in Prakrit, parole or the spoken vaak which is the synonym of mleccha. Prakrit was the term used in contradistinction to Samskṛtam: one denoted the early tongues and the other a refined, grammatically-correct, literary form of the spoken language of the people of Bharat, which was called bhāṣa by Panini or deśi by Hemacandra. This could be cognate with Nahali (<Nagari) an "Indo-Aryan" language -- with Dravidian and Munda substratum semantics -- on the banks of River Tapati, not far from the Bhimbhetka caves.

Ancient text of Panini also refers to two languages in *śikṣā*: Sanskrit and Prākṛt. Prof Avinash Sathaye provides a textual reference on the earliest occurrence of the word, 'Sanskrit':

triṣaṣṭiścatuh ṣaṣṭirvā varṇāh ṣambhumate matāh |

prākṛite samskṛte cāpi svayam proktā svayambhuvā || *(pāṇini's śikṣā)*

Trans. There are considered to be 63 or 64 varṇā-s in the school (mata) of shambhu. In Prakrit and Sanskrit by swayambhu (manu, Brahma), himself, these varṇā-s were stated.

This demonstrates that pāṇini knew both samskṛta and prākṛita as established languages. (Personal communication, 27 June 2010 with Prof. Shrinivas Tilak.) This is a good lead to equate mleccha vācas with Prākṛita.

Chapter 17 of Bharatamuni's *Nāṭyaśāstra* is a beautiful discourse about Sanskrit and Prakrit and the usage of *lingua franca* by actors/narrators in dramatic performances. Besides, Raja Shekhara, Kalidasa, Shudraka have also used the word Sanskrit for the literary language.[160] *Nāṭyaśāstra* XVII.29-30: *dvividhā jātibhāṣāca prayoge samudāhṛtā mlecchaśabdopacārā ca bhāratam varṣam aśritā* 'The jātibhāṣā (common language), prescribed for use (on the stage) has various forms. It contains words of mleccha origin and is spoken in Bhāratavarṣa only...'

Vātstyāyana refers to mlecchita vikalpa (lit. 'alternative writing of mleccha', i.e. cipher writing of mleccha) Vātstyāyana's Kamasutra lists (out of 64 arts) three arts related to language:

- *deśa bhāṣā jñānam* (knowledge of dialects)
- *mlecchita vikalpa* (cryptography used by mleccha) [cf. mleccha-mukha 'copper' (Skt.); the suffix –mukha is a reflex of mũh 'ingot' (Mu.)
- *akṣara muṣṭika kathanam* (messaging through wrist-finger gestures)

Thus, semantically, *mlecchita vikalpa* as a writing system relates to cryptography (perhaps, hieroglyphic writing or the Indus writing type) and to the work of artisans (smiths).

I suggest that this term *mlecchita vikalpa* of Vātstyāyana is a reference to Indian hieroglyphs.

It is not a mere coincidence that early writing attested during historical periods was on metal punch-marked coins, copper plates, two-feet long copper bolt used on an Aśokan pillar at Rampurva, Sohaura copper plate, two pure tingots found in a shipwreck in Haifa, and even on the Delhi iron pillar clearly pointing to the smiths as those artisans who had the competence to use a writing system. In reference to Rampurva copper-bolt: "Here then these signs occur upon an object which must have been made by craftsmen working for Asoka or one of his predessors."[161]

Mahābhārata also attests to mleccha -- as a dialect/language -- used in a conversation with Vidura. *Śatapatha Brāhmaṇa* refers to mleccha as language (with pronunciation variants) and also provides an example of such mleccha pronunciation by asuras. A Pali text, *Uttarādhyayana Sūtra* 10.16 notes: *ladhdhaṇa vimānusattaṇṇam āriattam puṇrāvi dullaham bahave dasyū milakkhuyā*; trans. 'though one be born as a man, it is rare chance to be an ārya, for many are the dasyu and milakkhu'. Milakkhu and dasyu constitute the majority, they are the many. Dasyu are milakkhu (mleccha speakers).

Gloss: mleccha

Milakkhu [the Prk. form (A -- Māgadhī, cp. Pischel, Prk. Gr. 105, 233) for P. milakkha] a non -- Aryan D iii.264; Th 1, 965 (°rajana "of foreign dye" trsl.; Kern, Toev. s. v. translates "vermiljoen kleurig"). As milakkhuka at Vin iii.28, where Bdhgh expls by "Andha -- Damil' ādi." Milāca [by -- form to milakkha, viâ *milaccha>*milacca> milāca: Geiger, P.Gr. 622; Kern, Toev. s. v.] a wild man of the woods, non -- Aryan, barbarian J iv.291 (not with C.=janapadā), cp. luddā m. ibid., and milāca -- puttā J v.165 (where C. also expls by bhojaputta, i. e. son of a villager). (Pali.lexicon) mlēcchá ' non -- Aryan ' ŚBr. [√mlēch]Pk. maleccha -- , milichha -- , meccha -- , miccha -- m. ' barbarian '; K. mī̃ch, dat. mī̃cas m. ' non -- Hindu ' (loss of aspiration unexpl.); P. milech, mal° m. (f. milechṇī, mal°) ' Moslem, unclean outcaste, wretch '; WPah.bhad, məle_ċh ' dirty '; B. mech ' a Tibeto -- Burman tribe ' ODBL 473; Si. milidu, miliñdu ' wild, savage ' (< MIA. *mlēcha -- or with H. Smith JA 1950, 186 X pulindá --),milis (< MIA. milichha --). -- Paš. mečə ' wretched, miserly ' rather < *mēcca -- ' defective '. -- With unexpl. -- kkh -- : Pa. milakkha -- , °khu -- ' non -- Aryan ', Si. malak ' savage ', malaki -- dū ' a Väddā woman '. -- X piśācá -- : Pa. milāca -- m. ' wild man of the woods, non -- Aryan '; Si. maladu ' wild, savage '.(CDIAL 10389)*mlēcchatva ' condition of a non -- Aryan '. [Cf. mlēcchatā -- f. VP. -- mlēcchá --]K. mīċuth, dat. °ċatas m. ' habit or life of an outcaste '. (CDIAL 10390)*mrēcchati ~ mlḗcchati ' speaks indistinctly ' ŚBr. [MIA. mr -- < ml -- ? See Add. -- √mlēch]K. briċhun, pp. bryuċhu ' to weep and lament, cry as a child for something wanted or as motherless child '.(CDIAL 10384)

Locus: mleccha

Excerpt from Gonzalo Rubio (Shulgi and the death of Sumerian, 2006)[embedded]:

"Line 211 uses the epithet 'black mountains' which may refer to Meluhha as in the Curse of Akkade (48): mu-luh-ha(ki) lu kur gi-ga-ke 'Meluhhans, men of the black mountains.' The same epithet kur gi 'black mountains' is used for Meluhha in Enki and the World Order (221). Thus, this may refer to the language of Meluhha. Torghar District (Pashto: تور غر) or Tor Ghar, was formerly known as The Black Mountain (or Kala Dhaka in Hindko).

A Sargonic seal mentions an interpreter from Meluhha: shu-i-li-shu eme-bal me-luh-ha(ki).[162]

Meluhha is the language of speakers from kur gi, 'black mountains'.

From the 'Praise of Gudea' a Sumerian text[163], we find the following references:

11 He purified the holy city and encircled it with fires . . . He collected clay in a very pure place; in a pure place he made silt into the bricks and put the bricks into the mould. He followed the rites in all their splendor: he purified the foundations of the temple, surrounded it with fires, anointed the platforms with an aromatic balm .

From Elam came the Elamites, from Susa the Susians. Magan and Muluhha collected timber from their mountains . . . and Gudea brought them together into his town Girsu.
Gudea, the great en-priest ooof Ningirsu, made a path into the Cedar mountains which nobody had entered before; he cut its cedars with great axes . . .like giant snakes, cedars were floating down the water (river) . . .
In the quarries that nobdoy had entered before, Gudea,, the great en-priest of Ningirsu, made a patyh and then the stones were delivered in large blocks . . . Many other precious metals were carried to the ensi. From the Copper mountinas of Kimash . . . its mountains as dust . . . For Gudea, the mined silver from its mountains, delivered red stone from Meluhha in great amount .

Was the red stone from Meluhha, *ancu* (Tocharian), that is amśu from Muztagh Ata, Mount Mujavat?

In Gudea's enumeration of the materials he brought from different countries to build his temples, copper came from the mountains of Kimash and from Meluhha (kur Me-luh-ha-ta) came ushu wood (ebony?). Gold was obtained from a mountain (har-sag), named Ha-hu-um and from Meluhha...Carnelian came from Meluhha.[164]

Was Meluhha from the eastern coast of Africa or was Meluhha a reference to the language of traders from Indus Valley civilization?

"The Assyrian king Tukulti-Ninurta uses in his titles the expression 'king of Dilmun and Meluhha'...There is a king of Dilmun by the name of Uperi, who paid tribute to Sargon II of Assyria. There is another king by the name of Hundaru, in whose days booty taken from Dilmun consisted of bronze, objects made of copper and bronze, sticks of precious wood, and large quantities of kohl, used as eye paint. In the days of Sennacherib, a crew of soldiers is sent from Dilmun to Babylon to help raze that city, and they bring with them bronze spades and spikes which are described as a characteristic product of Dilmun.[165] Tukulti-Ninurta I, reigned between 1243 BCE and 1207 BCE.

Landsberger suggested that Meluhha referred to in the Assyrian period may relate to Egypt-Ethiopia ('Southern Meluhha') because some materials such as gold and ivory earlier imported into Mesopotamia from 'Eastern Meluhha' were the same as those which came from 'Southern Meluhha'.[166] Gelb locates Magan on the southern shore of Arabia on the Persian Gulf, extending east from ancient Sumer up to and including Oman. He locates Meluhha on the north shore of the Gulf including Iran past Elam and Anshan and the region east of there upto and including the Indus Valley.[167]

Leemans notes that Meluhha and the word Mleccha show similarities in form.[168]

John Hansman (1973) postulates Meluhha > Baluhhu ? Baluch with m and b interchanging and with the Iranian ending ch replacing the non-Iranian ending of Baluhhu.

Identifying Telmun (Bahrain) as an entrepot for articles of commerce served during the reign of Rim-Sin (1822 to 1763 BCE) to continue supplies of copper, mesu-wood, carnelian and ivory which had been supplied earlier by Magan and Meluhha and explaining eastern Meluhha and southern Meluhha:

"The name Meluha or Miluha reappears in letters written by Rib-Addi, regent of Egypt at Gubla (Byblos), to Amenophis III (1411-1375 BCE) and to Amenophis IV (1375-1358 BCE). In a series of urgent messages, Rib-Addi pleads for troops from Misri (Egypt) and from Meluha to be dispathed to Gubla for the protection of Egyptian territorial conquests on the Eastern Mediterranean...in many letters he appears to have resorted to a substitute name, Meluha, for that of the indigenous toponym Kashi or Kush which he and and officials in neighbouring Palestine also knew and sometimes used in place of Meluha...After the period ofRib-Addi, an association of Meluhha with Nubia and the Sudan is next recorded in an Akkadian text from the Hittite royal archives at Boghazkoi. This relates that slaves of Meluhha were among gifts received from Egypt by an unnamed Hittite king. We hear next of Meluhha and Magan from inscriptions of the Assyrian king Tukulti-Ninurta I (1244-1208 BCE). In one text he styles himself King of Assyria, King of Telmun and Meluhha, King of the upper and the lower seas. The detailed Assyrian accounts of the conquests of Tukulti-Ninurta make no mention of his invading either the eastern or the souther Meluhha nor do they indicae that he at any time reached Telmun...Meluhha does not occur again in the historical texts for 500 years. It reappears in the annals of Sargon II (721-705 BCE) where, during an Assyrian advance on the rebellious state of Ashdod (in Palestine), the king of Ashdod fled to the side of Musur (Egypt), which is on the border of Meluhha. For the first time now there appears to be clear evidence of the association by the Assyrians of Meluhha with a district in the south near Egypt. An inscription of Sennacherib (704-681 BCE), successor of Sargon II, relates how rebels who rose against Assyrian rule in Palestine sought military assistance from the king of Musur (Egyp), and bowmen, chariots, and horses from the king of Meluhha. Sennacherib claims that he later captured the charioteers of Egypt and Meluhha. The succeeding Assyrian king, Esarhaddon (680-669 BCE)...advanced from Tyre to Musur and then toward Meluhha. This implies that Meluhha is to be found beyond Musur (Egypt), that is to say the country of Kush...It seems clear...that Kush and Meluhha are used alternatively to identify the same country...Lastly to be considered in the present survey are the annals of Assurbanipal (668-627 BCE). In editions B and D of this text Assurbanipal claims that 'on my first campaign I marched against Magan and Meluhha'...the passages which follow refer consistently to Musur and to Kusi. It is therefore reasonable to consider that Magan is used here as an alternative toponym for Musur and Meluhhaa for Kusi."[169]

In the Annexe to John Hansman's 'Periplus' H.W. Bailey[170] discusses three terms from the perspective of a linguistic area: *mleccha-, baloc,* and *Gadrosia.*
A. *mleccha-*; verbal *mlecchati, mliṣṭa-, mlecchita-*

1.1. Earliest reference is in the later Veda, *śatapathabrāhmaṇa*, 3.2.1.24: the noun mleccha-, used of Asura celestial beings who speak imprecise language whether ill-pronounced or foreign. The word *helayo*, variant *hailo*, is quoted. No vocalization is given for this mythic allusion.

2. Epic usage. *Mahābhārata* contrasts *mleccha-* with the *ārya-* and has the *mleccha-bhāṣā*, 'Mleccha language', and *mleccha-vāk* 'using Mleccha speech'. The Dharmasūtra text *Manu-smṛti*, 2.23, has the *mleccha-deśa-* 'Mleccha country' as unfit for Brahmanical sacrifices.

2. 1. The *Mahābhārata* places Mleccha loosely in east, north, and west.
The *Rāmāyaṇa* has Mleccha for the Matsya people of Rajputana[171]

2.2. Varāhamihira, c. 550 CE, placed the Mleccha in the *upara-* region, the western. His *upara*-region refers to the peoples beyond the Sindhu, Indus, for whom *Mahābhārata* had the epithet *pāre-sindhavah* 'beyond the Sindhu'. Varāhamihira has peoples reaching from *Vokkāṇa-* 'Wakhān', through Pancanada- 'Panjab', to the Pārata-, Pārada-, which is the Greek

Παραδηνή

'Parada-' placed by Ptolemy in Gedrosia. These Pārada- are named in the Paikuli inscription of the Sasanians and in the inscription of Shāpuhr I, Parthian text, line 2, in the list *krmn skstn twgrn mkwrn p'rtn hndstn* 'Kirmān, Sakastān, Tugrān, Pārtan, Hindastān. This position excludes Levi's proposal of the Panjab for the Pārata-.

These Indian localizations give only 'beyond the Indus'.

3. Linguistic evidence

1. (a) Later Veda, *mleccha-* and verbal *mlecchati*, with participle in the Scholiast to Pāṇini *mliṣṭa-*;*mlecchita-* is also cited. Patanjali has the infinitive *mlecchitavai.*

(b) Pali, in the oldest texts, *Dīgha-nikāya* and *Vinaya*, *milakkhu-, milakkhuka-, milakkha-, milakkha-bhāsā*, and later *milāca-*.

(c) Jaina older Ardha-māgadhī, milakkha- (with *Vokkāṇa-* and yavana- (Wakhān' and 'Greek'),*milakkhu-, milikkhu-, mileccha-*, and Māhārāṣṭrī *miliṭṭha-* 'speaking indistinctly'.

(d) Buddhist Sanskrit *mlecha-*, whence Saka Khotan *mīlaicha-*.

(e) New Indo-Aryan in R.L. Turner, *Comparative dictionary*, no. 10398, Kāśmīrī *mīch* (with *-ch* from older *-cch-*, not *-kṣ-*); Bengali *mech* of a Tibeto-Burmese tribe, Sinhalese *milidu, milindu* 'savage',*milis, maladu*, Panjābī *milech, malech.*

The Pali *-kkh-* was explained as secondary to *-cch-* by J. Wackernage, *Altindische Grammatik*, 1, 154; but was unexplained according to Turner, loc. cit.

2. The starting-point of the interpretation should be a form **mlekṣa-, mlikṣ-*. Within

the Veda there is a variation between *-cch- (-ch-)* and *-kṣ-* as in Atharva-veda *ṛccharā-* besides śukla-yajur-veda, Vājasneyi-samhitā *ṛkśalā-* 'fetter',and within the Atharva-veda in parikṣit- and variant paricchit- 'surrounding'. Hence *śatapathabrāhmaṇa mleccha-* may be traced to older **mlekṣa-*. The *kṣ* was replaced by *-kkh-* or by retroflex *-ch-* or by palatalized *-cch-* in different dialects. Within the Veda there was also variation *kśā-, kṣā-*, and *khyā-* from *kaś-*, corresponding to Avestan *xsā-* from *kas-*'to look at'.

If the oldest form had then *mlekṣa-, this -kṣ- could be accepted as a substitute for a foreign velar fricative χχ (the sound expressed in Arabic script by خ kh).

If the word *mlekṣ- was a foreign name, it was adapted to the usual Vedic verbal system, giving participle mliṣṭa- in the grammarians, supported by the Jaina Māhārāṣṭrī miliṭṭha-.

The vowel -e- of mleccha- was thus adapted into the ablaut system -e-: -i-.[172]

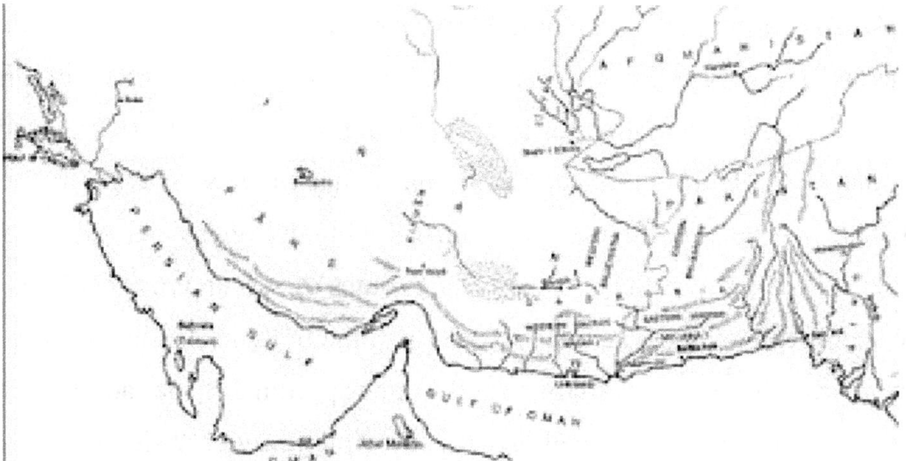

Sotka (Sokhta) Koh, Meluhha. On this map, Sokhta-koh is shown as a site in Meluhha. The coastal Harappan site at Sotka (Sokhta) Koh, 'burnt hill' was first surveyed by an American archaeologist George F Dales in 1960, while exploring estuaries along the Makran coast, Balochistan, Pakistan. The site is located about 15 miles north of Pasni. A similar site at Sutkagen-dor lies about 30 miles inland, astride Dasht River, north of Jiwani. Their position along a coastline (that was possibly much farther inland) goes well with evidence of overseas commerce in Harappan times. Based on pottery styles, it is estimated that the settlement belongs to the Mature Harappan (Integration) Era (2600-1900 BCE).

Meluhha as a trading outpost

Chris J D Kostman[173] in his paper, *The Indus Valley Civilization: In Search of Those Elusive Centers and Peripheries*, discusses: "A primary, if not the primary, rationale for long-range trade driving force would be a need for 'luxury goods,' raw materials, and other items not found in the riverine alluvial plain which made up the vast majority of the Indus Civilization. In the Indus Valley, sought-after materials included copper, gold, silver, tin, jasper and agate cherts, carnelian, azurite, lapis, fine shell, steatite, antimony, and ivory. Forays would have been made towards and beyond the civilization's peripheral areas to obtain these goods. At the minimum, then, there is an economic motive for inter-regional travel. Silvio Durante's study (1979) of marine shells from India and their appearance in the archaeological record in such distant sites as Tepe Yahya and Shahr-i-Sokhta in Iran, as well as in the Indus Valley, sheds light on the ancient trading routes of certain types of shells which are specifically and exclusively found along the Indian coastline proper. Durante primarily discusses the marine shell Xancus pyrum and the fact that it was traded whole and intact, then worked or reworked (into jewellery? sic) at its

destination site, perhaps then moving on to other locations. The importance of this specific shell is that Xancus pyrum has a very limited geographic distribution and thus has almost the same significance in the field of shells as that of lapis lazuli in the context of mineral resources (as regards the determination of the possible routes along which a locally unavailable raw material is transported from a well-defined place of origin to the place where it is processed and, as also in the case of Xancus pyrum, consumed). Perhaps, as these shells crossed so many cultural hands, they were left unworked in order for the final owner or consumer to work the raw material into a style and usage specific to their region. Durante offers four possible trade routes from their gathering zone along the west and northwest Indian coast to destinations west: sea route direct to the Iranian coastal area; sea route to Sutkagen-dor and Sotka-koh on the Makran coast, then overland westwards; overland through the Indus plain and then through the Makran interior to Sistan; overland through the Indus Valley and then through the Gomal Valley to Sistan."

A term cognate with *meluhha* is *mleccha* which is identified in an ancient text as a speech form.

The evidence which comes from Manu, dated to ca. 500 BCE. Manu (10.45) underscores the linguistic area: *ārya vācas mleccha vācas te sarve dasyuvah smṛtāh* [trans. "both ārya speakers and mleccha speakers (that is, both speakers of literary dialect and colloquial or vernacular dialect) are all remembered as dasyu"]. Dasyu is a general reference to people. Dasyu is cognate with dasa, whic in Khotanese language means 'man'. It is also cognate with daha, a word which occurs in Persepolis inscription of Xerxes, a possible reference to people of Dahistan, a region east of Caspian sea. Strabo[174] wrote :"Most of the scythians, beginning from the Caspian sea, are called Dahae Scythae, and those situated more towards the east Massagetae and Sacae." (Strabo, 11.8.1). Close to Caspian Sea is the site of Altyn-tepe which was an interaction area with Meluhha and where three Indus seals with inscriptions were found, including a silver seal showing a composite animal which can be called a signature glyph of Indus writing.

Dasyu are also ārya vācas (Manu 10.45), that is, speakers of Sanskrit. Both ārya vācas and mleccha vācas are dasyu [cognate *dahyu, daŋ́ha, daha* (Khotanese)], people, in general. दाशः 1 A fisherman; इयं च सज्जा नौश्चेति दाशाः प्राञ्ज- लयो$ब्रुवन्

Rām.7.46.32; Ms.8.48,49;1.34. दासः 'a fisherman' (Apte. Lexicon) Such people a re referred to in Rgveda by Viśvāmitra as 'Bhāratam janam.' Mahābhārata alludes to 'thousands of mlecchas', a numerical superiority equaled by their valour and courage in battle which enhances the invincibility of Pandava (MBh. 7.69.30; 95.36).

Excerpt from Encyclopaedia Iranica article[175] on cognate *dahyu* country (often with reference to the people inhabiting it): DAHYU (OIr. DAHYU-), attested in Avestan DAX́IIU-, DAŃHU- "country" (often with reference to the people inhabiting it; cf. AIRWB., cot. 706; Hoffmann, pp. 599-600 n. 14; idem and Narten, pp. 54-55) and in Old Persian DAHYU- "country, province" (pl. "nations"; Gershevitch, p. 160). The term is likely to be connected with Old Indian DÁSYU "enemy" (of the Aryans), which acquired the meaning of "demon, enemy of the gods" (Mayrhofer, DICTIONARY II, pp. 28-29). Because of the Indo-Iranian parallel, the word may be traced back to the root DAS-, from which a term denoting a large collectivity of men and women could have been derived. Such traces can be found in Iranian languages: for instance, in the ethnonym Dahae (q.v., i) "men" (cf. Av. ethnic name [fem. adj.] DĀHĪ, from DÅŃHA-; AIRWB., col. 744; Gk. Dáai, etc.), in Old Persian DAHĀ "the Daha people" (Brandenstein and Mayrhofer, pp. 113-14), and in Khotanese DAHA "man, male" (Bailey, DICTIONARY, p. 155).

Indian sprachbund: structural trait, 'reduplication'. Mirrored in antithetical or mirror image pictographs in writing system.

A distinguishing feature of writing systems of related languages are called isographs. The existence of reduplicated hieroglyphs on Indus writing can be related to the structural trait of reduplication in spoken phrases.

Reduplication of words is a structural trait of languages in the area of Indus script corpora (or Indian *sprachbund*).[176] Emeneau endorsed Jules Bloch's view that "Indo-Aryan had undergone, from the beginning of its presence in India, an Indianization through contact with Dravidian (and probably with other language families)." Indian sprachbund was defined by Emeneau[177]: 'an area which includes languages belonging to more than one family but showing traits in common which are found not to belong to the other members of (at least) one of the families.' This reduplication pattern gets reflected in the orthography of early writing systems of the area. One characteristic feature stands out among hundreds of cylinder seals and other artifacts of the area: depiction of picotraphs either in pairs or back-to-back. It is suggested that this depiction is related to the language repertoire of the inventors of the writing system.

A remarkable reduplicated phrase is evidenced in Pus'hto or Puk'hto language. پښت *pushṯ*, s.m. (2nd) The back. پښت به پښت *pushṯ bah pushṯ*, From generation to generation. pr̥ṣṭhyà 1 ' on the back ' RV. 4, 3, 10. [pr̥ṣṭhá --] Or. paṭhā ' boil on the back '.(CDIAL 8374). pr̥ṣṭí -- , °ṭī´ -- f. ' vertebrae ' RV., AV., ' back ' Kauś.com. [' ribs ' ŚBr. by association with párśu -- (cf. Av. parštī<-> f. ' back ' ~ Psht. puštaī ' rib ')] Pa. piṭṭhī̃ -- , °ṭhikā -- f. ' back ', Pk. piṭṭhī̃ -- , puṭṭhī -- , paṭṭhi -- f., Ash. piṣṭī, pṣṭī, Wg. yā̃ -- paṭī, Kt. pṭī, Shum. Gaw. piṣṭī´; S. puṭhi f. ' back, rear ', °ṭhī f. ' back '; L. puṭṭh f. ' back ', P. piṭṭh, puṭṭh f., WPah.mid.rudh. piṭṭhī, bhal. piṭṭh f., Ku. pīṭh, piṭhī, N. piṭh, piṭhyũ, A. Or. piṭhi, Mth. pī̃ṭhi, pīṭh, Bhoj. pīṭhi, OAw. pīṭhī, OH. pūṭhi, pū̃ṭh f., H. pīṭh, piṭṭhī, piṭhiyā f.; OG. pūṭhi f., pūṭhiiṁ ' after '; G. pīṭh, pūṭh f. ' back ', pũṭhiyũ n. ' rear '; M. pāṭh f. ' back ', Ko. pāṭi, Si. peṭa < *pāṭi (piṭi in cmpds. piṭi -- bim ' ground at the back ', he -- viṭi ' land by river ' ← Pa.). -- In absence of final -- i or distinction of gender altern. < pr̥ṣṭhá -- : Gy. pal. pišt ' back ', D. phīṭ, Kal.rumb. piṣṭ, Tor. pīḍ, B. Or.dial. piṭh, Aw.lakh. pīṭh. Addenda: pr̥ṣṭí -- : WPah.ktg. piṭṭh f. (obl. -- i), kc. pīṭh f. ' the back, support ', J. pīṭh f. ' back ', Garh. pīṭh (or < pr̥ṣṭhá --); -- read Ko. phāṭi, dial. pāṭi (S. M. Katre).(CDIAL 8370).

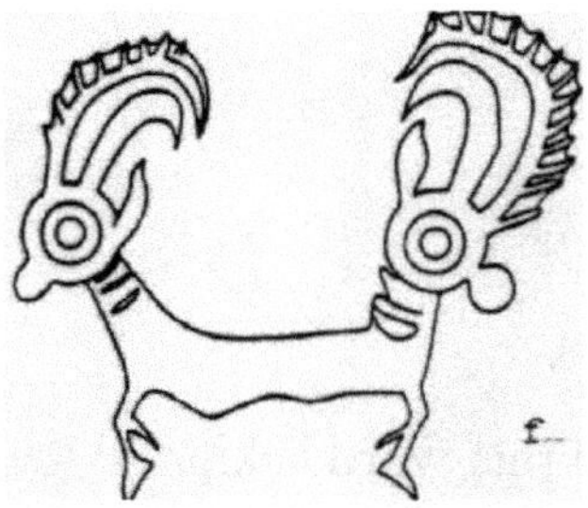

P پښت pushṯ, s.m. (2nd) The back (Pushto)

To denote the idea of 'generation' or 'lineage' the inventors of the writing system deploy pictographs back-to-back: *pus̲h̲t bah pus̲h̲t*. The rebus reading is representation of P پشت *pus̲h̲t*, 'progenitors, ancestry'; a prop, a second, an assistant. Pl. پشتونه *pus̲h̲tūnah*. . The artist is trying to convey the idea that the possessor of the seal or artificat is a progenitor with ancestry related to the artisanal competence denoted by the pictograph. If the pictograph denotes an antelope, the competence is that of a mint-merchant (artisan). That is, the owner of the seal or artifact with a pair of antelopes is of mint-merchant-lineage.
Antithetical antelopes of Ancient Near East, *harosheth hagoyim*

Antithetical antelopes. Failaka.[178]

Harosheth hagoyim is cognate with *kharoṣṭī gōya*
The gloss gōya (Prakrit) is cognate with Hebrew -goy in: hagoyim 'country, people'. The gloss *kharoṣṭī* is cognate with Hebrew *harosheth*. Etymology of *kharoṣṭī* = khār + *oṣṭ* ' blacksmith + lip. Thus the compound *kharoṣṭī* means 'lip (writing system) of blacksmiths'.

khār 1 खार् । लोहकारः m. (sg. abl. khāra 1 खार; the pl. dat. of this word is khāran 1 खारन्, which is to be distinguished from khāran 2, q.v., s.v.), a blacksmith, an iron worker (Kashmiri) ṓṣṭha m. ' lip ' RV. Pa. oṭṭha -- m., Pk. oṭṭha -- , uṭ°, hoṭṭha -- , huṭ° m., Gy. pal. ōšt, eur. vušt m.; Ash. ȫṣṭ, Wg. ṻṣṭ, wūṣṭ, Kt. yūṣṭ (prob. ← Ind. NTS xiii 232); Paš. lauṛ. ūṭh f. ← Ind. (?), gul. ūṣṭ ' lip ', dar. weg. uṣṭ ' bank of a river ' (IIFL iii 3, 22); Kal. rumb. ūṣṭ, uṣṭ ' lip '; Sh. ȭṭu m. ' upper lip ', ȭṭi f. ' lower lip ' (→ Ḍ ōṭe pl.); K. wuṭh, dat. °ṭhas m. ' lip '; L. hoṭh m., P. hoṭh, hõṭh m., WPah. bhal. oṭh m., jaun. hōṭh, Ku. ū̃ṭh, gng.ōṭh, N. oṭh, A. ȭṭh, MB. Or. oṭha, Mth. Bhoj. oṭh, Aw. lakh. ȭṭh, hȭṭh, H. oṭh, õṭh, hoṭh, hõṭh m., G. oṭh, hoṭh m., M. oṭh, õṭh, hoṭ m., Si.oṭa. WPah.poet. *oṭhḷu* m. ' lip ', *hoṭru*, kṭg. *hóṭṭh*, kc. *ōṭh*, Garh. *hoṭh*, *hȭṭ*. (CDIAL 2563).

gōtrá n. ' cowpen, enclosure ' RV., ' family, clan ' ChUp., *gōtrā* -- f. ' herd of cows ' Pāṇ. 2. gōtraka -- n. ' family ' Yājñ. [gṓ --] 1. Pa. *gotta* -- n. ' clan ', Pk. *gotta* -- , *gutta* -- , amg. *gōya* -- n.; Gau. *gū* ' house ' (in Kaf. and Dard. several other words for ' cowpen ' > ' house ': *gōśrayaṇa -- , gōṣṭhá -- , *gōstha -- (?), ghōṣa --); Pr. *gū´ṭu* ' cow '; S. *goṭru* m. ' parentage ', L. *got* f. ' clan ', P. *gotar*, *got* f.; Ku. N. *got* ' family '; A. *got* -- *nāti* ' relatives '; B. *got* ' clan '; Or. *gota* ' family, relative '; Bhoj. H. *got* m. ' family, clan ', G. *got* n.; M. *got* ' clan, relatives '; -- Si. *gota* ' clan, family ' ← Pa. 2. B. H. *gotā* m. ' relative '. (CDIAL 4279).

A locally made gold pendant of United Arab Emirates, from the Wadi Suq period. This is an evocation of a similar artifact of metal (perhaps gold or electrum 'gold-silver alloy') dated to ca. 2000 BCE. A unique metal artifact of ca. 3rd milennium BCE Ancient Near East, depicts antithetical antelopes with curling tails. Hieroglyphs of the metal artifact of ca. 2000 BCE Ancient Near East can be identified.[179]

What do the hieroglyphs signify? Read rebus, it is a calling card of an ancient professional artisan/merchant. The meaning conveyed: Lineage stone (ore, tin) mint merchant. The hieroglyphs are: 1. Antelope; 2. Mirror images joined back-to-back; 3. Curved mollusc as tail.

1, 2. *tagaru pus̱ẖt bah pus̱ẖt* 'antelope back-to-back'; rebus: *damgar* (mint-merchant) generation-to-generation (*pus̱ẖt bah pus̱ẖt*).

3. K. *hāngi* ' snail '; B. *sā̃khī* ' possessing or made of shells '. K. *hȭgiñ* f. ' pearl oyster shell, shell of any aquatic mollusc '.(CDIAL 12380). Rebus: S. L. P. *saṅgī* m. ' comrade; WPah.kṭg. (kc.) *sɔ́ṅgi* m. ' friend ', kṭg. *sɔ́ṅgəṇ*, kc. *sɔṅgiṇ* f., J. *saṅgī, saṅgu* m. (prob. ← H. Him.I 212). (CDIAL 13084). Thus, the antithetical antelope is a representation of a profession: associate/friend of mint-merchant lineage.

The patterns of joined animals are most vivid on Indus script corpora which have been explained as *sangaḍa* 'joined animals (allograph: standard device often shown in front of a young one-horned bull). Rebus reading explains this gloss as related to *jangaḍ* 'treasure entrusted to the treasury'. A linguistic depiction, in a writing system of the mint-worker-merchant-guild depositing metals/minerals/alloys into the common treasury.

Wooden Tablet Inscribed with Kharosthi Characters, Eastern Han Dynasty to Jin Dynasty (2nd - 3rd century AD), Excavated at the site of the Niya Ruins in the Xinjiang Uigher Autonomous Region, Collection of the Xinjiang Museum. Taken it at the Exhibition of Ancient Chinese Invention Artifacts.[180]

Paper strip with writing in Kharoṣṭhī. 2-5th century CE, Yingpan, Eastern Tarim Basin, XinjiangMuseum.[181]

Wooden plate with inscription in a Tocharian B language. Kucha, 5th-8th century.Tokyo National Museum.

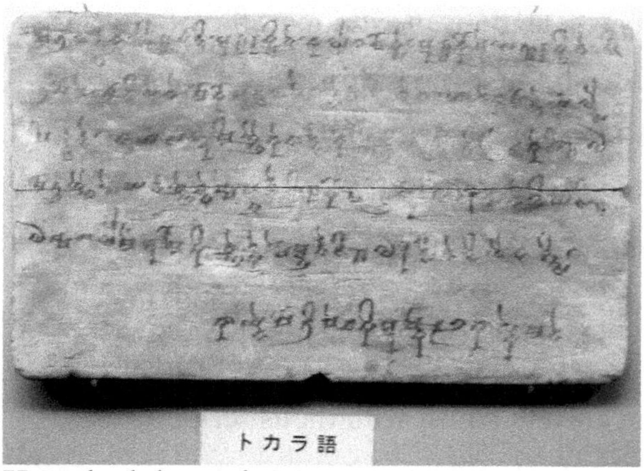

Harosheth hagoyim

The artisans' guild from Indus (Meluhha) assumed the form of a multi-national corporation, attested by *harosheth hagoyim*, [cognate: *kharoṣṭī goy* (Meluhha/mleccha)] 'smithy of nations' mentioned in the Old Testament. It appears that the Meluhhans were in contact with many interaction areas, Dilmun and Susa (elam) in particular. There is evidence for Meluhhan settlements outside of Meluhha. It is a reasonable inference that the Meluhhans with bronze-age expertise of creating arsenical and bronze alloys and working with other metals constituted the 'smithy of nations', Harosheth Hagoyim.

Harosheth (Hebrew: חרושת הגויים; pronounced *khar-o-sheth*?) of the Gentiles definition

(Judg. 4:2) or nations, a city near Hazor in Galilee of the Gentiles, or Upper Galilee, in the north of Palestine. It was here that Jabin's great army was marshalled before it went forth into the great battlefield of Esdraelon to encounter the army of Israel, by which it was routed and put to flight (Judg. 4). It was situated "at the entrance of the pass to Esdraelon from the plain of Acre" at the base of Carmel. The name in the Hebrew is _Harosheth ha Gojim_, i.e., "the smithy of the nations;" probably, as is supposed, so called because here Jabin's iron war-chariots, armed with scythes, were made. It is identified with el-Harithiyeh.[182]

Hieroglyphs of Indus script are rebus representations of workmanship of artisans (of the lapidaries and smiths) of the civilization - a veritable repertoire using over 400 signs and over 100 pictorial motifs to detail the items of the repertoire ranging from minerals, metals, alloys, ingots, furnaces, smelters, semi-precious stones, metallurgical techniques of gilding, turning, casting, forging. Hence, in effect,*harosheth hagoyim* 'smithy of nations'. This tradition survives into the historical periods of punch-marked coins using *kharoṣṭī* (cognate: *harosheth*) inscriptions, in many cases evidenced in ancient coins, with Indus script hieroglyphs together with the use of Greek/Brahmi/kharoṣṭī scripts.

Most likely,

חרשׁת

(haroshet) a noun meaning a carving. Hence, kharoṣṭī came to represent a 'carving, engraving' art, i.e. a writing system.

Hariti. Schist Stone, c 2nd century A.D.Skarah Dheri, Gandhara

Hariti was originally a demoness having five hundred sons. She was in the habit of killing and eating children of the city of Rajagriha. Gautama Buddha converted her to normal motherly behaviour and made her the caretaker of all the children of the world. Thus she became the mother goddess in Buddhism. Her male consort is Panchika. Usually Hariti and Panchika are shown together in art, along with some figures of children. However, a few individual images of either of them are also found in Gandhara Art. In the collection of the Museum, there is a unique image of Hariti with some children around. This image is inscribed with a date in an unspecified era. This image has not only some interesting stylistic and aesthetic features, but it also bears historical importance in the determination of the stylistic sequence in the evolution of Gandhara Art. Hariti, as also Panchika, represent the concept, upheld prominently in Buddhism, that sin should be despised, and not the sinner. Moreover, they together symbolise the tenderness of parental care that sustains the children, the core of any culture, through the ages.

Inscription in Kharoshti script

English Translation of the Kharoshti Inscription

The icon of Hariti bears an inscription of two lines engraved on the stone left unsculpted on the right (proper left) of the lower part of the standing figure of Hariti. It is written in the Kharoshti script and in North-western Prakrit.

Text:

Vash[e] eka-navati du-satima'e Ashadasa masasa divas(e) 20[+] 1 [? +] 1 (?)

sogapakho dasame bharadu

sharamitha rakhana'e

Translation:

"In the year two hundredth ninety one, on the day 22 of the month of Ashadha. Let the tenth carry up to (a) bright fortnight. I remember [Hariti] for the protection of this".

Apparently the donor of the image of Hariti, entreated the protectress of children for the delivery of his/her or someone else's child in a bright fortnight during the tenth month of pregnancy (i.e. after the full period of pregnancy). It was perhaps believed that a child born in a fair fortnight would be of fair or bright complexion. The donor also solicited for safety of the pregnancy. This interpretation is in complete agreement with a custom current in Gandhara, following which "the common folk" used to "offer sacrifices to obtain children from her" (i.e. Hariti).

If the date has been correctly read as "the year 291" (vash(e) ekanavatidusatimae) and attributed to the so-called Old Saka Era of c.170 B.C., the resultant date is c. A.D. 121.

(Dr. B.N. Mukherjee)[183]

Rondel with the Goddess Hariti[184] Description: The goddess Hariti is shown nursing a child and sitting on a throne flanked by lotuses and surmounted by auspicious geese (hamsa), the Buddha's messengers. Stylistically this roundel can be related to first-century finds from the Taxila city of Sirkap, a dating that would make it one of the earliest known representations of Hariti. Buddhist texts tell us that Hariti originally stole and devoured children, but with the Buddha's intervention she became their protector.

Meaning and etymology of the name Harosheth-hagoyim

HAROSHETH-HAGOYIM חרשת הגוים

Harosheth-hagoyim is the home of general Sisera, who was killed by Jael during the war of Naphtali and Zebulun against Jabin, king of Hazor in Canaan (Judges 4:2). The lead players of this war are the general Barak and the judge Deborah. The name Harosheth-hagoyim obviously consists of two parts. The first part is derived from the root , which HAW Theological Wordbook of the Old Testament treats as four separate roots (harash I, II, III, & IV). The verb (harash I) means to engrave or plough. HAW Theological Wordbook of the Old Testament reads, "The basic idea is cutting into some material, e.g. engraving metal or plowing soil." Derivatives of this verb are: (harash), meaning engraver; (haroshet) a noun meaning a carving. This word is equal to the first part of the name Harosheth-hagoyim; (harish), meaning plowing or plowing time; (maharesha) meaning ploughshare; (harishi), a word which is only used in Jona 4:8 to indicate a certain characteristic of the sun - vehement (King James) or scorching (NIV). The verb (harash II) most commonly denotes refraining from speech or response, either because one is deaf or mute, or because one doesn't want to respond. None of the sources indicates a relation with the previous root, and perhaps there is none, but on the other hand, perhaps deafness was regarded in Biblical as either being marked or else cut or cut off. The noun (horesh) from root (hrsh III) occurs only in Isaiah 17:9 and has to do with a wood or forest. The noun (heresh) from root (hrsh IV) occurs only in Isaiah 3:3 and probably means magical art or expert enchanter, or something along those lines. The second part of the name, hagoyim, comes from the definite article (ha plus the common word (goy) meaning nation, people, gentile. This word comes from the assumed root (gwh), which is not translated but which seems to denote things that are surpassed or left behind. Other derivatives are: (gaw a and gew), meaning back, as in "cast behind the back," i.e. put out of mind (1 Kings 14:9, Nehemiah 9:26, Isaiah 38:17); (gewiya), meaning body, either dead or alive (Genesis 47:18, Judges 14:8, Daniel 10:6). The meaning of the name Harosheth-hagoyim can be found as any combination of the above. NOBS Study Bible Name List reads Carving Of The Nations, but equally valid would be Silence Of The Gentiles or Engraving Of What's Abandoned. Jones' Dictionary of Old Testament Proper Names reads Manufactory for Harosheth and "of the Gentiles" for Hagoyim.[185]

The name Harosheth-hagoyim obviously consists of two parts. The first part is derived from the root חרש , which HAW Theological Wordbook of the Old Testament treats as four separate roots (HARASH I, II, III, & IV).

The verb חרש (HARASH I) means to engrave or plough. HAW Theological

Wordbook of the Old Testament reads, "The basic idea is cutting into some material, e.g. engraving metal or plowing soil." Derivatives of this verb are:

חרשׁ (HARASH), meaning engraver;

חרשׁת (HAROSHET) a noun meaning a carving. This word is equal to the first part of the name Harosheth-hagoyim;

חרישׁ (HARISH), meaning plowing or plowing time;

מחרשׁה (MAHARESHA) meaning ploughshare;

חרישׁי (HARISHI), a word which is only used in Jona 4:8 to indicate a certain characteristic of the sun - vehement (King James) or scorching (NIV).

The verb חרשׁ (HARASH II) most commonly denotes refraining from speech or response, either because one is deaf or mute, or because one doesn't want to respond. None of the sources indicates a relation with the previous root, and perhaps there is none, but on the other hand, perhaps deafness was regarded in Biblical as either being marked or else cut or cut off.

The noun חרשׁ (HORESH) from root חרשׁ (HRSH III) occurs only in Isaiah 17:9 and has to do with a wood or forest. The noun חרשׁ (HERESH) from root חרשׁ (HRSH IV) occurs only in Isaiah 3:3 and probably means magical art or expert enchanter, or something along those lines.

The second part of the name, HAGOYIM, comes from the definite article (HA plus the common word גוי (GOY) meaning nation, people, gentile. This word comes from the assumed root גוה (GWH), which is not translated but which seems to denote things that are surpassed or left behind. Other derivatives are: גו (GAW a and GEW), meaning back, as in "cast behind the back," i.e. put out of mind (1 Kings 14:9, Nehemiah 9:26, Isaiah 38:17); גויה (GEWIYA), meaning body, either dead or alive (Genesis 47:18, Judges 14:8, Daniel 10:6).

The meaning of the name Harosheth-hagoyim can be found as any combination of

the above. NOBS Study Bible Name List reads *Carving Of The Nations*, but equally valid would be *Silence Of The Gentiles* or*Engraving Of What's Abandoned.*
Jones' Dictionary of Old Testament Proper Names reads *Manufactory* for Harosheth and "*of the Gentiles*" for Hagoyim.[186]

Another reconstruction of Harosheth Hagoyim (Darrell Pursiful, 2008)reads as follows, citing reference to the manual of Kikkuli for training chariot horses (which has often been cited as a link with Indian civilization):

[quote]Jabin and Sisera

...battle described in the Bible involving chariots occurs during the judgeship of Deborah a few generations after the Israelite conquest/settlement of Canaan. At this time, Israel's oppressor was Jabin, a Canaanite king whose capital was Hazor. The commander of Jabin's army was Sisera, whose name has been interpreted to be either Hittite or Hurrian in origin, fitting for a man who lived in the "woodland of the gentiles" (Harosheth-ha-goyim).

Both Hittites and Hurrians were noted innovators in chariotry. The Hittites, in fact, seem to have been the first nation to capitalize on the military potential of chariot-mounted archers as early as the Middle Bronze Age (Robert Drews, The Coming of the Greeks [Princeton University Press, 1994] 105-106). The Hurrians were noted charioteers who, evidently led by an Indo-Aryan ruling class, had established the kingdom of Mitanni in northern Mesopotamia. Kikkuli, a Hurrian, wrote an important manual for training chariot horses.

It may be, then, that Sisera was a foreigner hired by Jabin for his expertise in chariot warfare. Such chariot warriors dominated many Ancient Near Eastern societies and were collectively known as maryan(n)u. Sisera is said to have commanded 900 chariot teams, although once again I think Edgecomb is correct to read ninety (and only 1,000 foot soldiers for the Israelites). Either way, once again the chariots are numbered and clearly described as being the principal threat an enemy brought to bear against Israel:

Then the Israelites cried out to the LORD for help; for [Sisera] had nine hundred chariots of iron, and had oppressed the Israelites cruelly twenty years. (Jdg 4:3)

Unlike the exodus story, here we can actually read some of the details of how the battle unfolded:

When Sisera was told that Barak son of Abinoam had gone up to Mount Tabor, Sisera called out all his chariots, nine hundred chariots of iron, and all the troops who were with him, from Harosheth-ha-goiim to the Wadi Kishon. Then Deobrah said to Barak, "Up! For this is the day on which the LORD has given Sisera into your hand. The LORD is indeed going out before you." So Barak went down from Mount Tabor with ten thousand warriors following him. And the LORD threw Sisera and all his chariots and all his army into a panic before Barak; Sisera got down from his chariot and fled away on foot, while Barak pursued the chariots and the army to Harosheth-ha-goiim. All the army of Sisera fell by the sword; no one was left. (Jdg 4:12-16) [unquote][187]

Cognate lexemes (relatable to the semantics: engraving, ploughing) from the Indian linguistic area:

karṣá m. ' dragging ' Pāṇ., ' agriculture ' Āp. [Cf. kā´rṣi -- ' ploughing ' TS., karṣí -- Kapiṣṭh.: √kr̥ṣ] Pk. karisa -- m. ' dragging ', kassa -- m. ' mud '; Paš. kaṣ ' pulling '; Or. kāsa ' time or turn of ploughing a field '. <-> Poss. Wg. koṣ ' snake ', Ash. kəreš ' snake ', Wg. koṣ (< ' dragging or trailing on the ground ') or < kr̥śá -- . karṣaka ' cultivating ', m. ' husbandman ' Yājñ. [karṣá -- : √kr̥ṣ] Pa. kassaka -- m. ' ploughman ', Pk. karisaya -- , kāsaya -- , °sava -- m.; Si. kasayā ' peasant ', kasu -- kama ' ploughing, agriculture '; -- H. kassā m. ' mattock ', °sī ' small do. ', kussī f. (X kus < kuśī´ --).karṣaṇa n. ' tugging, ploughing, hurting ' Mn., ' cultivated land '

MBh. [kárṣati, √kr̥ṣ] Pk. karisaṇa -- n. ‘ pulling, ploughing ’; G. karsaṇ n. ‘ cultivation, ploughing ’; OG. karasaṇī m. ‘ cultivator ’, G. karasṇī m. -kárṣati ‘ draws, pulls ’ RV. [√kr̥ṣ]Pa. kassatē ‘ ploughs ’; Pk. karisaï, kāsaï ‘ pulls ’; Gy. pal. kšal -- ‘ to drag, pull, lead ’, arm. kaš -- ‘ to pull ’; Ash. keṣawā -- ‘ to draw out ’; Wg. kaṣ -- ‘ to pull ’, kaṣā -- ‘ to take away by force ’; Kt. kṣō -- ‘ to creep ’; Pr. -- kṣə -- ‘ to pull ’, Dm. kaṣāy -- ; Kal. kaṣalém ‘ I creep ’; S. kasaṇu ‘ to tighten ’, L. kassaṇ, awāṇ. kassuṇ, WPah. bhad. kaśṇū, P. kassṇā (→ Ku. kasṇo, N. kasnu, B. kasā; Or. kasā ‘ close -- fisted ’; Mth. kasab ‘ to tighten ’, OAw. kasaï, H. kasnā; OMarw. kasaï ‘ harnesses, binds ’; G. kasvũ ‘ to tighten ’, M. kasṇẽ); OM. kāsaṇeṁ ‘ to tie fast ’. -- See kr̥ṣáti. Addenda: kárṣati [Cf. Ir. in Shgh. kirā̤x̌t ‘ to drag, remove ’, Rosh. kirēx̌t EVSh 41 < *krāršaya -- < *kāršaya --]WPah.kṭg. (kc.) kɔ́śṇõ ‘ to tighten, tie ’, J. kaśṇu.karṣí ‘ furrowing ’ Kapiṣṭh. [Cf. kā´rṣi -- ‘ ploughing ’ VS., karṣū´ -- f. ‘ furrow, trench ’ ŚBr.: √kr̥ṣ] Pr. kṣe_ ‘ plough -- iron ’, Paš. kaṣí ‘ mattock, hoe ’; Shum. káṣi ‘ spade, pickaxe ’; S. kasī f. ‘ trench, watercourse ’; L. kass m. ‘ catch drain, ravine ’, kassī f. ‘ small distributing channel from a canal ’; G. kā̃s m. ‘ artificial canal for irrigation ’ -- Dm. Phal. khaṣī´ ‘ small hoe ’ perh. X khánati. Addenda: karṣí -- (kaṣī̄ -- f. ‘ spade ’ lex.). [Like Av. karšivant<-> ‘ cultivator ’ < IE. *kworsi -- with alternative development of IE. o ~ kā´rṣi -- , kārṣīvaṇa -- ‘ cultivator ’ T. Burrow, BSOAS xxxviii 63, 70; cf. karṣū´ -- ~ †*kārṣū -- Turner BSOAS xxxvi 425](CDIAL 2905 to 2909). -oṣṭ- cognate ?): Gu {V} ``to ^engrave (cut incised designs)''. !literally. {V} ``to ^engrave (cut incised designs)''. !literally. @V0282. #25401.(Munda etyma) krāv क्राव् ।

कृष्यारम्भः f. the harvesting, usufruct, or collection of crops, fruit, flowers, etc. (YZ. 31, 254; Śiv. 269, 526, 172, 181); the final reaping of a harvest (K.Pr. 247); the village festival on the first day of spring, on which farmers commence to plough their fields for the new crop (Paṇḍit's explanation of kr̥ṣyârambhaḥ).(Kashmiri)

Harosheth Hebrew: הגויים חרושת; is pronounced khar-o-sheth? Most likely, (haroshet) a noun meaning a carving. Hence, kharoṣṭī came to represent a 'carving, engraving' art, i.e. a writing system. Harosheth-hagoyim See: Haroshet [Carving]; a forest; agriculture; workmanship;Harsha [Artifice: deviser: secret work]; workmanship; a wood.[188] Cognate with haroshet: karṣá m. ' dragging ' Pāṇ., ' agriculture ' Āp.(CDIAL 2905). karṣaṇa n. ' tugging, ploughing, hurting ' Mn., ' cultivated land ' MBh. [kárṣati, √kr̥ṣ] Pk. karisaṇa -- n. ' pulling, ploughing '; G. karsaṇ n. ' cultivation, ploughing '; OG. karasaṇī m. ' cultivator ', G. karasṇī m. -- See *kr̥ṣaṇa -- .(CDIAL 2907).

It is suggest that the semantics of the word *kharoṣṭī* (engraving)(and hence, the cognate *harosheth*Heb.) is relatable, etymologically, to, and derivable from the root phoneme: kr̥ṣṭiḥ कृष्टिः 'drawing, pulling'; 'inhabitants'. (See Monier-Williams lexicon entry given below). This is clearly relatable to the act of engraving by a scribe on a punch-marked coin, a copper plate or seal/tablet. Hence the name for the kharoṣṭī writing system. कृष्टि m. a teacher , learned man or Pandit Hariv. 3588 SkandaP.(Skt.)

कृष्टि f. pl. (once only sg. RV. iv , 42 , 1) men , races of men (sometimes with the epithet म्/आनुषीस् [i , 59 , 5 and vi , 18 , 2] or न्/आहुषीस् [vi , 46 , 7] or मानव्/ईस् [AV. iii , 24 , 3] ; cf. चर्षण्/इ ; originally the word may have meant cultivated ground , then an inhabited land , next its inhabitants , and lastly any race of men ; इन्द्र and अग्नि have the N. र्/आजा or प्/अतिः कृष्टीन्/आम् ; the term प्/अञ्च कृष्ट्/अयस् , perhaps originally designating the five Aryan tribes of the यदुs , तुर्वशs , द्रुह्युs , अनुs , and पूरुs , comprehends the whole human race , not only the Aryan tribes) RV. AV. (Monier-Williams, p. 306).

kr̥ṣṭiḥ कृष्टिः [कृष्-क्तिन्] A learned man. -f. 1 Drawing, attracting. -2 Ploughing, cultivating the soil. कृष्ट a. [कृष् कर्मणि क्त] 1 Drawn, pulled, dragged, attracted &c. -2 Ploughed; न हि तस्मात्फलं तस्य सुकृष्टादूष- रादिव Pt.1.47. -Comp. -उप्त a. sown on cultivated ground. -ज a. grown in cultivated ground; Ms.11. 144. -पच्य, -पाक्य a. 1 ripening in cultivated ground; यो हि कृष्टे पक्तव्यः कृष्टपाक्यः स भवति Mbh. on P.III.1.114; cf. अकृष्टपच्य; न कृष्टपच्यमश्नीयादकृष्टं चाप्यकालतः Bhāg.7.12. 18. -2 cultivated. -फलम् the product of a harvest. अकृष्ट a. [न. त.] Not tilled; not drawn. -Comp. -पच्य a. [अकृष्टे क्षेत्रे पच्यते] growing or ripening in un- ploughed land, growing exuberant or wild; °च्या इव सस्य- संपदः Ki.1.17; so °च्या ओषधयः; °च्यम् अशनं धान्यम्, &c. -पच्या (applied especially to) the earth yielding food grains, fruit etc. without being tilled; very fertile; अकृष्टपच्या पृथिवी विबभौ चैत्यमालिनी Mb. Crit. Ed.12.29.21; 12.216.16. -रोहिन् = °पच्य; बीजं च बालेयमकृष्टरोहि R.14.77. कृषक a. [कृष्-क्वन्] 1 Attractive, drawing. -2 Ploughing. -कः 1 A ploughman, husbandman. कच्चिन्न भक्तं बीजं च कर्षकस्यावसीदति Mb.2.5.78. -2 An ox. -कम् A ploughshare. (also m.). कृषाणः कृषिकः [कृष्-आनक्-किकन् वा] A ploughman, husbandman. కృష్టము [kṛṣṭamu] kṛishṭamu. [Skt.] adj. That which is drawn. ఈడ్వబడిన. అనుకర్షము [anukarṣamu] anu-karshamu. [Skt.] n. A piece of wood at the end of a cart pole, to which the yoke is fixed. Invoking, summoning by incantation.మొగకింది కోడిపీట. ఆకర్షణము. కర్షకుడు [karṣakuḍu] karshakuḍu. [Skt. కృషి.] n. A cultivator, a farmer. సంకర్షణుడు [saṅkarṣaṇuḍu] san-karshaṇuḍu. [Skt.] n. A name of Balarāma, బలరాముడు. కృషి [kṛṣi] kṛishi. [Skt.] n. Cultivation, husbandry, agriculture, ploughing, cultivating the soil. సేద్యము. Labour, exertion ప్రయాసము, శ్రమ. కృషికుడు or కృషీవలుడుkṛiṣhī-kuḍu. n. A cultivator, a husbandman. సేద్యకాడు.

A scribe! Hence, early semantics of kharoṣṭī should be: 'engraving'. The word kharoṣṭī (cognate harosheth) should therefore have meant 'smithy-engraving'. The word hagoyim had meant 'nations'. Thus, the phrase *harosheth hagoyim* (kharoṣṭīgoi 'smithy engraving guilds') can be translated as 'smithy engraving nations' as was the engraving of a woman's face (Hariti's face) on the chariot linchpin.

Pillar capital, Kushan dynasty, 1st CE[189]. See the use of molluscs and śrivatsa, on the capital of the pillar. Read rebus, refer to hangi 'shell, mollusc'; rebus: sanga 'priest, community (guild)'. ayira 'fish'; rebus: metath. ayira 'noble'. The hieroglyphic composition held between the pair of lions can thus be read as: *ariya sangha.*[190]

The inscription details donors and donations to Mahasanghikas.

Transcript.

A. I.[2]

1. Mahachhatravasa Rajulasa
2. agramaheshia[3] Yasia
3. Kamudhaa dhitra
4. Kharaostasa yuvarana
5. matra Nadasia Kasaye[4]

A. II.[5]

1. sadha matra A[b]uholaa
2. pi[ta]mahi-Pishpasria bhra-
3. [t]ra Hayuarana sadha Hana-dhi[tra][6]
4. a[te]urena[7] [a]rakapa-[8]
5. rivarena iśe praḍhavipra[de]-
6. śe nisime śarira pra[ti]ṭhavito[9]
7. bhakavata-Śakamunisa Budhasa [| *]
8. mukihitaya saspae bhusati [| *]
9. Thuva cha sagharamo cha chat[u]-
10. diśasa saghasa Sarva-
11. stivadana parigrahe [|| *].

Translation.

I.

By *Nadasi Kasa*, the first queen of the great Satrap Rajula, the daughter of *Yasi Kamudha*, the mother of the Cæsar (*yuvarâja*) *Kharaosta*,

II.

(*Who is associated*) with her mother *Abuhola*, her grandmother *Pishpasri* (*Viśvaśrî ?*), her brother *Hayuara*, her daughter *Hana*, (and) with the crowd of the women of the harem, has deposited in this spot of the earth, in the Stûpa (*nisima*), a relic of divine Śâkyamuni Buddha; it will conduce to eternal welfare (*viz.*) liberation. Both the Stûpa (*thuva*) and the monastery (*are*) for the acceptance of the community of Sarvâstivâda (*monks*) that belongs to the four quarters (*of the world*).

Transcript.

B.[1]

1. Mahachhatravasa
2. Rajulasa putre
3. Śuḍase chhatrave [|| *]

[1] Incised on the neck of the lion to the right, in large characters.

Translation.

Kharaosta, the Cæsar,
Jalamasa the prince (?),
-maja the youngest.
A funeral monument for a monk has been erected.[6]

Transcript.

H.[7]

Guhavihare [|| *].

Translation.

In the Guha-monastery.

Transcript.

I.[1]

1. Veyaudino kadhavaro [b]usapa-
2. ro[2] kadha-
3. varo
4. viyaa [|| *].

Translation.[3]

The army started in haste; the army (*is*) intent on wealth: victory!

Transcript.

J.[4]

1. -[śamana]- P[u]lishṭena
2. [n]is[i]mo karita niyadido[5]
3. Sarvastivadana parigraho [|| *].[6]

Translation.

By the monk (?) Pulishṭa a Stûpa (*nisima*) was ordered to be made and given in the possession of the Sarvâstivâdas.

Transcript.

N.[6]

1. Ayariasa Budhilasa Nakarakasa bhikhu-
2. sa Sarvastivadaśa pagasa- [7]
3. na Mahasaghiana pra-
4. ñavida [8] v[a]khalulasa [9] [|| *].

Translation.

(P.) In honour of the whole Sakastana,
(Q.) Of the Satrap Khardaa,
(R.) Of Koḍina (*Kauṇḍinya*), a native of Tachhila.

"A Buddhist gold coin from India was found in northern Afghanistan at the archaeological site of Tillia Tepe, and dated to the 1st century CE. On the reverse, it depicts a lion with a nandipada, with the Kharoṣṭī legend "Sih[o] vigatabhay[o]" ("The lion who dispelled fear"). On the obverse, an almost naked man only wearing an Hellenistic chlamys and a petasus hat (an iconography similar to that of Hermes/ Mercury) rolls a Buddhist wheel. The legend in Kharoṣṭī reads "Dharmacakrapravata[ko]" ("The one who turned the Wheel of the Law"). It has been suggested that this may be an early representation of the Buddha."[191]

kharoṣṭī 'a kind of written character or alphabet', Lalit.x,29; kharoṭṭī, Jain.(Monier-Williams, p. 337).

This hypothesis is confirmed by harosheth, (cognate *kharoṣṭī*) tradition. *kharoṣṭī* was a syllabic writing system with intimations of contacts with Aramaic writing system. Though early evidences of *kharoṣṭī* documents are dated to ca. 6th century BCE, it is likely that between 15th century BCE (c. date of Daimabad which yielded a 'rim-of-jar' hieroglyph seal) and 6th century BCE, some form of contract documentation using a proto-form of *kharoṣṭī* (in combination with cuneiform or Indus writing systems) was perhaps used by artisan and traders, across a vast interaction area which covered a wide geographic area from Kyrgystan (Tocharia) to Haifa (Israel, Seaport on Mediterranean Ocean) – across Sarasvati-Sindu river-basins, Tigris-Euphrates doab, Caspian Sea, and Mediterranean Ocean – of three civilizations Indus, Mesopotamia and Egypt. The evidence of about 6000 Indus script inscriptions provides the details of products traded in this *harosheth hagoyim*, a smithy of nations, indeed. Harosheth is spelt in pronunciation: *khar-o'-sheth. Harosheth* and cognate *kharoṣṭī* may mean 'workmanship' or 'art of writing', apart from connoting specifically blacksmiths' writing system. Artisans had invented early writing systems necessitated by the economic imperative of bronze-age trade. In this smithy of nations, language was not a barrier. The barrier had been bridged by the invention and use of hieroglyphic and syllabic writing systems to record guild production and sea-faring or land-caravan trade transactions.

Since Harosheth denoted 'smithy of nations', kharoṣṭī users of the Indian linguistic area should have been the smiths who were the Shardana tribe of the Sea-Peoples. The ancestors of these kharoṣṭī script users had used Indus script hieroglyphs (which survived in the kharoṣṭī inscriptions of punch-marked coins). The users of Indus script hieroglyphs were also Sea-Peoples moving from a maritime, riverine civilization area across the Persian Gulf into and beyond the fertile crescent. It is notable that the finds of two pure tin ingots from a shipwreck in Haifa can be explained as the artifacts created by the Sea-Peoples since the ingots contained Indus script hieroglyphs. The inscriptions on these ingots have been discussed.[192] Based on this intense interconnection, it may be hypothesised, that the Shardana tribe of the Sea-Peoples recognized in Harosheth Hagoyim (kharoṣṭī...) were the smiths and traders of the civilization who used Indus script inscriptions to identify their artisanal repertoire, in an extensive area which ranged from Rakhigrhi (near Delhi) to Haifa (Israel), from Tepe Yahya to Harosheth Hagoyim (in the context of supplying trademrk linchipins for chariots in warfare).

The Hebrew word 'goy' is comparable to the Sanskrit word 'gotra'. Gotra is based on the Guru for the family or one of the ancestors. Lit. 'cattle shed', the lineage acted as a joint family, holding possessions in common. Seven Rishis (saptarshi) are recognized as the mind born sons of the creator Brahma. The *śathapatha brāhmaṇa* gives their names as: Atri, Bharadwaja, Gautama, Jamadagni, Kashyapa, Vasishtha, Vishwamitra. This is comparable to the Hebrew tradition of Menorah with seven candles signifying seventy nations.

Israeli archaeologists have uncovered one of the earliest depictions of a menorah, the seven-branched candelabra that has come to symbolize Judaism, the Israel Antiquities Authority[193] said. The menorah was engraved in stone around 2,000 years ago and found in a synagogue recently discovered by the Sea of Galilee.

See: cognate Prakrit lexeme: gōya (The word denotes descent from a common ancestor, with a common occupation): Gotta (nt.) [Vedic gotra, to go] ancestry, lineage. There is no word in English for gotta. It includes all those descended, or supposed to be descended, from a common ancestor. A gotta name is always distinguished from the personal name, the name drawn from place of origin or residence, or from occupation, and lastly from the nick -- name. It probably means agnate rather than cognate. About a score of gotta names are known. They are all assigned to the Buddha's time. See also Rh. D. Dialogues i.27, 195 sq. -- jāti gotta lakkhaṇa Sn 1004; gotta salakkhaṇa Sn 1018; Ādiccā nāma gottena, Sākiyā nāma jātiyā Sn 423; jāti gotta kula J ii.3; jātiyā gottena bhogena sadisa "equal in rank, lineage & wealth" DhA ii.218. -- evaŋ -- gotta (adj.) belonging to such & such an ancestry M i.429; ii.20, 33; kathaŋ° of what lineage, or: what is your family name? D i.92; nānā° (pl.) of various families Pv ii.916. -- With nāma (name & lineage, or nomen et cognomen): nāmagottaŋ Vin i.93; ii.239; D i.92 (expl. at DA i.257: paññatti -- vasena nāmaŋ paveṇi -- vasena gottaŋ: the name for recognition, the surname for lineage); Sn 648; Vv 8445 (with nāma & nāmadheyya; expl. at VvA 348<-> 349: nāmadheyya, as Tisso, Phusso, etc.; gotta, as Bhaggavo Bhāradvājo, etc.). -- gottena by the ancestral name: Vin i.93; D ii.154; Sn 1019; Dh 393; gottato same J i.56. Examples: Ambaṭṭha Kaṇhāyana -- gottena D i.92; Vipassī Koṇḍañño g°; Kakusandho Kassapo g°; Bhagavā Gotamo g° D ii.3; Nāgito Kassapo g° DA i.310; Vasudevo Kaṇho g° PvA 94. -- thaddha conceited as regards descent (+jāti° & dhana°) Sn 104; -- pañha question after one's family name Sn 456; -- paṭisārin (adj.) relying on lineage D i.99 (cp. Dialogues i.122); A v.327 sq.; -- bandhava connected by family ties (ñāti°+) Nd2 455; -- rakkhita protected by a (good) name Sn 315; VvA 72; -- vāda talk over lineage, boasting as regards descent D i.99. (Pali)

gōtrá n. ‘ cowpen, enclosure ’ RV., ‘ family, clan ’ ChUp., gōtrā -- f. ‘ herd of cows ’ Pāṇ. 2. gōtraka -- n. ‘ family ’ Yājñ. [gṓ --]1. Pa. gotta -- n. ‘ clan ’, Pk. gotta -- , gutta -- , amg. gōya -- n.; Gau. gū ‘ house ’ (in Kaf. and Dard. several other words for ‘ cowpen ’ > ‘ house ’: *gōśrayaṇa -- , gōṣṭhá -- , *gōstha -- (?), ghōṣa --); Pr. gū´ṭu ‘ cow ’; S. goṭru m. ‘ parentage ’, L. got f. ‘ clan ’, P. gotar, got f.; Ku. N. got ‘ family ’; A. got -- nāti ‘ relatives ’; B. got ‘ clan ’; Or. gota ‘ family, relative ’; Bhoj. H. got m. ‘ family, clan ’, G. got n.; M. got ‘ clan, relatives ’; -- Si. gota ‘ clan, family ’ ← Pa.2. B. H. gotā m. ‘ relative ’.Garh. got ‘ clan ’; -- A. goṭāiba ‘ to collect '(CDIAL 4279). (Z) [kORa] {N} ``^sun ^clan''. #17410.(Z) {N} ``^girl of the ^sun ^clan''. | `child', cf. `daughter'. #17420. (Munda etyma) gōtrin m. ' relative ' Vet., gōtrika -- ' relating to a family ' Jain. [gōtrá --]Pk. gotti -- , °ia -- , guttiya -- m. ' kinsman '; S. goṭrī ' related ', P. gotī; N. goti, gotiyā bhai ' kinsman ', Or. goti; H. gotī ' belonging to the same clan ', G. gotrī, M. gotī; -- N. goyā, guĩyā bhai ' very close friend ', H. goiyā̃, guiyā m.f. ' companion ' (cf. Pk. amg. gōya -- < gōtrá --)?(CDIAL 4281) Goy (Hebrew: גוי, regular plural goyim גוים or גויים) is a Hebrew biblical term for "nation". .. In the Torah/Hebrew Bible, goy and its variants appear over 550 times in reference to Israelites and to Gentile nations. The first recorded usage of goy occurs in Genesis10:5 and applies innocuously to non-Israelite nations. The first mention in relation to the Israelites comes in Genesis 12:2, when God promises Abraham that his descendants will form a goy gadol ("great nation"). On one occasion, the Jewish people are referred to as a goy kadosh, a "holy nation." While the earlier books of the Hebrew Bible often use goy to describe the Israelites, the later ones tend to apply the term to other nations…The Rabbinic literature conceives of the nations (goyim) of the world as numbering seventy, each with a distinct language.[194]

"It is such a wide variety of peoples that Herodotus writes about in his *History*, painting a vivid picture of their social makeup, their vocations and pursuits of life and their close relationship with the Achaemenian State. It was a result of this mixing that the Aramaean merchants spread out in Central Asia and that Aramaic writing led to the evolution of other alphabetic writings, such as Sogdian and kharoṣṭī. Iranian-speaking people moved eastward and their language exerted considerable influence on older languages of this region. Herodotus talks a lot about gold tribute, and narrates fantastic stories of gold-digging ants."[195]
Aramaic-kharoṣṭī interactions was noticed and recorded precisely by Monier-Williams: "Perhaps a more likely conjecture is that Hindu traders, passing up the Persian Gulf, had commercial dealings with Aramaean traders in Mesopotamia, and, becoming acquainted with their graphic methods, imported the knowledge and

use of some of their phonetic signs into India. This view was first propounded in the writings of the learned Professor A. Weber of Berlin, and has recently been ably argued in a work on 'Indische Palaeographie', by the late Professor Buhler of Vienna (published in 1896). If Indian Pandits will consult that most interesting standard work, they will there find a table exhibiting the most ancient of known Phoenician letters side by side with the kindred symbols used in the Moabite inscriptions of King Mesha -- which, as before intimated, is known to be as old as about 850 BCE -- while in parallel columns, and in a series of other excellent tables, are given the corresponding phonographic symbols from the numerous inscriptions of King Asoka scattered everywhere throughout Central and Northern India."[196]

"Kharoshti (Bactrian) was the ancient north Afghan language which is a derivative of Aramaic, which in turn is a derivative of Hebrew. It was unique among the Iranian language in the sense it is written using Greek scripts, a legacy which Alexander the Great had left behind after his victory over Bactrian in the fourth century BC. Soon after the conquest of Bactria by the nomadic people, Greek was the official language and script for administrative purposes. It's new rulers (Kushanas) Kujula Kadphises, Vima Takto (Kujula's son), Vima Kadphises continued the usage of Greek script to write the local language. It is Kanishka who adopted Bactrian as the language on his coins, thus became a cause for Greek language to disappear slowly. Kanishka introduced the Iranian title, Shaonanoshao - "King of Kings" in place of Greek form Basileos Basileon. Bactrian emerged as the most important language throughout the Kushana empire at least for six centuries even after the fall of Kushanas. Certain Brahmi letters seems to have distinguished in the coins of successive rulers."[197]

Bronze coin of Agathocles. Bactrian, about 190-180 BCE. Minted in Begram, Afghanistan

"Agathocles was a king of Bactria, an ancient Greek kingdom in central Asia (about 200-145 BC). From 200 BC the kingdom extended its control south of the Hindu Kush into Gandhara (modern Pakistan). The resulting direct contact with India influenced the design of the kingdom's coinage. On the coins intended for circulation south of the Hindu Kush, Indian deities and typical Indian images such as elephants and humped bulls, were often used. This bronze coin depicts the Indian goddess Subhadra (Krishna's sister) and also imitates the conventional square shape of Indian coins. The reverse has the more traditional Greek image of a panther and a legend in Greek, 'Basileos Agathokleous' ('of King Agathocles'). More significantly, this was the earliest bilingual Indo-Greek coin issue, for the obverse (front) carries an Indian translation of the same legend in Prakrit (the local language): 'Rajane Agathuklayasa'. It is written in Brahmi, one of the earliest Indian scripts, which was first deciphered in the 1830s. The realization that the legends on Indo-Greek coins were bilingual led to the decipherment of another ancient Indian script, Kharoṣṭī, which was adopted instead of Brahmi for all the issues of Agathocles' successors."[198]

"This study traces the development of the Kharoṣṭhī script primarily through the data made available by the recent discoveries of Kharoṣṭhī manuscripts. Epigraphic and numismatic sources are also taken into account to fill in the gaps in the history of the script.Part one summarizes opinions on the development of this writing system, and presents a new hypothesis. Foot marks, which are characteristic of many letters in the script have been presented systematically. This is followed by a description of the writing tools used to write the manuscripts. In part two, all of the individual signs of the script are discribed and illustrated at various stages of development. An appendix includes detailed charts illustrating the full range of signs used in several of the most important manuscripts."[199]

Excerpts from the Andrew Glass work[200]:

Coins with legends in Kharosthi have been found from almost all chronological span of the script, including issues of the Indo-Greeks, Indo-Scythians, Indo-Parmians, Kusanas, Ksatrapas, Audumbaras, Kulutas, Kunindas, Rajanyas, Vemakis and Vrsns. Many of these coins have been catalogued and illustrated in Gardner 1886, Hill 1906, Smith 1906, Rapson 1908, Whitehead 1914, and Allan 1936. A few Sino-Kharosthi coins, bearing inscriptions in both Chinese and Kharosthi, have been discovered in and around Hotan. The attribution and dates of these coins are discussed in Gribb 1984, 1985.

British Library has a collection of twenty-nine birch bark fragments containing the work of twenty-one different scribes, reportedly found in Hadda, Afganistan.

Geographical extent of the Kharoṣṭhī script

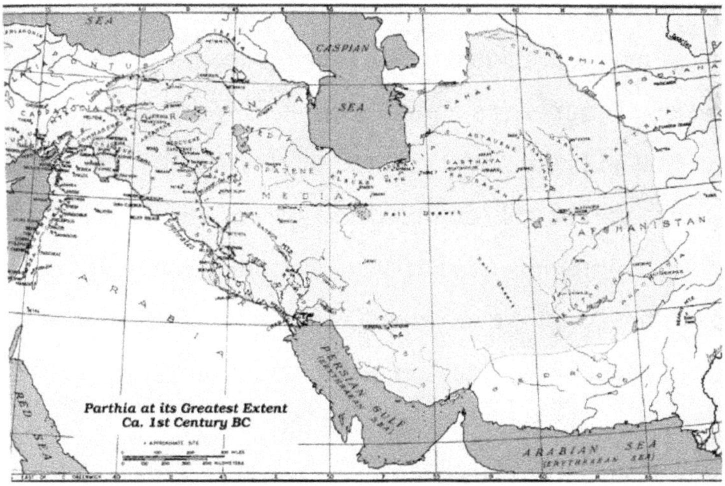

Parthia at its Greatest Extent
Ca. 1st Century BC

1-st c. BCE Parthian map

The kharoṣṭī signs for a, ca, da, na, ya, ra, va, s'a, sa, za and ha present little difficulty as they can be derived more or less directly from their Aramaic counterparts alep, sadeh, dalet, nun, bet, yod, res, waw, het, samek, zayin and he.

The letters ka, kha, ga, ta and pa do not match the Aramaiv letters kap, qop, gimel, taw, and peh, which show a closer resemblance to Kharosthi da, sa, ya, pa and a respectively. Probably each form da, sa, ya, pa and a was created before ka, kha, ga, ta and pa.

Table kharoṣṭī and Aramaic

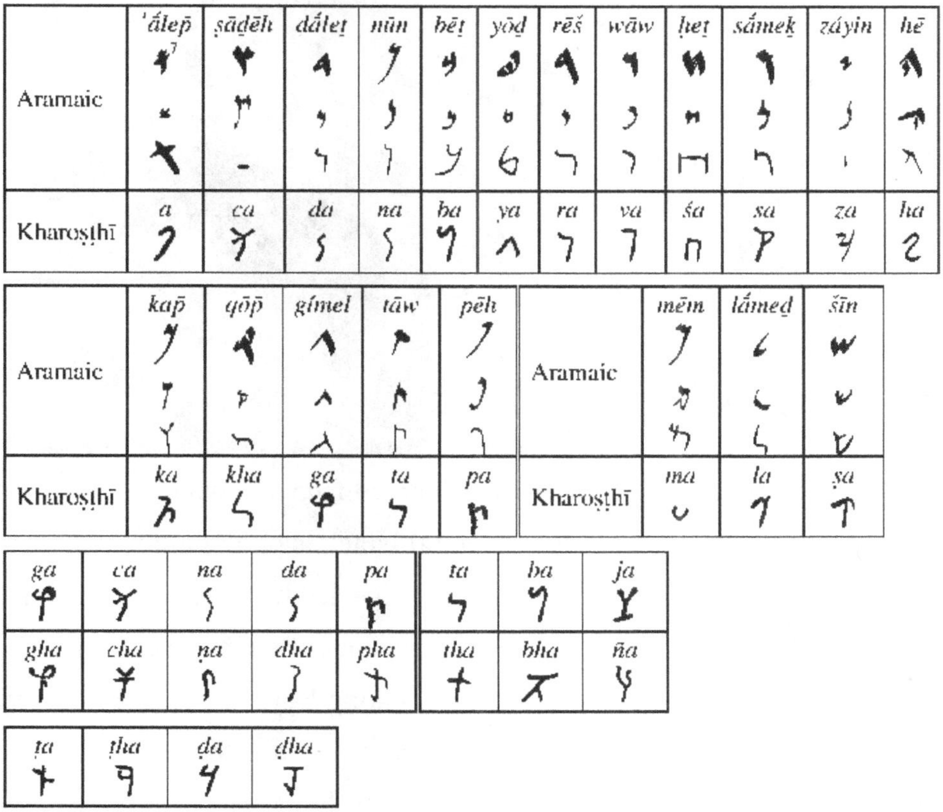

Use of kharoṣṭī script spread along trade routes. Hence, the interactions with metalsmiths of Harosheth Hagoyim. Since metalsmiths deployed Indus Script hieroglyphs, these were used together with kharoṣṭī script on early punch-marked coins and later, also on Sohgaura copper plate (together with Brahmi script).

A news report on the find of a lynchpin of a chariot[201]:

A 3,200-year-old round bronze tablet with a carved face of a woman, found at the El-Ahwat excavation site near Katzir in central Israel, is part of a linchpin that held the wheel of a battle chariot in place. This was revealed by scientist Oren Cohen of the Zinman Institute of Archaeology at the University of Haifa. "Such an identification reinforces the claim that a high-ranking Egyptian or local ruler was based at this location, and is likely to support the theory that the site is Harosheth Hagoyim, the home town of Sisera, as mentioned in Judges 4-5," says Prof. Zertal.

The El-Ahwat site, near Nahal 'Iron, was exposed by a cooperative delegation excavating there during 1993-2000 from the Universities of Haifa and Cagliari (Sardinia), headed by Prof. Zertal. The excavated city has been dated back to the end of the Bronze Age and early Iron Age (13th-12th centuries B.C.E.). The city's uniqueness - its fortifications, passageways in the walls, and rounded huts - made it foreign amidst the Canaanite landscape. Prof. Zertal has proposed that based on these unusual features, the site may have been home to the Shardana tribe of the Sea-Peoples, who, according to some researchers, lived in Harosheth Hagoyim, Sisera's capital city. The city is mentioned in the Bible's narratives as Sisera's capital, and it was from there that the army of chariots set out to fight the Israelites, who were being led by Deborah the prophetess and Barak, son of Avinoam. The full excavation and its conclusions have been summarized in Prof. Zertal's book "Sisera's Secret, A Journey following the Sea-Peoples and the Song of Deborah" (Dvir, Tel Aviv, 2010 [Hebrew]).

One of the objects uncovered at the site remained masked in mystery. The round, bronze tablet, about 2 cm. in diameter and 5 mm. thick, was found in a structure identified as the "Governor's House". The object features a carved face of a woman wearing a cap and earrings shaped as chariot wheels. When uncovered in 1997, it was already clear that the tablet was the broken end of an elongated object, but Mr. Cohen, who included the tablet in the final report of the excavations, did not manage to find its parallel in any other archaeological discoveries.

Now, 13 years later, the mystery has been solved. When carrying out a scrutinizing study of ancient Egyptian reliefs depicting chariot battles, Mr. Cohen discerned a unique decoration: the bronze linchpins fastening the chariot wheels were decorated with people's faces - of captives, foreigners and enemies of Egypt. He also noticed that these decorations characterized those chariots that were used by royalty and distinguished people.

“This identification enhances the historical and archaeological value of the site and proves that chariots belonging to high-ranking individuals were found there. It provides support for the possibility, which has not yet been definitively established, that this was Sisera’s city of residence and that it was from there that the chariots set out on their way to the battle against the Israelite tribes, located between the ancient sites of Taanach and Megiddo,” Prof. Zertal concludes.

Photos:

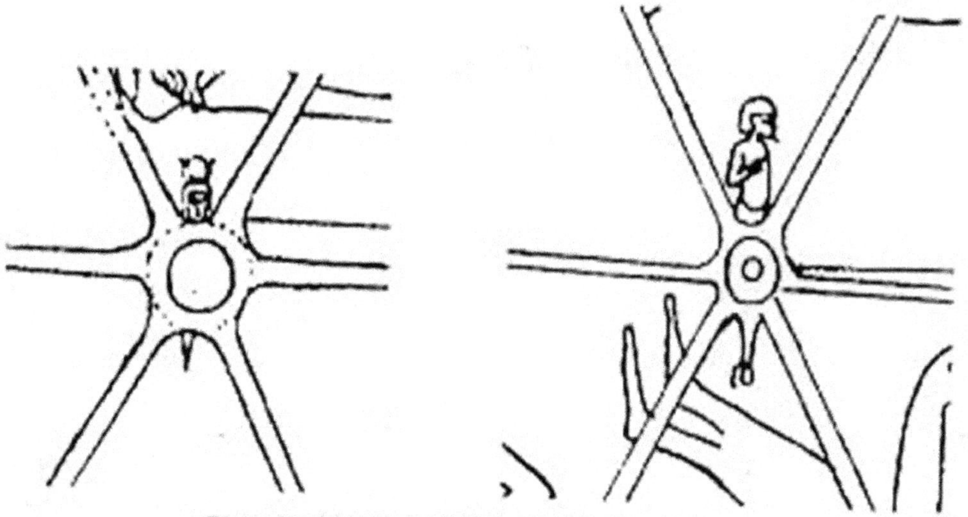

Fig. 1-2. Hubs of chariot wheels

Chariot linchpin (Moshe Einav)

Postulating Proto-Indian

The cultural contacts among languages of Indian *sprachbund* because of geographical proximity render the postulate a falsifiable hypothesis. While the languages may be genetically unrelated, or only distantly related and where genetic affiliations are unclear, caution in evaluating the formation and evaluation of languages is warranted, since the sprachbund characteristics might give a false appearance of relatedness.

In a classic 1956 paper titled "India as a Linguistic Area", Emeneau[202] laid the groundwork for the general acceptance of the concept of a *sprachbund.* In the paper, Emeneau observed that the subcontinent's Dravidian and Indo-Aryan languages shared a number of features that were not inherited from a common source, but were areal features, the result of diffusion during sustained contact." Common features of a group of languages in a Sprachbund are called 'areal features'. In linguistics, an areal feature is any typological feature shared by languages within the same geographical area. An example refers to retroflex consonants in the Burushaski[203], Nuristani[204], Dravidian, Munda[205] and Indo-Aryan language families of the Indian subcontinent.

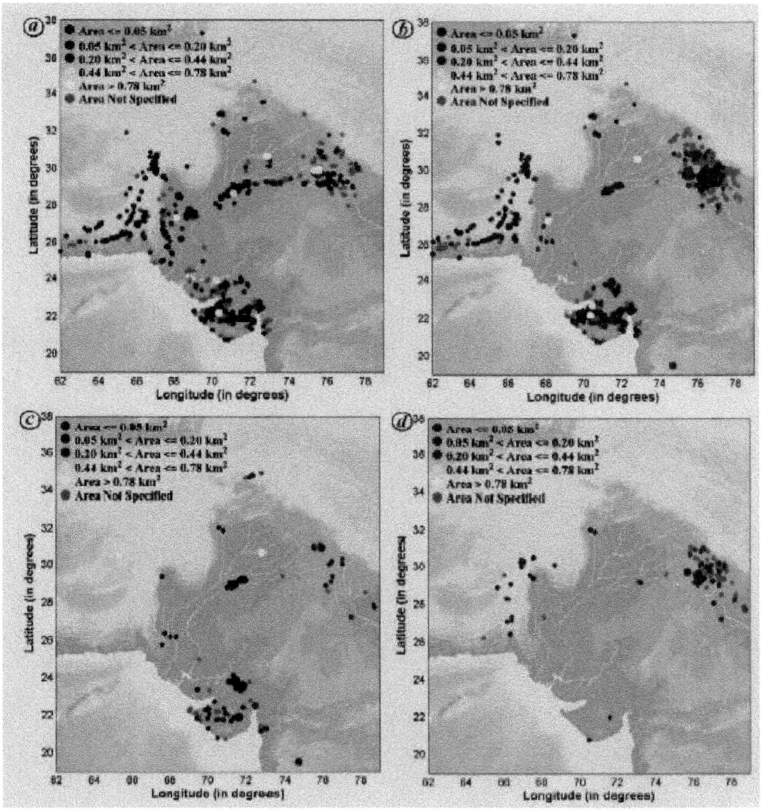

In addition to studies in the evolution of and historical contacts among Indian languages, further researches are also needed in an archaeological context. Karl Menninger[206] cites a remarkable instance. In the Indian tradition, finger signals were used to settle the price for a trade transaction. Finger gestures were a numeric cipher!

Further work on the nature of the contacts between Indian artisans and their trade associates, say, in Meluhhan settlements in the Persian Gulf region, or minewworkers in Muztagh Ata (Tushara) may unravel the the nature of long-distance contacts between India and neighbouring civilization areas such as Kyrgystan, Bactria-Margiana-Archaeological Complex, Persian Gulf, Elam, Sumer, Mesopotamia. Could it be that the Indus language and writing were Indus Artisans' cryptographic messaging system for specifications of artifacts made in and exported from Meluhha?

Location of Meluha. Interaction areas.[207]

Plots of the distribution of archaeological sites in the greater Indus valley at (a) 5000 BCE; (b) 4000 BCE; (c) 3700 BCE; (d) 3200 BCE. Sites are color coded by area according to the legend. Large area sites are emphasized by increasing their symbol size.

Plots of the distribution of archaeological sites in the greater Indus valley at (a) 2500 BCE; (b) 1900 BCE; (c) 1500 BCE; (d) 1000 BCE. Sites are color coded by area according to the legend. Large area sites are emphasized by increasing their symbol size.[208]

Sarasvarti river basin and Gujarat have about 2000 (80%) of archaeological sites of the civilization.

The principal interaction areas were within Meluhha and in the regions identified as Turan towards the Caspian Sea, Magan, Dilmun and Mesopotamian cultural zones across the Persian Gulf and the Tigris-Euphrates doab, Western Asia showing Mesopotamia, Turan, Dilmun, Meluhha.[209]

The interaction is evidenced by the finds of Indus script epigraphs as shown in the map which takes Meluhhan sea-faring artisans/merchants across the Persian Gulf.

Tanana mleccha

A Jaina text, Avasyaka Churani notes that ivory trade was managed by tanana mleccha, who also traveled from Uttaravaha to Dakshinapatha.[210] Guttila Jataka (ca.4th cent.) makes reference to itinerant ivory workers/traders journeying from Varanasi to Ujjain.[211] The word, tanana in tanana mleccha may be related to: (i) tah'nai, 'engraver' mleccha; or (ii) tana, 'of (mleccha) lineage'. 1. See Kuwi. tah'nai 'to engrave' in DEDR and Bsh. then, thon, 'small axe' in CDIAL: DEDR 3146 *Go.* (Tr.) tarcana , (Mu.) tarc- to scrape; (Ma.) tarsk- id., plane; (D.) task-, (Mu.) tarsk-/tarisk- to level, scrape (*Voc.*1670).

Notes on Indian linguistic area: pre-aryan,pre-Munda and pre-dravidian in India

It will be a hasty claim to make that Old Tamil or Proto-Munda or Santali or Prakṛt or Pali or any other specific language of the Indian linguistic area, by itself (to the exclusion of other languages in contact), explains the language of the Indus civilization. In this context, the work by Sylvan Levi, Jules Bloch and Jean Przyluski published in the 1920's (cited elsewhere) continues to be relevant, even today, despite some advances in studies related to formation of Indian languages and the archaeological perspectives of and evidences from the civilization.

Emeneau[212] notes: "In fact, promising as it has seemed to assume Dravidian membership for the Harappa language, it is not the only possibility. Professor W. Norman Brown has pointed out (The United States and India and Pakistan, 131-132, Cambridge, Harvard University Press, 1953) that Northwest India, i.e. the Indus Valley and adjoining parts of India, has during most of its history had Near Eastern elements in its political and cultural make-up at least as prominently as it had true Indian elements of the Gangetic and Southern types. The passage is so important that it is quoted in full: 'More ominous yet was another consideration. Partition now would reproduce an ancient, recurring, and sinister incompatibility between Northwest and the rest of the subcontinent, which, but for a few brief periods of uneasy cohabitation, had kept them politically apart or hostile and had rendered the subcontinent defensively weak. When an intrusive people came through the passes and established itself there, it was at first spiritually closer to the relatives it had left behind than to any group already in India. Not until it had been separated from those relatives for a fairly long period and had succeeded in pushing eastward would I loosen the external ties. In period after period this seems to have been true. In the third millennium B.C. the Harappa culture in the Indus Valley was partly similar to contemporary western Asian civilizations and partly to later historic Indian culture of the Ganges Valley. In the latter part of the next millennium the earliest Aryans, living in the Punjab and composing the hymns of the Rig Veda, were apparently more like their linguistic and religious kinsmen, the Iranians, than like their eastern Indian contemporaries. In the middle of the next millennium the Persian Achaemenians for two centuries held the Northwest as satrapies. After Alexander had invaded India (327/6-325 B.C.) and Hellenism had arise, the Northwest too was Hellenized, and once more was partly Indian and partly western. And after Islam entered India, the Northwest again was associated with Persia, Bokhara, Central Asia, rather than with India, and considered itself Islamic first and Indian second. The periods during which the Punjab has been culturally assimilated to the rest of northern India are ew if any at all. Periods of political assimilation are almost as few; perhaps a part of the fourth and third centuries B.C. under the Mauryas; possibly a brief period under the Indo-Greek king menander in the second century B.C.; another brief period under the Muslim kingdom of Delhi in the last quarter of the twelfth century A.D.; a long one under the great Mughals in the sixteenth and seventeenth centuries A.D.; a century under the British, 1849-1947.'

"Though this refers to cultural and political factors, it is a warning that we must not leap to linguistic conclusions hastily. The early, but probably centuries-long condition in which Sanskrit, a close ally of languages of Iran, was restricted to the northwest (though it was not the only language there) and the rest of India was not Sanskritic in speech, may well have been mirrored earlier by a period when some other language invader from the Near East-a relative of Sumerian or of Elamitic or what not-was spoken and written in the Indus Valley-perhaps that of invaders and conquerors-while the indigenous population spoke another language-perhaps one of the Dravidian stock, or perhaps one of the Munda stock, which is now represented only by a handful of languages in the backwoods of Central India.

"On leaving this highly speculative question, we can move on to an examination of the Sanskrit records, and we find in them linguistic evidence of contacts between the Sanskrit-speaking invaders and the other linguistic groups within India...the early days of Indo-European scholarship were without benefit of the spectacular archaeological discoveries that were later to be made in the Mediterranean area, Mesopotamia and the Indus Valley... This assumption (that IE languages were urbanized bearers of a high civilization) led in the long run to another block-the methodological tendency of the end of the nineteenth and the beginning of the twentieth century to attempt to find Indo-European etymologies for the greatest possible portion of the vocabularies of the Indo-European languages, even though the object could only be achieved by flights of phonological and semantic fancy...

very few scholars attempted to identify borrowings from Dravidian into Sanskrit...The Sanskrit etymological dictionary of Uhlenbrck (1898-1899) and the Indo-European etymological dictionary of Walde and Pokorny (1930-1932) completely ignore the work of Gundert (1869), Kittel (1872, 1894), and Caldwell (1856,1875)... It is clear that not all of Burrow's suggested borrowings will stand the test even of his own principles.. 'India' and 'Indian' will be used in what follows for the subcontinent, ignoring the political division into the Republic of India and Pakistan, and, when necessary, including Ceylong also... the northern boundary of Dravidian is and has been for a long time retreating south before the expansion of Indo-Aryan... We know in fact from the study of the non-Indo-European element in the Sanskrit lexicon that at the time of the earliest Sanskrit records, the R.gveda, when Sanskrit speakers were localized no further east than the Panjab, there were already a few Dravidian words current in Sanskrit. This involves a localization of Dravidian speech in this area no lather than three millennia ago. It also of course means much bilingualism and gradual abandonment of Dravidian speech in favor of IndoAryan over a long period and a great area-a process for which we have only the most meagre of evidence in detail. Similar relationships must have existed between Indo-Aryan and Munda and between Dravidian and Munda, but it is still almost impossible to be sure of either of these in detail... The Dravidian languages all have many Indo-Aryan items, borrowed at all periods from Sanskrit, Middle Indo-Aryan and Modern Indo-Aryan. The Munda languages likewise have much Indo-Aryan material, chiefly, so far as we know now, borrowed rom Modern Indo-Aryan, thogh this of course inlcudes items that are Sanskrit in form, since Modern Indo-Aryan borrows from Sanskrit very considerably. That Indo-Aryan has borrowed from Dravidian has also become clear. T. Burrow, The Sanskrit Language, 379-88 (1955), gives a sampling and a statement of the chronology involved. It is noteworthy that this influence was spent by the end of the pre-Christian era, a precious indication for the linguistic history of North India: Dravidian speech must have practically ceased to exist in the Ganges valley by this period... Most of the languages of India, of no matter which major family, have a set of retroflex, cerebral, or domal consonants in contrast with dentals. The retroflexes include stops and nasal certainly, also in some languages sibilants, lateral, tremulant, and even others. Indo-Aryan, Dravidian, Munda and even the far northern Burushaski, form a practically solid bloc characterized by this phonological feature... Even our earliest Sanskrit records already show phonemes of this class, which are, on the whole, unknown elsewhere in the Indo-European field, and which are certainly not Proto-Indo-European. In Sanskrit many of the occurrences of retroflexes are conditioned; others are explained historically as reflexes of certain Indo-European consonants and consonant clusters. But, in fact, in Dravidian it is a matter of the utmost certainty that retroflexes in contrast with dentals are Proto-Dravidian in origin, not the result of conditioning circumstances... it is clear already that echo-words are a pan-Indic trait and that Indo-Aryan probably received it from non-Indo-Aryan (for it is not Indo-European)... The use of classifiers can be added to those other linguistic traits previously discussed, which establish India as one linguistic area ('an area which includes languages belonging to more than one family but showing traits in common which are found not to belong to the other members of (at least) one of the families') for historical study. The evidence is at least as clear-cut as in any part of the world... Some of the features presented here are, it seems to me, as 'profound' as we could wish to find... Certainly the end result of the borrowings is that the languages of the two families, Indo-Aryan and Dravidian, seem in many respects more akin to one another than Indo-Aryan does to the other Indo-European languages. (We must not, however, neglect Bloch's final remark and his reasons therefor: *'Ainsi donc, si profondes qu'aient ete les influences locales, elles n'ont pas conduit l'aryen de l;inde... a se differencier fortement des autres langues indo-europeennes.'*)"[213]

Swaminatha Iyer[214] posits a genetic relationship between Tamil and Sanskrit. He cites GU Pope to aver that several Indo-European languages are linguistically farther away from Sanskrit than Dravidian. He cites examples of Tamil and Sanskrit forms of some glosses: hair: mayir, s'mas'ru; mouth: vāya, vā c; ear: s śevi, śrava; hear: kēḷ keṇ (Tulu), karṇa; walk: śel, car; mother: āyi, yāy (Paiśāci). Evaluating this work, Edwin Bryant and Laurie Patton[215] note: "It is still more simple and sound to assume that the words which need a date of contact of the fourth millennium BCE on linguistic grounds as loan words in Dravidian might be words originally inherited in Dravidian from the Proto-speech which was the common ancestor of both Dravidian and Indo-Aryan...It will be simpler to explain the situation if both Indo-Aryan and Dravidian are traced to a common language family. In vocables they show significant agreement. In phonology and morphology the linguistic structures agree significantly. It requires a thorough comparative study of the two language families to conduct a fuller study. "

Proto-Munda continuity and Language X

- Sources of OIA agricultural vocabulary based on Masica (1979)

	Percentage
IE/IIr	40%
Drav	13%
Munda	11%
Other	2%
Unknown	34%
Total	100%

- Hence, a Language X is postulated; Language 'X' to explain a large number of agriculture-related words with no IE cognates: Colin Masica, 1991, Indo-Aryan Languages, Cambridge Univ. Press
- Since there is cultural continuity in India from the days of Sarasvati civilization, it is possible to reconstruct Language X by identifying isoglosses in the linguistic area.

Contributions of the following language/archaeology scholars[216] have followed upon these insights of Sylvan Levi, Jules Bloch and Jean Przyluski published over 90 years ago: Emeneatu, MB, Kuiper, FBJ, Masica, CP, Southworth F.

Resemblances between two or more languages (whether typological or in vocabulary) can be due to genetic relation (descent from a common ancestor language), or due to borrowing at some time in the past between languages that were not necessarily genetically related. When little or no direct documentation of ancestor languages is available, determining whether a similarity is genetic or areal can be difficult.

These observations provide the framework for postulating Proto-Indian which can explain 1) the large percentage of words (said to be from Language 'X') in Proto-Indoaryan and Indo-aryan which cannot be explained by links with Proto-Indo-European or Indo-European; and 2) the large number of Munda words in Sanskrit demonstrated by Kuiper.

"While Prof. Thomson maintained that a Munda influence has probably been at play in fixing the principle regulating the inflexion of nouns in Indo-Aryan vernaculars, such influence appeared to be unimportant to Prof. Sten Konow... Prof. Przyluski in his papers, translated here, have tried to explain a certain number of words of the Sanskrit vocabulary as fairly ancient loans from the Austro-Asiatic family of languages. He has in this opened up a new line of enquiry. Prof. Jules

Bloch in his article on Sanskrit and Dravidian, also translated in this volume, has criticised the position of those who stand exclusively for Dravidian influence and has proved that the question of the Mnn<j& substratum in Indo-Aryan cannot be

overlooked...In 1923, Prof. Levi, in a fundamental article on Pre-Aryen et PrJ-Draviditn dans VInde tried to show that some geographical names of ancient India like Kosala-Tosala, Anga-Vanga, Kalinga-Trilinga, Utkala-Mekala and Pulinda-Kulinda, ethnic names which go by pairs, can be explained by the morphological system of the Austro-Asiatic languages. Names like Accha-Vaccha, Takkola-

Kakkola belong to the same category. He concluded his long study with the following observation, " We must know whether the legends, the religion and the philosophical thought of India do not owe anything to this past. India has been too exclusively examined from the Indo-European standpoint. It ought to be remembered that India is a great maritime country... the movement which carried the Indian colonization towards the Far East... was far from inaugurating a new route...Adventurers, traffickers and missionaries profited by the technical progress of navigation and followed under better conditions of comfort and efficiency, the way traced from time immemorial, by the mariners of another race, whom Aryan or Aryanised India despised as savages." In 1926, Przyluski tried to explain the name of an ancient people of the Punjab, the Udumbara, in a similar way and affiliate it to the Austro-Asiatic group. (cf. Journal Asiatique, 1926, 1, pp. 1-25, Un ancicn peuple du Pendjables Udumbaras : only a portion of this article containing linguistic discussions has been translated in the Appendix of this book.) In another article, the same scholar discussed some names of Indian towns in the geography of Ptolemy and tried to explain them by Austro-Asiatic forms...Dr. J. H. Hutton, in an interesting lecture on the Stone Age Cult of Assam delivered in the Indian Museum at Calcutta in 1928, while dealing with some prehistoric monoliths of Dimapur, near Manipur, says that " the method of erection of these monoliths is very important, as it throws some light on the erection of prehistoric monoliths in other parts of the world. Assam and Madagascar are the only remaining parts of the world where the practice of erecting rough stones still continues....The origin of this stone cult is uncertain, but it appears that it is to be mainly imputed to the Mon-Khmer intrusion from the east In his opinion the erection of these monoliths takes the form of the lingam and yoni. He thinks that the Tantrik form of worship, so prevalent in Assam, is probably due to " the incorporation into Hinduism of a fertility cult which preceded it as .the religion of the country. The dolmens possibly suggest distribution from South India, but if so, the probable course was across the Bay of Bengal and then back again westward from further Asia. Possibly the origin was from Indonesia whence apparently the use of supari (areca nut) spread to India as well as the Pacific." (From the Introduction by PC Bagchi and SK Chatterjee, 1

May 1929).

On 'Sanskrit and Dravidian', comments by Jules Bloch: "There is, therefore, nothing to justify the assertion that Indo-Aryan cerebrals are of indigenous origin. The local pronunciation has rendered the development of this class possible ; and in this sense the action of the substratum is undeniable. But it is necessary at once to insist upon the fact that the Munda languages have dentals and cerebrals just like Dravidian, and nothing, therefore, stands in the way of attributing theoretically the origin of the Sanskrit pronunciation to the action of a substratum of either Munda or some other language connected with it, if not of a fourth linguistic family still unknown...A curious fact that might be noted here is the continuous character of the Sanskrit sentences, which has given rise to the rules of sandhi, because Tamil and Canarese admit a rigorous sandhi in writing, But the same languages in their spoken form ignore it; Gondi and Kurukh also ignore it. In so far as these literary languages admit this tandhi, it is certainly due to the influence of Sanskrit ; and even in Sanskrit it is probable that the use of the rules in question has very much surpassed in extension the real use ; Aśoka ignores them absolutely. There is, therefore, no clear phonetic proof of the action of Dravidian on Indo-European, at any rate, in ancient times...The facts of a substratum result from the unconscious blending of two systems existing amongst the same people ; the loan results from a willing effort to add elements taken from outside to the mass of the vocabulary. The loan proves the contact of the two languages and not the substitution of the one by the other. On the other hand it is often difficult to recognise in what sense the borrowing is made between two given languages and to make sure that it has not been made by each of the two languages from a third one, known or unknown... Perhaps the principal interest for ourselves in the study of ancient loans (and it would be necessary to try both ways since Dravidian has borrowed much from Aryan) would be to form an idea of prehistoric Dravidian ; because even those Dravidian languages which have a past are only attested in a definite way, for the first time, a few centuries after the Christian Era. Moreover the complications we have met with, suggest that Dravidian like Sanskrit may have taken loans of vocabulary from Munda, which must be at least as ancient as Dravidian in India." (pp. 40-59).

Kuiper[217] notes: " ...a very considerable amount (say some 40%) of the New Indo-Aryan vocabulary is borrowed from Munda, either via Sanskrit (and Prākṛt), or via Prākṛt alone, or directly from Munda; wide-branched and seemingly native, word-families of South Dravidian are of Proto-Munda origin; in Vedic and later Sanskrit, the words adopted have often been Aryanized, resp. Sanskritized. "In view of the intensive interrelations between Dravidian, Munda and Aryan dating from pre-Vedic times even individual etymological questions will often have to be approached from a Pan-Indic point of view if their study is to be fruitful. It is hoped that this work may be helpful to arrive at this all-embracing view of the Indian languages, which is the final goal of these studies."

Parasher provides an impressionistic account of the social status of mleccha[218]. Excerpts/blurb: "Exploring Identity and the Other in Ancient India. Mleccha (and its equivalent milakkha) are usually translated as foreigner or barbarian. A translation which is inadequate in so many ways but not least because it implies that it was a word used by Indians to describe non-Indians. In fact it is a term used by some writers who lived in certain parts of India to describe people native to what we think of as India but who lacked some important criteria the writer felt defined his cultural identity (language, religion, geographical location, ancestry etc.). Most often it was used by Brahmanical writers to describe those outside of the aryavarta... Parsher begins with a discussion of the etymology of Mleccha. As the earliest reference occurs in the Śathapathabrāhmaṇa, which is part of an oral tradition dating to before 500 BC, scholars have usually looked for various origins in the bronze age societies of the first and second millennium BCE... In fact in early texts it is clear that mleccha status was defined largely in terms of language (either the inability to use Sanskrit, or the inability to use it correctly). Language was central to identity in ancient India, as evidence by the process of Sanskritization in the early centuries AD, the importance of the Grammarians from Panini onwards. Readers interested in this aspect should also consult the very good collection of essays by Madhav M Deshpande, *Sanskrit & Prakrit: Sociolinguistic Issues* (Mohilal Banarsidass, 1993)…Arthaśāstra suggests that mleccha would make valuable mercenaries, in fact it prescribes their use for a number of activities (assassination, espionage, poisoning) which might be considered beneath arya. This is a not entirely positive view, but it is a pragmatic one. The epics, which Parsher takes as generally later in tone, also portray the mleccha as valuable mercenaries. On the other hand, the Dharmaśāstra literature generally takes a theoretical (but not consistent) view of non-contact with the mleccha, and the Mudraraksasa a similar position, portraying Malayaketu as depending on mleccha mercenaries in contrast to Chandragupta. If the sources are taken in this order, they suggest a shift towards a rhetoric (if not reality) of mleccha exclusion… The assertion that 'aboriginals were apparently ostracized because of their backwardness and repulsive habits'… Parasher vacillates '... they were all listed together as mlecchas. This is not difficult to understand and can be explained by the fact that to the brahmin writers these people were all outside the varnāśramadharma' (p. 214)."

A milakkhu (Pali) is disconnected from vāc and does not speak Vedic; he spoke Prakrt. " *na* ā*ry*ā *mlecchanti bh*āṣā *bhir māyay*ā *na caranty uta:* aryas do not speak with crude dialects like mlecchas, nor do they behave with duplicity (MBh. 2.53.8). a dear friend of Vidura who was a professional excavator is sent by Vidura to help the Pāṇḍavas in confinement; this friend of Vidura has a conversation with Yudhisthira, the eldest Pāṇḍava: "*kṛṣṇapakṣe caturdasyām ṛtāv asya purocanah, bhavanasya tava dvāri pradāsyati hutāsanam, mātrā saha* *pradagdhavyāh Pāṇḍavāh puruṣ arṣabhāh, iti vyavasitam pārtha dhārtaā ṣṭrrāsya me śrutam, kiñcic ca vidurenkoto mleccha-vācāsi Pāṇḍava, tyayā ca tat tathety uktam etad visvāsa kāraṇam*: on the fourteenth evening of the dark fortnight, Purocana will put fire in the door of your house. 'The Pandavas are leaders of the people, and they are to be burned to death with their mother.' This, Pārtha (Yudhiṣṭ ira), is the determined plan of Dhṛtarāṣṭra's son, as I have heard it. When you were leaving the city, Vidura spoke a few words to you in the dialect of the mlecchas, and you replied to him, 'So be it'. I say this to gain your trust.(*MBh.* 1.135.4-6). This passage shows that there were two Aryans distinguished by language and ethnicity, Yudhiṣṭira and Vidura. Both are aryas, who could speak mlecchas' language; Dhṛtarāṣṭra and his people are NOT aryas only because of their behaviour.

Melakkha, island-dwellers

According to the great epic, Mlecchas lived on islands: "*sa sarvān mleccha nṛpatin sāgara dvīpa vāsinah, aram āhāryām āsa ratnāni vividhāni ca, andana aguru vastrāṇi maṇi muktam anuttamam, kāñcanam rajatam vajram vidrumam ca mahā dhanam:* (Bhima) arranged for all the mleccha kings, who dwell on the ocean islands, to bring varieties of gems, sandalwood, aloe, garments, and incomparable jewels and pearls, gold, silver, diamonds, and extremely valuable coral… great wealth." (*MBh.* 2.27.25-26).

A series of articles and counters had appeared in the *Journal of the Economic and social history of the Orient,* Vol.XXI, Pt.II, Elizabeth C.L. During Caspers and A. Govindankutty countering R.Thapar's dravidian hypothesis for the locations of Meluhha, Dilmun and Makan; Thapar's A Possible identification of Meluhha, Dilmun, and Makan appeared in the journal Vol. XVIII, Part I locating these on India's west coast.

Bh. Krishnamurthy defended Thapar on linguistic grounds in Vol. XXVI, Pt. II: *mel-u-kku =3D highland, west; *teLmaN (=3D pure earth) ~ dilmun; *makant =3D male child (Skt. vi_ra =3D male offspring.[219]

Meluhha trade was first mentioned by Sargon of Akkad (Mesopotamia 2370 B.C.) who stated that boats from Dilmun, Magan and Meluhha came to the quay of Akkad.[220] The Mesopotamian imports from Meluhha were: woods, copper (ayas), gold, silver, carnelian, cotton. Gudea sent expeditions in 2200 B.C. to Makkan and Meluhha in search of hard wood. Seal impression with the cotton cloth from Umma[221] and cotton cloth piece stuck to the base of a silver vase from Mohenjodaro[222] are indicative evidence. Babylonian and Greek names for cotton were: sind, sindon. This is an apparent reference to the cotton produced in the black cotton soils of Sind and Gujarat.

Milakku, Meluhha and copper

Copper-smelting had to occur on the outskirts of a village. Hence, the semantic equivalence of milakkha as copper. Mleccha in Pali is milakkha or milakkhu to describe those who dwell on the outskirts of a village.[223]

"Gordon Childe refers to the 'relatively large amount of social labour' expended in the extraction and distribution of copper and tin', the possession of which, in the form of bronze weaponry, 'consolidated the positions of war-chiefs and conquering aristocracies' (Childe 1941: 133)... With the publication of J.D. Muhly's monumental *Copper and Tin* in 1973 (Muhly 1973: 155-535; cf. 1976: 77-136) an

enormous amount of data on copper previously scattered throughout the scholarly literature became easily accessible... cuneiform texts consistently distinguish

refined (urudu-luh-ha) [cf. loha = red, later metal (Skt.)] from unrefined copper (urudu) strongly suggests that it was matte (impure mixture of copper and copper sulphide) and not refined copper that was often imported into the country. Old

Assyrian texts concerned with the import of copper from Anatolia distinguish urudu from urudu-sig, the latter term appearing when written phonetically as dammuqum, 'fine, good' (CAD D: 180, s.v. dummuqu), and this suggests that it is not just 'fine quality' but actually 'refined' copper that is in question... TIN. In antiquity tin (Sum. nagga/[AN.NA], Akk.annaku) was

important, not in its own right, but as an additive to copper in the production of the alloy bronze (Sum. sabar, Akk. siparru) (Joannes 1993: 97-8)... In some cases, ancient recipes call for a ratio of tin to copper as high as 1: 6 or 16.6 per cent, while other texts speak of a 1:8 ratio or 12.5 per cent (Joannes 1993: 104)... 'there is little or no tin bronze' in Western Asia before c. 3000 B.C. (Muhly 1977: 76; cf. Muhly 1983:9). The presence of at least four tin-bronzes in the Early Dynastic I period... Y-Cemetery at Kish signals the first appearance of tin-bronze in southern Mesopotamia... arsenical copper continued in use at sites like Tepe Gawra, Fara, Kheit Qasim and Ur (Muhly 1993: 129). By the time of the Royal Cemetery at Ur (Early Dynastic IIIa), according to M.Muller-Karpe, 'tin-bronze had become the dominant alloy' (Muller-Karpe 1991: 111) in Southern Mesopotamia... Gudea of Lagash says he received tin from Meluhha... and in the Old Babylonian period it was imported to Mari from Elam... *Abhidhāna Cintāmaṇi* of Hemachandra states that mleccha and mleccha-mukha are two of the twelve names for copper: tāmram (IV.105-6: tāmram mlecchamukham śulvam raktam dvaṣṭamudumbaram;

mlecchaśāvarabhedākhyam markatāsyam kanīyasam; brahmavarddhanam variṣṭham sīsantu sīsapatrakam). Theragāthā in Pali refers to a banner which was dyed the colour of copper: milakkhurajanam (The Thera and Theragāthā PTS, verse 965: milakkhurajanam rattam garahantā sakam dhajam; tithiyānam dhajam keci dhāressanty avadātakam; K.R.Norman, tr., Theragāthā : Finding fault with their own banner which is dyed the colour of copper, some will wear the white banner of sectarians).[224]

An excellent introduction to the introduction of writing system by Meluhha traders is provided by Massimo Vidale[225]: "In Mesopotamia and in the Gulf, the immigrant Indus families maintained and trasmitted their language, the writing system and system of weights of the motherland (known in Mesopotamia as the "Dilmunite" standard) as strategic tools of trade. Their official symbol of the gaur might have stressed, together with the condition of living in a foreign world, an ideal connection with the motherland. Nonetheless, they gradually adopted the use of foreign languages and introduced minor changes in the writing system for tackling with new, rapidy evolving linguistic needs."

Two great inventions of 4th millennium BCE: alloying and writing

The artisans of the bronze age not only mined for precious minerals but also experimented with alloying of minerals to attain hard metals for tools and weapons. Matching this invention of alloying was the invention of the writing system known as 'Indus script' during ca. 4th millennium BCE.

The writing system of smiths and mine-workers reported on their repertoire of minerals and furnaces used to create surplus goods for long-distance trade between Meluhha and Mesopotamia.[226]

The writing system is called, 'mlecchita vikalpa' that is, cryptography, an alternative mode of representing mleccha language words. The phrase 'mlecchita vikalpa' is used as one of the 64 arts to be learnt by youth in Vatsyayana's *Kamasutra.* The technique used is hieroglyphs -- homonyms read rebus. Hence, the appearance of many pictorial motifs in over 400 glyptic signs and over 100 pictorial motifs in the corpus of inscriptions.

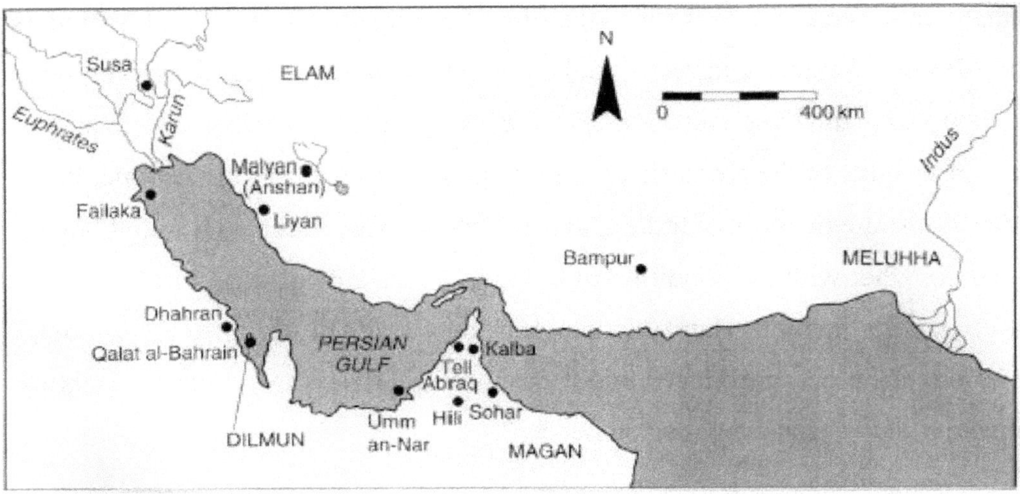

Map by D.T. Potts 2003 "Anshan, Liyan, and Magan circa 2000 BCE." N.F. Miller, K. Abdi and W.M. Summer (eds.) *Yeki Bud, Yeki Nabud: Essays on the Archaeology of Iran in Honor of William M. Sumner (Monographs Series (Cotsen Institute of Archaeology at Ucla), 48,)*, pp.156-160.

Massimo Vidale[227] refutes the Harappan 'illiteracy' claim made by some alleging that Indus script was NOT a writing system: "Should we be surprised by this announced 'collapse'? From the first noun in the title of their paper, Farmer, Sproat and Witzel are eager to communicate to us that previous and current views on the Indus script are naïve and completely wrong, and that after 130 years of illusion, through their paper, we may finally see the truth behind the dark curtains of a dangerous scientific myth."

Vidale identifies Meluhhan villages in Mesopotamia.[228] These Meluhhans were the speakers of mleccha vācas and inventors of Indus writing, using hieroglyphs as devices – devices, read rebus, which continue into the historical periods on punch-marked coins produced in mints from Gandhara to Karur in Sarasvati civilization area.

Cul-de-sac (dead-end) of Aryan movement postulates

The present status can be summarized by two quotes.

Quote 1: "To conclude the discussion of the data, then, while the horse and chariotevidence cannot be simply brushed aside, it will only be the decipherment of thescript that will prove decisive in this whole issue to the satisfaction of most scholars,since the recent discovery suggests that the script could go back to 3500 BCE (providing, of course, that it encapsulates the same language throughout). If itturns out to be a language other than Indo-Aryan, then obviously the Indigenist position need no longer detain the consideration of Indologists or serious scholarsof ancient history. In my opinion, this eventuality will be the only development that will convince a large number of scholars that the Aryans were, indeed, immigrants into India. On the other hand, an Indo-Aryan decipherment will radicallyalter the entire Indo-European homeland-locating landscape, not just the proto-history of the subcontinent. If it is Indo-Aryan, everything will need to be recon-sidered – Indo-Aryans, Indo-Iranians, and Indo-Europeans. We can note thatVentris, the decipherer of Linear B script from Crete, was amazed to see Greek emerge from Linear B – he was expecting to see a pre-Indo-European language,the consensus gentium of his day. The answer, after all is said and done, is writtenon the seals. If it is not Indo-Aryan, then the standard Migrationist scenario willlikely remain an excellent rendition of events which can always be updated and improved as new evidence surfaces." (Edwin Bryant, Page 511)

Quote 2: Barring any new discoveries, neither internal evidence from the Veda, nor archaeological evidence, nor linguistic substrata alone can make the turning point in anygiven hypothesis. This situation should be the most persuasive case of all for schol-ars to allow the questions to unite them in interdependence, rather than suspicions todivide them in monistic theory-making. It is far too early for scholars to begin taking positions and constructing scenarios as if they were truths. Rather, it is time for scholars to rewrite and then share a set of common questions, such as the ones artic-ulated earlier. Then, a lack of conclusive evidence can be a spur for further research,rather than a political bludgeon which wastes precious intellectual resources. (Laurie Patton, Page 30).[229]

The term Proto-Indian is used as a linguistic category.

The idea of a Linguistic Area is linked with the term Sprachbund which was introduced in April 1928 in the 1st Intl. Congress of Linguists by Nikolai Trubetzkoy. He made a distinction between Sprachfamilien and Sprachbunde:

Gruppen, bestehend aus Sprachen, die eine große Ähnlichkeit in syntaktischer Hinsicht;
eine Ähnlichkeit in den Grundsätzen des morphologischen Baues aufweisen; und eine
große Anzahl gemeinsamer Kulturwörter bieten, manchmal auch äussere Ähnlichkeit
im Bestande der Lautsystem, — dabei aber keine systematischen Lautentsprechungen keine Übereinstimmung in der lautlichen Gestalt der morphologischen Elemente, und
keine gemeinsamen Elementarwörter besitzen, — solche Sprachgruppen nennen wir
Sprachbünde.[230]

The distinction in classifying languages was suggested by Trubetzkoy in order to avoid 'missverstandnisse und fehler' (trans. misunderstandings and errors).

Burrow[231] attempted to identify Proto-Indoaryans using the Mitanni textual evidence of Rigvedic terms: “It is now generally agreed by most authorities on the subject that the Aryan linguistic vestiges in the Near East are to be connected specifically with Indo-Aryan, and not with Iranian, and also that they do not represent a third, independent Aryan group, and are not to be ascribed to the hypothetically reconstructed Proto-Aryan. This conclusion is incorporated in the title of M. Mayrhofer's bibliography of the subject, *Die Indo-Arier im alten Vorderasien* (Wiesbaden, 1966), and it can now be taken as the commonly accepted view. It is based on the fact that where there is divergence between Iranian and Indo-Aryan, and where such elements appear in the Near Eastern record, the latter always agrees with Indo-Aryan. Such items are *aika* “one” and *šuriyaš* “sun”, and the colour names *parita-nnu* and *pinkara-nnu* which correspond to Sanskrit palita- "grey" and *piṅgala-* "reddish". The evidence of vocabulary is supported by that of the four names of gods appearing in the Hittite-Mitanni treaty, where the Vedic gods Mitra and Varuṇa, Indra, and the Nāsatyas can be clearly recognized. This combined evidence is sufficient to establish the conclusions of Mayrhofer and others beyond reasonable doubt, and the arguments of A. Kammenhuber, who later attempted to resuscitate the theory that the Aryans of the Near East were Proto-Aryans, cannot be said to have been successful."

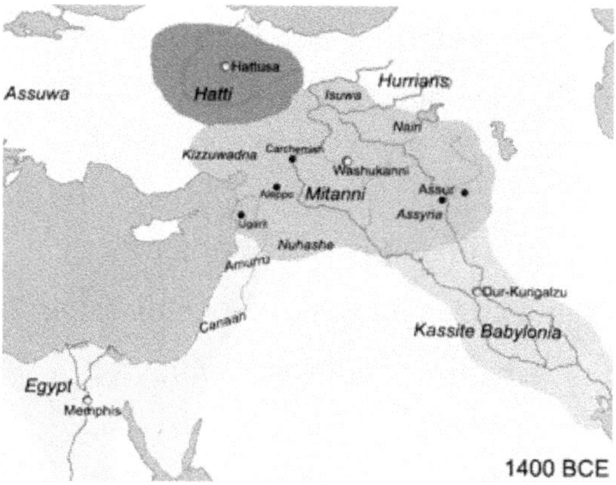

Loction map of *Waššukhani*

Thieme[232] had demonstrated that the divinities of Mitanni treaties are Vedic divinities. Burrow explains the semantics of Waššukanni, capital of the Mitanni state as vasu 'wealth' + khani 'mine', thus meaning 'mine of wealth (i.e. precious metals' in the context of Proto-Indoaryans of an age 'when prospecting for metals, precious or otherwise, was being actively pursued, and the Aryans were as much interested in this activity as anybody else…Since the 'Aryan' of the Near east is to be connected with Indo-Aryan it follows that the division of Proto-Aryan into two branches, Indo-Aryan and Iranian, must have taken place before those languages were established in their eventual homes, and not merely be due to developments which took place within each of the two groups after the Indo-Aryans had settled in India and the Iranians in Iran…A further conclusion following from this is that the date of the Proto-Aryan period must be pushed back further than has often been thought, and probably it cannot be brought down below 2000 BCE at the latest.' (p.124). Burrow also notes the concordance between usig- 'a priestly title' (Avestan) with usij- 'a certain class of priest' (Vedic); kavi 'a proto-Indoaryan priesthod' (Avestan.Vedic); karapan 'mumbler' (Avestan) connected with kalpa- 'rite' (Sanskrit).

This evaluation of Burrow has been taken further to identify Proto-Indian as a language category in the context of the new evidences such as the Tocharian *ancu* (concordant with Rigvedic *amśu* discussed in this monograph.)

Conclusions

The challenge has been partially, provisionally met, to outline a few structural features (principally, lexical glosses) of Proto-Indian language (with two dialects: Vedic and Mleccha/Meluhha) in the context of *harosheth hagoyim*, 'smithy of nations', from ca. 4th millennium BCE.

This monograph has demonstrated the reality of Proto-Indian, as a language category, principally in the context of the cultural continuum in India evidenced by lexical isoglosses among Munda, Indo-Aryan, Dravidian *sprachfamilien*. The Proto-Indoaryan discussed by Burrow was part of Indian *sprachbund* as evidenced by over 1240 semantic clusters included in the *Indian Lexicon* for over 25 languages of the *sprachfamilien*..

The presence of Shu-ilishu as a Meluhhan merchant reinforces the evidence of Meluhhan villages of Mesopotamia of the third millennium.

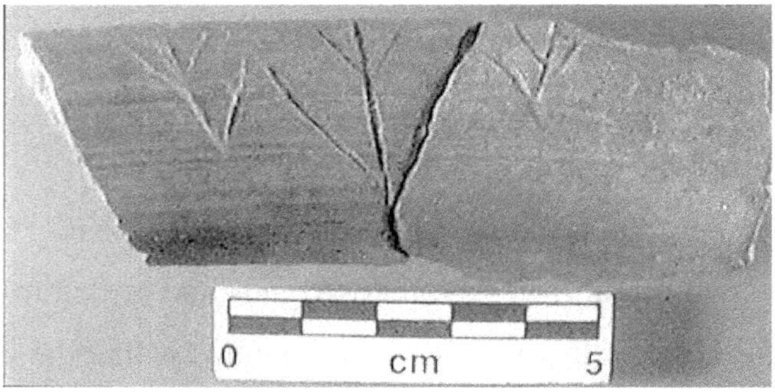

The evidence of *ancu* 'iron' (Tocharian) concordant with *amśu* (Rigveda) reinforces 1) identification of soma as 'metallic mineral'; and 2) Sumerian/Akkadian and Tocharian speakers, were in contact with Proto-Indian speakers, since substrate glosses of Sumerian/Akkadian and Tocharian have cognates in Indian *sprachbund.* This evidence is concordant with a cultural parallel found in Mesopotamian myth of *Anzu*, the lion-headed eagle which fetches the Tablets of Destinies and Rigvedic legend of *śyena* which fetches soma breaking the ayo-jālāni 'iron grid or iron net'. A provisional assessment of the current status of language studies and intimations

from archaeological finds point to Proto-Indian (with some loan words from Munda and one of the lost sources, such as Language 'X') evolved as a language with two dialectical forms: Vedic, the literary form and Mleccha, the vernacular form.

Mleccha is concordant with Meluhha of Mesopotamian texts.That a significant percentage of Indo-Aryan glosses are related by linguistic studies to Language X and to Munda, is indicative of the reality of mleccha (meluhha) as a language which co-existed with the Vedic. Mleccha-speakers are attested by Manu and in the Great Epic. The excursus of identifying some isoglosses has led to the reality of lexical isoglosses of Tocharian, Proto-Indo-Iranian, Proto-Indoaryan.

h1522 The invention of writing was necessitated by the inventions of alloys during the Bronze Age. This potsherd with Indus writing is dated to ca. 3500 BCE by the discovery of a potsherd in Harappa by archaeologists of HARP (Harvard Archaeology Project). Citing this find, the report quoted one of the excavators, Richard Meadow: "...these primitive inscriptions found on pottery may pre-date all other known writing."[233] A decipherment attempt has been made in Kalyanaraman (2012). This work is premised on the hypothesis that glosses of Indian *sprachbund* hold the key to unravel the semantics in rebus readings of hieroglyphs in Indus script inscriptions. Ta'anach 'cult' stand dated to 10th century BCE has hieroglyphs comparable to Mesopotamian and Indus artifacts which yield a link with *ṭaṅka* 'mint' (Indian *sprachbund*) and in the context of *damgar* 'mint-merchant' (Akkadian).

The reconstruction of glosses and other language features of Proto-Indian will help evaluate, conclusively, the claims of decipherment of Indus writing.

This monograph has not attempted to resolve the polemics of dating and relative chronology of Rigveda and Avestan and directions of migrations of Proto-Indian people.

Further studies in the identification of isoglosses, demarcating several linguistic features relatable Indian *sprachbund* will complement the contributions by studies in Proto-Indo-European and help delineate the cultural framework of the formation and evolution of languages in Indian *sprachbund.* The apparent semantic links between Tocharian and Indian *sprachbund* call for a rethink of Proto-Indo-European (PIE) dispersal theories and of PIE Urheimat theories.

References

Abbe, Jean Antoine. 1825. Moeurs, institutions et ceremonies des peuples de l'Inde. Paris.

Aitchison, J.E.T. 1888. Transactions of the Linnean Society of London. 2nd Ser. Botany. Vol. III, Part I: The Botany of the Afghan Delimitation Commission. London: The Linnean Society.

Anquetil-Duperron, Abraham-Hyacinthe. 1771. Zend-Avesta, ouvrage de Zoroastre, contenant les idees theologiques, physiques & morales de ce legislateur, ... Paris: Tilliard.

Apollinaire, Guillaume. 1913. Alcools. Lecture accompagnee par Henri Scepi. Paris: Gallimard, 1999.

Bartholomae, Christian. 1904. Altiranisches Woerterbuch. Nachdruck: Berlin: Walter de Gruyter, 1961.

Bergaigne, Abel. 1889. "Recherches sur l'histoire de la liturgie vedique." Journal asiatique, Janvier: 5-32, Fevrier-Mars: 121-197.

van den Bosch, Lourens P. 1985. "The AprI hymns of the .Rgveda and their interpretation." Indo-Iranian Journal 28: 95-122, 169-189.

Brough, John. "Soma and Amanita muscaria." Bulletin of the School of Oriental and African Studies (1971): 331-362. Reprinted in Brough (1996: 336-97).

--. Collected Papers. Eds. Minoru Hara and J. C. Wright. London: School of Oriental and African Studies, 1996.

Brough, John. 1973. "Problems of the <Soma-mushroom> theory." Indologica Taurinensia 1: 21-32.

Burnell, A.C. 1878. Elements of South Indian Palaeography. Reprinted Delhi 1968.

Burnouf, Eugene. 1844. Etudes sur la langue et les textes zends. IV: Le Dieu Homa. Journal Asiatique, 8e serie, no. 4, Decembre, p. 449-505.

van Buitenen, J.A.B. 1968. The Pravargya: An ancient Indian iconic ritual, described and annotated. Poona: Deccan College.

Caland, W. (ed.). 1915. De Open-Deure tot het Verborgen Heydendom van Abraham Rogerius. Uitgegeven door W. Caland. 's-Gravenhage: Martinus Nijhof.

(Re-edition of Rogerius 1651.)

Caland, W. and V. Henry. 1906. L'AgniSToma: description complete de la forme normale du sacrifice de soma dans le culte vedique. Tome premier. Paris: Ernest Leroux.

Caland, W. and V. Henry. 1907. L'AgniSToma: description complete de la forme normale du sacrifice de soma dans le culte vedique. Tome II. Paris: Ernest Leroux.

Cardona, George. 1988. Panini: His work and its traditions. Vol. 1: Background and Introduction. Delhi. Motilal Banarsidass.

CDIAL. Turner, RL. 1962-85. A comparative dictionary of Indo-Aryan languages, London, Oxford University Press.

Curzon, George N. The Pamirs and the Source of the Oxus. London: The Royal Geographical Society, 1896.

Dandekar, R.N. (Translator) 1973. *Śrautakośa, encyclopaedia of Vedic sacrificial ritual, Vol.2. English section. The Agnistoma, part 1.* Poona.

DEDR. Burrow, TA and MB Emeneau, 1984. A Dravidian Etymological Dictionary, 2nd ed. Oxford, Clarendon Press.

Doniger, Wendy. "'Somatic' Memories of R. Gordon Wasson." The Sacred Mushroom Seeker. Essays for R. Gordon Wasson. Ed. Thomas J. Riedlinger. Foreword by Richard Evans Schultes. Portland, Ore.: Dioscorides Press, 1990: 55-9.

Doniger O'Flaherty, Wendy. "The Post-Vedic History of the Soma Plant." Soma. Divine Mushroom of Immortality. R. Gordon Wasson. New York: Harcourt Brace Jovanovich, Inc., 1968. Part II: 95-147.

--. The Rig Veda. An Anthology. Harmondsworth: Penguin Books, 1981.

Durante, Sylvio. 1979 "Marine Shells from Balakot, Shahr-i Sokhta and Tepe Yahya: Their Significance for Trade Technology in Ancient Indo-Iran." In South Asian Archaeology 1977, Naples.

Eggeling, Julius. 1885. /Satapatha-BrAhmaNa according to the text of the mAdhyandina school. Part II: Books III and IV. Oxford: Clarendon Press.

Elizarenkova, Tatjana. 1996. "The problem of Soma in the light of language and style of the Rgveda." In: Langue, style et structure dans le monde Indien. Colloque international pour le Centenaire de la Naissance de Louis Renou (ed. par N. Balbir et G.-J. Pinault): 13-31. Paris: Unite de Recherche Associe 1058 "LACMI".

Elst, Koenraad. 1999. Update on the Aryan Invasion debate. Aditya Prakashan, New Delhi. http://koenraadelst.bharatvani.org/books/ait/index.htm

Emeneau, MB, 1956, India as a linguistic area, Language 32, 1956, 3-16.

Falk, Harry, "Soma I and II." Bulletin of the School of Oriental and African Studies 52 (1989): 77-90.

Falk, Harry. 1993. Schrift im alten Indien. Ein Forschungsbericht mit Anmerkungen. Tuebingen: Gunter Narr Verlag.

Flattery, David Stophlet, and Martin Schwartz. Haoma and Harmaline: The Botanical Identity of the Indo-Iranian Sacred Hallucinogen "Soma" and Its Legacy in Religion, Language, and Middle Eastern Folklore. Berkeley: University of California Press, 1989.

Furst, Peter T. (ed.) 1972. Flesh of the gods: the ritual use of hallucinogens. New York: Praeger Publ. Reissued with changes Waveland Press, Prospect Heights, Illinois, 1990.

Gardner, Robert, and Frits Staal, producers. Altar of Fire. Directed by Robert Gardner. 1976. Videocassette. Mystic Fire Video, 2000.

Geldner, Karl F. 1926. Die Zoroastrische Religion <Das AvestA>. Tubingen: J.C.B. Mohr.

Geldner, Karl F. 1928. Vedismus und Brahmanismus. Religionsgeschichtliches Lesebuch, 9. Tubingen: Mohr.

Geldner, Karl F. 1951. Der Rig-Veda: aus dem Sanskrit ins deutsche ubersetzt und mit einem laufendem Kommentar versehen. Teil I-III.Cambridge, Mass.: Harvard University Press.

Geldner, Karl F. 1957. Der Rig-Veda: aus dem Sanskrit ins deutsche ubersetzt und mit einem laufendem Kommentar versehen. Vierter Teil: Namen-und Sachregister zur Uebersetzung dazu Nachtraege und Verbesserungen. Ed.Johannes Nobel. Cambridge, Mass.: Harvard University Press.

Gnoli, Gherardo (2000). *Zoroaster in History*. New York: Oxbow.
Gonda, Jan. 1963. The Vision of the Vedic Poets. The Hague: Mouton.
Gonda, Jan. 1975. Vedic Literature. Wiesbaden: Harrassowitz.
Gonda, Jan. 1978. Hymns of the .Rgveda not employed in the solemn ritual. Amsterdam: North-Holland Publishing Company.
Halbfass, Wilhelm. 1988. India and Europe: An Essay in Understanding. Albany: SUNY-Press.
Halbfass, Wilhelm. 2001. "Mescaline and Indian Philosophy: Aldous Huxley and the Mythology of Experience." In: Barfoot 2001: 221-235.
Hansman, John. 1973. A "Periplus" of Magan and Meluḫḫa, in: Bulletin of the School of Oriental and African Studies, 36 , pp 553-587
Hillebrandt, Alfred. 1891. Vedische Mythologie. I: Soma und verwandte Goetter. Breslau: Koebner.
Hillebrandt, Alfred. 1927. Vedische Mythologie. Breslau: M. & H. Markus.
Houben, Jan E.M. 1991. The Pravargya BrAhmaNa of the TaittirIya AraNyaka: an ancient commentary on the Pravargya ritual. Delhi: Motilal Banarsidass.
Houben, Jan E.M. 2000. "The ritual pragmatics of a Vedic hymn: the 'riddle hymn' and the Pravargya ritual." Journal of the American Oriental Society 120.4: 499-536.
J.E.M. Houben. 2003. The Soma-Haoma problem: Introductory overview and observations on the discussion.
http://www.ejvs.laurasianacademy.com/ejvs0901/ejvs0901a.txt
Hummel, Karl. 1997. Review of Wasson 1969. Studien zur Indologie und Iranistik 21: 79-90.
Huxley, Aldous. 1932. Brave New World. London: Chatto and Windus.
Huxley, Aldous. 1959. Brave New World Revisited. London: Chatto and Windus.
Huxley, Aldous. 1977. Moksha: Writings on Psychedelics and the Visionary Experience, 1931-1963 (ed. by M. Horowitz and C. Palmer). London: Chatto and Windus.
Ingalls, Daniel H. H. "Remarks on Mr. Wasson's Soma." Journal of the American Oriental Society 91 (1971): 188-191.

Kalyanaraman, S. 1995. Indian Lexicon. www.scribd.com/doc/2232617/Lexicon
Kalyanaraman, S. 2000. *Rgvedic Soma as a metallurgical allegory; soma, electrum is deified.* http://www.docstoc.com/docs/96454517/Rgvedic-Soma-as-a-metallurgical-allegory-soma-electrum-is-deified----S-Kalyanaraman-(2000)
Kalyanaraman, S. 2012. Indian hieroglyphs. Herndon, Sarasvati Research Center. Amazon.com http://tinyurl.com/8dhqsd8
Kashikar, C.G. 1990. Identification of Soma. Pune: Tilak Maharashtra Vidyapeeth.
Kashikar, C.G. and Asko Parpola. 1983. "Śrauta Traditions in Recent Times." In: Staal 1983, Vol. II: 199-251.
Kashikar, C.G. (Editor and translator) 1964. The Śrauta, Paitṛmedhika and Pariśeṣa Sūtras of Bharadvāja. Part II. Translation. Poona.
Katz, Steven T. (ed.) 1978. Mysticism and Philosophical Analysis. London: Sheldon Press.
Katz, Steven T. (ed.) 1983. Mysticism and Religious Traditions. New York: Oxford University Press.
Katz, Steven T.(ed.) 1992. Mysticism and Language. New York: Oxford University Press.
Katz, Steven T. (ed.) 2000. Mysticism and Sacred Scripture. Oxford: Oxford University Press.
Kazanas, Nicholas. 2009a. Indo-European linguistics and Indo-Aryan indigenism in: *Indo-Aryan origins and other Vedic issues*, Aditya Prakashan, New Delhi.
Kazanas, Nicholas. 2009b. The RV pre-dates the Sindhu-Sarasvati Culture, Conf. The Sindhu-Sarasvati valley civilization, a reappraisl, Los Angeles, Feb. 2009.
Kazanas, Nicholas. 2002. Indigenous Indoryans and the Rigveda, JIES, 2002.
Kazanas, Nicholas. 2000. A new date for the Rigveda, in: GC Pande & D Krishna, Philosophy and Chronology, Journal of Indian Council of Philosophical Research, June 2001.
Kazanas, Nicholas & Klostermaier Klaus. 2012. Vedic civilization and its spread. in: *Vedic Venues* Vol.1 (2012).

KEITH, A.B., The Religion and Philosophy of the Veda and the Upanisads, 2 Vols, *1925*.

Kellens, Jean. 1989. "Avesta." In: Encyclopaedia Iranica (ed. by Ehsan Yarshater), Vol. III, p. 35-44.

Kotwal, Dastur Firoze M. and James W. Boyd. 1991. A Persian Offering: the Yasna: A Zoroastrian high liturgy. Paris: Association pour l'avancement des etudes iraniennes.

Kramrisch, Stella. 1972. Review of Wasson 1969. Artibus Asiae, 34: 263-267.

Kramrisch, Stella. 1975. "The mahAvIra vessel and the plant pUtika [sic]." Journal of the American Oriental Society 95.2: 222-235. [Reprinted as chapter 3 in Wasson et al. 1986.]

Kuhn, Adalbert. 1859. Die Herabkunft des Feuers und des Goettertranks. Berlin: Ferd. Duemmler's Verlagsbuchhandlung.

Kuiper, FBJ, 1948, Proto-Munda words in Sanskrit, Amsterdam

Kuiper, FBJ. 1967, The genesis of a linguistic area, IIJ 10, 1967, 81-102

Kuiper, F. B. J. Review of Soma. Divine Mushroom of Immortality, by R. Gordon Wasson. Indo-Iranian Journal 12 (1970): 279-285.

Kuiper, F.B.J. 1984. "Was the Puutiika a mushroom?." In: Am.rtadhaaraa: Professor R.N. Dandekar Felicitation Volume (ed. by S.D. Joshi): 219-227.Delhi: Ajanta.

Lal, B.B. 2009. How deep are the roots of Indian civilization. Aryan Books International. Delhi.

Lal, B.B. 2007. Let not the 19th century paradigms continue to haunt us! Inaugural Address delivered at the 19th International Conference on South Asian Archaeology, held at University of Bologna, Ravenna, Italy on July 2-6, 2007. http://www.archaeologyonline.net/artifacts/19th-century-paradigms.html

Lehmann, 2000. "Die urspruengliche rigvedische Somapflanze war weder gruene Pflanze noch Pilz: Gepresst wurden Bienenwaben. Sicht eines Entomologen." In: Indoarisch, Iranisch unddie Indogermanistik: Arbeitstagung der Indogermanischen Gesellschaft vom 2. bis 5. Oktober 1997 in Erlangen (herausg. v. B. Forssman und

Robert Plath): 295-314. Wiesbaden: Reichert Verlag.
Lewin, L. 1927. Phantastica: Die Betaeubenden und erregenden Genussmittel -- fuer Aerzte und Nichtaerzte. Berlin: Georg Stilke.
Lexicons used: Digital dictionaries of South Asia Languages: dsal.uchicago.edu/dictionaries
Lowie, Robert H. 1954. Indians of the Plains. New York: McGraw-Hill.
Mair, Victor H., ed. The Bronze Age and Early Iron Age Peoples of Eastern Central Asia. Vols. I-II. Washington: Institute for the Study of Man and Philadelphia: University of Pennsylvania Museum Publications, 1998.
Malamoud, Charles. Cuire le monde. Rite et pensee dans l'inde ancienne. Paris: Editions de la Decouverte, 1989. Cooking the World. Ritual and Thought in Ancient India. Trans. David White. Delhi: Oxford University Press, 1996.
Mallory, J. P., and Victor H. Mair. The Tarim Mummies. Ancot China and the Mysteries of the Earliest Peoples from the West. London: Thames and Hudson, 2000.
Manandhar, N.P. 1980. Medicinal plants of Nepal Himalaya. Khatmandu.
Marcantonio, Angela (ed). 2009. The Indo-European Language Family: Questions about its Status Monograph series 55, *Journal of Indo-European Studies.* Washington DC: Institute of Man (2009)
Marcantonio, Angela. & Brady, R.M. 2012. The evidence to support Verner's Law in: *Vedic Venues* Vol.1 (2012).
Marshall, John. (ed.) 1931. *Mohenjo-Daro and the Indus Civilization*. London. Trubner.
Masica, CP, 1971, Defining a Linguistic area. South Asia. Chicago: The University of Chicago Press.
Mayrhofer, Manfred. 1992. Etymologisches Woerterbuch des Altindoarischen. Heidelberg: Carl Winter Universitaetsverlag.
Misra, Satish & Ravilochanan Iyengar, Pre-Rgvedic Mitanni? in: *Vedic Venues* Vol.1 (2012).

Modi, Jivanji Jamshedji. 1922. The Religious Ceremonies and Customs of the Parsees. Bombay. Reprint: New York, 1979.
Mueller, Friedrich Max. 1855. "Die Todtenbestattung bei den Brahmanen." Zeitschrift der Deutschen Morgenlaendischen Gesellschaft, 9: I-LXXXII.
Mueller, Friedrich Max. 1888. Biographies of Words and the Home of the Aryans. London: Longmans, Green & Co.
Muhly, J.D., 1973. Coper and Tin. Conn.: Archon., Hamden; Transactions of Connecticut Academy of Arts and Sciences, vol. 43)
Mukherjee, Braja Lal. 1921. "The Soma Plant." The Journal of the Royal Asiatic Society of Great Britain and Ireland for 1921: 241-244.
Mukherjee, Braja Lal. 1922. The Soma Plant. Calcutta: Weekly Notes Printing Press.
Munda Etyma. Stampe DM. (ed.) 1985. Comparative Munda (mostly North), rough draft ed. Stampe, based on Heinz-Jürgen Pinnow's *Versuch einer historischen Lautlehre der Kharia-Sprache* (Wiesbaden: Harrassowitz, 1959) and Ram Dayal Munda's *Proto-Kherwarian Phonology*, unpublished MA thesis, University of Chicago, 1968. Other resources downloadable as a zip archive munda-archive.zip http://www.ling.hawaii.edu/austroasiatic/
Murr, Sylvia (ed.). 1987. L'Inde philosophique entre Bossuet et Voltaire - I: Moeurs et coutumes des indiens (1777). Un inedit du Pere G.-L. Coeurdoux s.j. dans la version de N.-J. Desvaulx. Paris: Ecole Francaise d'Extreme Orient.
Needham, Joseph. 1985. Science and Civilisation in China Volume 5: Chemistry and Chemical Technology. Cambridge University Press.
Nyberg, Harry. "The Problem of the Aryans and the Soma: The Botanical Evidence." The Indo-Aryans of Ancient South Asia. Ed. George Erdosy. Berlin and New York: Walter de Gruyter, 1995.
Oberlies, Thomas. 1995. Review of Wasson 1969. Wiener Zeitschrift fuer die Kunde Suedasiens, 39: 235-238.

Oberlies, Thomas. 1998. Die Religion des .Rgveda. Erster Teil: Das Religiose System des .Rgveda. Wien: Institut der Indologie der Universitat Wien.

Oberlies, Thomas. 1999. Die Religion des .Rgveda. Zweiter Teil: Kompositionsanalyse der Soma-Hymnen des .Rgveda. Wien: Institut der Indologie der Universitat Wien.Parpola, Asko. Deciphering the Indus Script. Cambridge: Cambridge University Press, 1994

Oldenberg, Herman. 1894. Die Religion des Veda. Berlin: Hertz. (2nd, revised edition 1917: Stuttgart, Cotta.)

Parpola, Asko. 1995. "The problem of the Aryans and the Soma: Textual-linguistic and archaeological evidence." In: The Indo-Aryans of Ancient South-Asia: Language, Material Culture and Ethnicity (ed. by George Erdosy): 353-381. Berlin: Walter de Gruyter.

Pinault, Georges-Jean. 2006. Further links between the Indo-Iranian substratum and the BMAC language in: Bertil Tikkanen & Heinrich Hettrich, eds., 2006, *Themes and tasks in old and middle Indo-Aryan linguistics—Papers of the World Sanskrit Conference held in Helsinki, Finland, 13-18 July 2003, Vol. 5*, Delhi, Motilal Banarsidass, pp. 167 to 196.

Przyludski, J., 1929, Further notes on non-aryan loans in Indo-Aryan in: Bagchi, P. C. (ed.), Pre-Aryan and Pre-Dravidian in Sanskrit. Calcutta : University of Calcutta: 145-149

Rappaport, Roy A. 1999. Ritual and Religion in the Making of Humanity. Cambridge: Cambridge University Press.

Rau, Wilhelm. "The Earliest Literary Evidence for Permanent Vedic Settlements." Inside the Texts/Beyond the Texts. New Approaches to the Study of the Vedas. Ed. Michael Witzel. Cambridge: Harvard University Press, 1997: 20345.

Renou, Louis. Religions of Ancient India. University of London: The Athlone Press, 1953.

Renou, Louis. 1962. "Recherches sur le rituel vedique: la place du Rig-Veda dans l'ordonnance du culte." Journal asiatique 250: 161-184.

Rogerius, Abraham. 1651. De Open-Deure tot het Verborgen Heydendom Ofte Waerachtig vertoogh van het Leven ende Zeden, mitsgaders de Religie ende Godsdienst der Bramines op de Cust Chormandel, ende de Landen daar ontrent. Leyden. Second edition: Caland 1915.
Said, Edward W. Orientalism. New York: Vintage Books, 1978.
Sarianidi, Victor. 1994. "New Discoveries at ancient Gonur." Ancient Civilizations from Scythia to Siberia 2.3: 289-310.
Sarianidi, Victor. 1998. Margiana and Proto-Zoroastrism. Athens: Kapon Editions.
SARVA. Indian Substratum: South Asia Residual Vocabulary Assemblage (SARVA), a compilation of ancient Indian words lacking apparent Indo-Aryan, Dravidian, or Austroasiatic origins, in progress by Franklin Southworth and Michael Witzel, with David Stampe.
Shreshtha, K. 1979. Nepali names for plants. Kathmandu.
Shulgin, Alexander T., and David E. Nichols. 1978. "Characterization of three new psychomimetics." The Psychopharmacology of Hallucinogens (Proceedings of a two-day workshop held in Bethesda, Maryland, Dec. 21-22,1976) (ed. by Richard C. Stillman and Robert E. Willette): 74-83. New York: Pergamon Press.
Singh, M., S. Malla, S. Rajbhandari and A. Manandhur. 1979. 'Medicinal plants of Nepal: retrospects and prospects.' Economic Botany 33, 185-198.
Skjaervo, Oktor P. 1997. "The State of Old Avestan Scholarship." Journal of the American Oriental Society, 117.1: 103-114.
Smith, Huston. Cleansing the Doors of Perception: The Religious Significance of Entheogenic Plants and Chemicals. New York: Jeremy P. Tarcher/ Putnam, 2000.
Southworth, F., 2005, Linguistic archaeology of South Asia, London, Routledge-Curzon.
Spess, David L. 2000. Soma: The Divine Hallucinogen. Rochester (Vermont):Inner Traditions. (Reference according to http://www.innertraditions.com/titles/soma.htm).
Staal, Frits. Exploring Mysticism: A Methodological Essay. Berkeley: University of California Press, 1988. New York: Penguin Books, 1975.

--. "Vedic Mantras." Understanding Mantras. Ed. Harvey Alper. Albany: State University of New York Press, 1989: 48-95.

--. Rules without Meaning: Ritual, Mantras and the Human Sciences. Toronto Studies in Religion 4. New York: Peter Lang, 1993 [1989].

--. "Greek and Vedic Geometry." Journal of Indian Philosophy 27 (1999): 105-27.

--. "Article One." Etudes de Lettres/Etudes Asiatiques (Lausanne), 2001a, forthcoming.--. "Noam Chomsky between the Human and Natural Sciences." Janus Head. Supplement. 6/2 (2001b): 25-56 <www.janushead.org/ gwu-2001/staal.cfm>.

--. "The Indian Sciences: 1. The Science of Language." The Blackwell Companion to Hinduism. Ed. Gavin Flood. Oxford: Blackwell, 2001c, forthcoming.

--. "Squares and Oblongs in the Veda." Journal of Indian Philosophy 29 (2001d): 257-73.

Staal, Frits, in collaboration with C. V. Somayajipad and M. Itti Ravi Nambudiri. Agni: The Vedic Ritual of the Fire Altar. Photographs by Adelaide de Menil. 2 vols. Berkeley: Asian Humanities Press, 1983. Reprint. Delhi: Motilal Banarsidass, 2001.

Staal, Frits. 2001. "How a psychoactive substance becomes a ritual: the case of Soma." Social Research, vol. 68.3: 745-778.

Staal, Frits. 1979. Agni: the Vedic ritual of the fire altar. 2 vols. Berkeley.

Stein, Aurel. 1931. "On the ephedra, the Hum plant, and the Soma." Bulletin of the School for Oriental and African Studies 6:501-14.

Stevenson, John. 1842. Translation of the sanhita of the Sama Veda. London: Allen.

Stuhrmann, Rainer. 1985. "Worum handelt es sich beim Soma?" Indo-Iranian Journal 28: 85-93.

Taillieu, Dieter. (2002). "Haoma: Bontany". *Encyclopaedia Iranica*. New York: Mazda Pub.

Taillieu, Dieter (1995). "Old Iranian *haoma*: A Note on Its Pharmacology". *Acta Belgica* 9.

van Gulik, R. H. Sexual Life in Ancient China. A Preliminary Survey of Chinese Sex and Society from ca. 1500 B.C. till 1644 A.D. Leiden: E.J. Brill, 1961.

Talageri, Shrikant G. 2000. The Rigveda - A Historical Analysis. Adity Prakashan. New Delhi. http://voiceofdharma.org/books/rig/

Talageri, Shrikant G. 2009. Rigveda and the Avesta: the final evidence. Aditya Prakashan. New Delhi.

Wasson, Valentina Pavlovna and Robert Gordon Wasson. 1957. Mushrooms, Russia and History. New York: Pantheon Books.

Wasson, R. Gordon. [1969.] Soma: Divine Mushroom of Immortality. [New York:] Harcourt, Brace, Jovanovich. [No publication date is indicated on the title or copyright page of the book available to me; in Wasson 1972a Wasson gives 1969 as the date of publication; we often also find the book mentioned as appearing in 1968.]

Wasson, R. Gordon. 1970. "Soma: comments inspired by Professor Kuiper's Review." Indo-Iranian-Journal, 12.4: 286-298.

Wasson, Robert Gordon.1972a. Soma and the Fly-Agaric; Mr. Wasson s Rejoinder to Professor Brough. Cambridge: Botanical Museum of Harvard University.

Wasson, R. Gordon. 1972b. "What was the Soma of the Aryans?" In: Furst 1972: 201-213.

--. "Soma Brought Up-to-Date." Journal of the American Oriental Society 99 (1979): 100-104.

Wasson, R. Gordon et al. 1986. R. Gordon Wasson, Stella Kramrisch, Jonathan Ott, and Carl P. Ruck. Persephone's Quest: Entheogens and the Origins of Religion. New Haven: Yale University Press.

Wezler, Albrecht. 2001. "'Psychedelic' drugs as a means to mystical experience: Aldous Huxley versus Indian reality." In: Barfoot 2001: 191-220.

Wilbert, Johannes. 1972. "Tobacco and Shamanistic Ecstasy Among the Warao Indians of Venezuela." In: Furst 1972: 55-83.

Wilkins, Charles. 1785. The Bhagavat-geeta, or, Dialogues of Kreeshna and Arjoon : in Eighteen Lectures, with Notes, Translated from the original, in the Sanskreet, or Ancient language of the Brahmans. London: C. Nourse.

Windischmann, Fr. 1846. Ueber den Somacultus der Arier. Abhandlungen der

Philosoph.-philologischen Classe der Koeniglich Bayerischen Akademie der Wissenschaften. IV.2: 125-142.
Witzel, Michael. "Early Eastern Iran and the Atharvaveda." Persica 9 (1980): 86-128.
--. "Early Sanskritization. Origins and Development of the Kuru State." Recht, Staat und Verwaltung im klassischen Indien. (The State, the Law, and Administration in Classical India). Ed. B. Kolver. Munchen: R. Oldenbourg, 1997a: 27-52. [Electronic Journal of Vedic Studies 1.4 (1995) www.shore.net/~india/ejvs].
--. "The Development of the Vedic Canon and Its Schools: The Social and Political Milieu." Inside the Texts/Beyond the Texts. New Approaches to the Study of the Vedas. Ed. Michael Witzel. Cambridge: Harvard University Press, 1997: 257-345.
--. "Aryan and Non-Aryan Names in Vedic India. Data for the Linguistic Situation, c.1900-500 B.C." Aryan and Non-Aryan in South Asia: Evidence, Interpretation and Ideology. Eds. Johannes Bronkhorst and Madhav M. Deshpande. Cambridge: Harvard University Press, 1999: 337-404.
Wujastyk, Dominik. The Roots of Ayurveda. New Delhi: Penguin Books, 1998.

A

agate 166
Akkadian 10, 14, 63, 64, 65, 94, 96, 97, 103, 104, 108, 111, 114, 115, 118, 119, 123, 128, 129, 162, 221
allograph 172
alloy 3, 26, 27, 55, 71, 75, 76, 77, 78, 100, 105, 115, 119, 126, 171, 214
alloying 4, 124, 126, 215
Ancient Near East 3, 4, 99, 170, 171, 179
antelope 75, 97, 111, 114, 117, 118, 119, 122, 123, 138, 170, 172
arrow 92, 109
Arthaśāstra 26, 27, 61, 68, 211
artifact 118, 170, 171
artifacts 8, 14, 85, 94, 102, 111, 118, 124, 125, 126, 130, 169, 189, 200, 221, 228, 241
artisan 3, 5, 10, 65, 99, 170, 171, 188
artisan guild 3, 99
artisan guilds 3, 99
Austro-Asiatic 132, 133, 150, 207, 208
awl 124
axe 24, 124, 125, 133, 201
ayas 89, 91, 92, 93, 130, 213
ayo 56, 92, 117, 221

B

backbone 110
Bagchi 208, 231
beads 8, 61, 106, 110
Bhirrana 8, 9, 12
Bible 3, 4, 6, 115, 177, 179, 191, 197, 241
bird 39, 63, 124
bison 122, 128
blacksmith 5, 24, 93, 94, 95, 114, 116, 119, 120, 170
boar 138
boat 104
body 8, 38, 61, 79, 88, 123, 130, 141, 142, 177, 178
branch 72, 81, 82
brass 22, 52, 55, 64, 66, 119, 131
bronze 3, 4, 6, 7, 8, 12, 13, 23, 29, 91, 92, 100, 102, 104, 105, 109, 118, 124, 130, 131, 161, 173, 188, 193, 196, 197, 211, 213, 214, 215
bucket 96
buffalo 53, 121, 122, 128
bull 41, 64, 65, 73, 75, 93, 95, 111, 112, 119, 120, 121, 122, 130, 143, 147, 172
Burrow 152, 181, 204, 218, 219, 220, 224

C

Campbell 127
canal 54, 113, 181
carnelian 101, 106, 107, 108, 126, 161, 166, 213
carpenter 94
carpenters 55
Caspian Sea 4, 81, 167, 188, 201
cast 64, 110, 119, 123, 177, 178
casting 3, 131, 174
Chatterjee 208
cipher 147, 157, 199
citadel 112
community 5, 93, 184
composite animal 167
copper 110, 114, 117, 157
copper tablet 110
copper tablets 110
coppersmith 94
corner 58, 101
curve 122
curved 117

D

decoded 93
deer 139
deśi 123, 156
dotted circle 123
drill 110

E

Egyptian 7, 8, 11, 12, 13, 75, 78, 105, 128, 154, 162, 196, 197
El-Ahwat 3, 4, 6, 7, 8, 9, 10, 11, 196, 197, 241
Emeneau 148, 152, 168, 199, 202, 224, 225
engraver 128, 176, 178, 201
eraka 98

F

Failaka 122, 170
fish 92, 112, 117, 123, 130, 184
fishes 121
forge 3, 65
furnace 93, 110

G

gloss 13, 94, 127, 145, 170, 172

glosses 13, 50, 94, 111, 116, 117, 205, 220, 221, 222
glyph 62, 110, 117, 167
glyptic 128, 215
goat 27, 54, 97, 114, 115, 120, 139
goats 111, 112, 113, 114, 119
gold 8, 18, 22, 23, 26, 27, 28, 29, 33, 35, 49, 52, 55, 60, 61, 63, 64, 66, 67, 68, 72, 73, 75, 76, 77, 78, 79, 82, 89, 91, 101, 103, 106, 108, 119, 122, 127, 128, 130, 131, 136, 138, 161, 166, 171, 187, 191, 212, 213
gold pendant 171
guild 5, 93, 172, 173, 184, 188

H

Haifa 3, 4, 100, 105, 157, 188, 189, 196, 197
Harosheth hagoyim 1, 3, 4, 5, 6, 7, 9, 170, 173
head-dress 96
Hermeneutics 14
hieroglyph 10, 11, 97, 111, 117, 119, 121, 123, 130, 188
hieroglyphic 65, 157, 184, 188
hieroglyphs 157
hill 114, 138, 166
horns 31, 112, 117, 119, 121, 122, 128

I

ibex 8, 10
Indo-European 13, 14, 18, 62, 80, 82, 91, 130, 131, 132, 140, 148, 150, 203, 204, 205, 207, 208, 209, 217, 222, 227, 229
ingot 11, 105, 110, 111, 112, 119, 122, 123, 138, 157
inscription 117, 167
iron 4, 8, 9, 14, 18, 22, 52, 55, 56, 58, 62, 67, 71, 76, 78, 82, 88, 91, 92, 93, 110, 114, 115, 127, 143, 157, 170, 174, 180, 181, 221, 241
iron ore 89, 93
isogloss 16, 59, 91, 141
isoglosses 13, 15, 18, 65, 140, 141, 148, 206, 220, 221, 222

J

jar 102, 120, 188
joined 85, 171, 172

K

Kalyanaraman 1, 18, 148, 221, 227, 241
Kazanas 15, 227
kharoṣṭī 4, 5, 12, 170, 173, 174, 181, 188, 189, 191, 195, 196
Kish 102, 106, 107, 125, 214
Kuiper 90, 132, 133, 148, 206, 207, 210, 228, 234

L

Language X 111, 206, 221
lapidaries 174
lapis lazuli 25, 101, 106, 125, 126, 166
Levi 164, 201, 206, 207
ligatured 119, 120
lion 18, 62, 63, 65, 118, 187, 221

M

Mahābhārata 66, 85, 86, 158, 163, 168
markhor 117
Marshall 106, 107, 229
Masica 148, 206, 229
Meadow 221
Meluhha 13, 96, 97, 100, 101, 106, 111, 118, 120, 124, 125, 126, 128, 130, 147, 159, 160, 161, 162, 166, 167, 173, 200, 201, 212, 213, 214, 215, 220, 221
merchant 14, 80, 94, 95, 97, 102, 103, 108, 110, 111, 114, 115, 116, 117, 119, 170, 171, 172, 220, 221
metal 93, 110, 123, 130, 157
metalsmith 45, 119
mineral 13, 14, 18, 56, 58, 66, 67, 69, 77, 91, 105, 109, 119, 124, 127, 166, 221
mine-worker 215
mleccha 14, 55, 82, 84, 97, 98, 111, 112, 140, 147, 148, 154, 155, 156, 157, 158, 159, 163, 164, 167, 173, 201, 210, 211, 212, 214, 215, 216, 221
mountain 15, 25, 30, 57, 61, 68, 69, 70, 72, 79, 80, 82, 83, 103, 114, 139, 146, 148, 160
Mt. Mustagh Ata 4
Munda 98, 111, 132, 133, 142, 148, 149, 150, 152, 156, 181, 191, 199, 201, 203, 204, 206, 207, 209, 210, 220, 221, 228, 230

N

Narmer 121
native metal 91
neck 28
Nippur 21
numerals 58

O

offering 14, 41, 42, 79, 96, 131, 144

ore 14, 18, 23, 27, 29, 31, 35, 36, 45, 60, 61, 63, 67, 68, 69, 73, 77, 82, 89, 91, 92, 93, 110, 127, 128, 131, 134, 136, 171, 241

P

Pande 227
Pāṇini 92, 164
Parpola 96, 106, 227, 231
penance 21
Persian Gulf 4, 105, 161, 188, 191, 199, 201
phonetic97, 120, 130, 141, 151, 152, 153, 192, 209
pictograph 170
pictorial motif 93, 118, 119, 120, 174, 215
Pinault 18, 54, 88, 91, 131, 132, 225, 231
platform 34
Prakrit 156, 157, 170, 175, 189, 193, 211
Prākṛt 5, 13, 156, 210
priest 23, 38, 41, 42, 54, 70, 80, 94, 96, 116, 132, 139, 141, 144, 160, 184, 219
Proto-Aryan 218, 219
Proto-Dravidian 205
Proto-Indian 4, 5, 12, 13, 14, 15, 98, 99, 100, 141, 155, 198, 207, 217, 220, 221, 222
Proto-Indo-European 14, 18, 140, 205, 207, 222
Przyludski 148, 231
pun 61, 67
punch-marked 147, 157, 174, 182, 188, 196, 216

R

Rakhigarhi 4
ram 10, 114, 115, 117, 119, 120
Rāmāyaṇa 56, 85, 155, 163
Rampurva 157
rebus 93, 95, 114, 124
reduplicated 168, 169
reduplication 91, 168, 169
Rigveda 14, 18, 22, 24, 27, 77, 92, 97, 109, 132, 141, 221, 222, 227, 234

S

Sarasvati 1, 2, 4, 9, 33, 45, 68, 73, 98, 99, 143, 149, 150, 151, 188, 206, 216, 227, 241
Sarasvati river basin 99
scarf 119
scribe 182
semantic 3, 13, 14, 56, 59, 130, 148, 149, 150, 151, 152, 153, 154, 203, 213, 220, 222
semantic cluster 148, 150, 152, 153, 154, 220
semantic clusters 3, 13, 148, 152, 153, 154, 220
serpent 21
silver 8, 18, 24, 26, 27, 29, 33, 35, 52, 55, 61, 63, 64, 71, 73, 74, 75, 76, 77, 78, 82, 89, 103, 106, 107, 108, 118, 119, 123, 127, 128, 131, 160, 166, 167, 171, 212, 213
slope 114, 146
smelt 3
smelter 119
smelting 4, 8, 27, 35, 75, 82, 93, 104, 110, 213
smith 18, 94, 95
smiths 5, 18, 104, 109, 157, 174, 188, 189, 215
smithy 3, 4, 5, 6, 12, 13, 100, 109, 173, 174, 184, 188, 220
Sohgaura 196
Southworth 147, 148, 206, 232
spade 181
spear 106
spokes 12, 65
sprachbund 3, 5, 12, 13, 14, 94, 97, 99, 111, 115, 116, 120, 122, 141, 147, 168, 198, 199, 220, 221, 222
spy 155
śrivatsa 184
standard device 172
star 41, 164
steel 52
stone 8, 15, 22, 23, 25, 47, 61, 70, 72, 73, 92, 100, 103, 109, 110, 118, 121, 123, 127, 139, 160, 171, 175, 189, 208
substrate 94, 111, 114, 119, 131, 132, 221
Sumerian 10, 63, 94, 99, 101, 102, 107, 108, 111, 114, 116, 118, 119, 120, 121, 141, 159, 203, 221
summit 22, 36
Susa 97, 103, 107, 108, 124, 125, 130, 160, 173
svastika 106
Swaminatha Iyer 205

T

tail54, 171
Tepe Yahya 12, 62, 125, 126, 166, 189, 224
Tewari 9
tiger 118, 119
Tilak 156, 227
tin 4, 27, 65, 77, 78, 91, 100, 101, 102, 103, 104, 105, 106, 114, 115, 117, 119, 120, 124, 125, 126, 127, 166, 171, 188, 213, 214
tin ingot 4, 120, 188
Tocharian 4, 12, 13, 14, 15, 17, 18, 22, 54, 55, 56, 59, 62, 81, 82, 87, 88, 91, 127, 131, 132, 134, 141, 143, 160, 173, 220, 221, 222
Tolkāppiyam 92, 151
trader 10, 61, 94
tree 31, 52, 57, 72, 111, 114, 119, 123, 126
trough 22

Turkmenistan 4, 87
turner 114

U

Ur 21, 26, 96, 105, 107, 108, 121, 214
Uruk 105, 118, 120, 121

V

Valdiya 99
Veda 16, 20, 30, 31, 33, 140, 145, 155, 163, 164, 202, 217, 224, 225, 228, 231, 233
Vedic 13, 14, 15, 16, 17, 23, 28, 30, 43, 44, 45, 46, 81, 87, 88, 98, 127, 131, 132, 140, 148, 151, 165, 189, 210, 211, 219, 220, 221, 224, 226, 227, 229, 231, 233, 235
vessel 21, 33, 34, 73, 118, 121, 122, 228
Vidale 215, 215
vikalpa 110, 147, 157, 215

W

warehouse 124
weights 101, 108, 215
wheel 7, 12, 65, 187, 196
wing 65
Witzel 80, 131, 132, 133, 216, 231, 232, 235
workshop 45, 65, 96, 122, 140, 232
writer 210

Z

zebu 93
zinc 55, 77, 78

End Notes

[1] Source: http://jeffemanuel.net/201/03/sardinians-in-central-israel-the-excavator-of-El-Ahwat-makes-his-final-case/ Mirror: http://tinyurl.com/8cantj4

[2] *Journal of Indo-Judaic Studies*, Vol. 1, Number 11 (2010) -- The Bronze Age Writing System of Sarasvati Hieroglyphics as Evidenced by Two "Rosetta Stones" By S. Kalyanaraman (Editor of JIJS: Prof. Nathan Katz) http://www.indojudaic.com/index.php?option=com_contact&view=contact&id=1&Itemid=8

[3] http://concordances.org/hebrew/2800.htm

[4] 'NOBS Study Bible Name List reads Carving Of The Nations, but equally valid would be Silence Of The Gentiles orEngraving Of What's Abandoned. Jones' Dictionary of Old Testament Proper Names reads Manufactory for Harosheth and "of the Gentiles" for Hagoyim.' http://www.abarim-publications.com/Meaning/Harosheth.html)

[6] Photo by Moshe Einav Courtesy of Prof. Adam Zertal Source: http://tinyurl.com/ctd8wya)

[7] Cast in high relief, depicting a youthful face rising from a plaque. Dimensions - Height: 5.8 cm. Width: 5.0 cm. http://buckinghamcollections.com/v/asian/gandhara/pilgrim/PG018.jpg.html

[4] http://www.israel-a-history-of.com/naphtali.html http://biblicalorigins.wordpress.com/tag/deborah/

[8] Philistine Kin Found in Early Israel, Adam Zertal, BAR 28:03, May/Jun 2002.

Links: http://cojs.org/articles/BAR%202002%20May-Jun/Philistine%20Kin%20Found%20in%20Early%20Israel.pdf

http://cojs.org/cojswiki/Philistine_Kin_Found_in_Early_Israel,_Adam_Zertal,_BAR_28:03,_May/Jun_2002.

[9] Source: http://tinyurl.com/9md35rq

[10] Source: http://www.archaeologyonline.net/artifacts/iron-ore.html

[11] "The dwelling pits whose inside walls are mud plastered and which have average diameter of 2.30 m are mostly circular at Bhirrana…" (B.R. Mani, 2006, Kashmir Neolithic and early Harappan: a linkage **http://archaeology.up.nic.in/doc/kneh_brm.pdf**)

[12] Source: http://tinyurl.com/8ggubm2

[13] After El-Ahwat near kibuts Katsir-Harish find at The megalithic portal: http://tinyurl.com/925eudx

[14] Courtesy of Prof. Adam Zertal http://tinyurl.com/8boprtd

[17] Image after Diwiyana

[18] http://asi.nic.in/images/exec_bhirrana/thumbnails/017.jpg

[19] Renou, Louis, *Etudes Vediques et Panineens*, *Tome IX*, Paris 1961, p. 8.

[20] Gadamer 1976: xii). Gadamer, Hans-Georg. 1976, Philosophical Hermeneutics, ed. and trans. by David E. Linge, Berkeley: University of California Press.

[21] Alfred Hillebrandt, 1927, *Vedische Mythologie*, tr.Sreeramula Rajeswara Sarma, 1980, *Vedic Mythology*, 2 vols. Delhi, Motilal Banarsidass, p16.

[22] Lecture on "The collapse of the Aryan Invasion Theory" delivered by Nicholas Kazanas, on 31 December 2010, organized by Wider Association for Vedic Studies (WAVES) An affiliate of "World Association for Vedic Studies, USA. https://sites.google.com/site/kalyan97/sarasvati-hindu-civilization) Mirror: Nicholas Kazanas, 2010, The collapse of the AIT and the prevalence of Indigenism: archaeological, genetic, linguistic and literary evidences. http://www.docstoc.com/docs/68174185/The_Collapse_of_the_AIT_h_res_for_publication

[23] Ibid.

[24] Douglas Q. Adams, The position of Tocharian among the other Indo-European Languages, JAOS 104.3 (1984). http://azargoshnasp.net/history/Tocharian/positionoftocharian.pdf

[25] Christensen, A.,1932, *Les Kayanides*. Det Kgl. Danske Videnskabernes Sellskab, Hist.-Filos. Meddelelser XIX.2. Copenhagen).

[26] David M. Knipe, 1967. The Heroic Theft: Myths from Ṛgveda IV and the Ancient near East in: *History of Religions* Vol. 6, No. 4 (May, 1967), pp. 328-360, Univ. of Chicago Press.

[27] Si. Ara Svaminathan, Indira Gandhi National Centre for the Arts, 2000, *Kaanvashatapathabraahmanam*, volume 3, Motilal Banarsidass, Sanskrit text with English translation, IV.6.2.4-5). Source: http://tinyurl.com/ceepqj3

[28] http://www.zeitlin.net/EndEnchantment/images/Nippur.gif

[29] Langdon, *Semitic Mythology*, p. 170 (fig. 65).

[30] AK Coomaraswamy, Rama P. Coomaraswamy, 2004, 'The Myth' in: The essential Ananda K. Coomaraswamy, World Wisdom, Inc., p.267.

[31] J.P. Mallory, Douglas Q. Adams, 2006, *The Oxford introduction to Proto-Indo=European and the Proto-Indo-European world*, OUP, p. 241.

[32] J.Gonda, 1991, *The Functions and Significance of Gold in the Veda*, Leiden, E.J.Brill, p. 5.

[33] Text 1, Bab. K. 713; A. Leo Oppenheim, RA, 60, 1966, pp. 29-45.

[34] http://www.livius.org/a/1/maps/persia_map.gif

[35] http://www.livius.org/da-dd/darius/darius_i_t08.html

[36] Diodorus—III,14,3-4; loc. cit. Harry Falk, *Refining gold in ancient India* : ad JUB 3.17,3 in: *Acta Orientalia* 1997: 58, 47-51.

[37] Healy, John F. (1978): *Mining and Metallurgy in the Greek and Roman World*, Thames and Hudson, London, p. 154.

[38] Notton, J. H. F. 1974. Ancient Egyptian Gold Refining: A reproduction of early techniques. *Gold Bulletin.* 2 (7) 50–56.

[39] R.N.Dandekar, *Śrautakośa*, vol.II, pt. I, p. 129.

[40] J.F.Fleet, Corpus Inscriptionum Indicarum, Vol. III, p.200, no.41, Pl. XXVII.

[41] M.N.Banerjee, "On Metals and Metallurgy in Ancient India", *Indian Historical Quarterly*, Vol. III, March 1927, no. 1, p. 123.

[42] Soma I and II, 1989, *BSOAS*, LII, Pt. 1, pp. 77-90.

[43] Elizarenkova, T. Y. 1996. "The problem of Soma in the light of language and style of the Rgveda." In Language, style et structure dans le monde Indien.

Colloque international pour le Centenaire de la Naissance de Louis Renou (ed. par N. Balbir et G.-J. Pinault). Paris. 1996. 13-31.

[44] http://www.iranica.com/articles/v11f6/v11f6059a.html#i

[45] K Suresh – Venkatrama Sharma, 2003, *Camaka*, Chennai http://ghanapati.com/chamaka.htm

[46] Alfred Hillebrandt, 1927, *Vedische Mythologie*, tr. Sreeramula Rajeswara Sarma, 1980, *Vedic Mythology*, 2 vols. Delhi, Motilal Banarsidass, p184.
[47] Falk, p.79.

[48] Brough, John, 1971, "Soma and Amanita muscaria". *Bulletin of the School of Oriental and African Studies* (BSOAS) 34.

[49] *Flattery, David Stophlet and Schwarz, Martin (1989). Haoma and Harmaline.*
[50] L.H. Gray, *The foundations of the Iranian religions, in: Journal of the K.R. Cama Oriental Institute*, XV,1929.
[51] G. Watt, *Dictionary of the Economic Products of India*, III, 246-7

[52] Mary Boyce, Haoma, priest of the sacrifice, in: *W. B. Henning Memorial Volume* , 1970, London, Lund Humphries, pp. 62-80.

[53] C.G. Kashikar, 1964, The Vedic sacrificial rituals through the ages, in: *Indian Antiquary*, Vol. 1, No.2, Bombay, Popular Prakashan, p.88. See parhaoma ritual (Ab-Zohr).

[54] C.C. Bakels, Report concerning the contents of a ceramic vessel found in the "white room" of the Gonur Temenos, Merv Oasis, Turkmenistan. EJVS Vol.9, 2003.

[55] *Bakels, Corrie C. (May 5, 2003). "*Report concerning the contents of a ceramic vessel found in the "white room" of the Gonur Temenos, Merv Oasis, Turkmenistan*". Electronic Journal of Vedic Studies 9/1c.*

[56] David Stophlet Flattery and Martin Schwartz, 1989, *Haoma and Harmaline: The botanical identity of the Indo-Iranian sacred hallucinogen 'Soma' and its legacy in religion, language, and middle eastern folklore*, Berkeley, Univ. of California Press, p. 4.

[57] Haoma/Soma: the plant, in: Acta Iranica 25 (= Papers in Honour of Professor Mary Boyce, *Hommages et Opera Minora*, 11) (Leiden, 1985), 699-726, see pp. 703, 707.

[58] H.D. Griswold, 1923, *The Religion of the Rigveda*, London, Oxford University Press, p. 14.

[59] Asko Parpola, 1995, The problem of the Aryans and the Soma: Textual-linguistic and archaeological evidence, in: George Erdosy, ed., T*he Indo-Aryans of Ancient South Asia,* Berlin, Walter de Gruyter & Co., p. 371. [Note: Hari Nyberg, 1995, The problem of the Aryans and the Soma: the botanical evidence, p. 401, ibid., notes that theevidence from the Togolok 21 finds are not conclusive: 'In1991, I received some samples from the site,which were subjected to pollen analysis at the Department of Botany, University of Helsinki. However, upon analysis,it was evident that most of the pollen in the sampleshad been destroyed...in most cases only pollen of the family Caryophyllaceae was found, along with some pollen remains from the families Chenopodiaceae and Poaceae (grain crops?)...No pollen from ephedras or poppies was found...Thus, further archaeological investigations are necessary to add weight to the existing, but scarce, archaeological evidence for the early use of ephedras.']

[60] *Gōttingische Gelehrte Anzeigen* 1875, p. 568

[61] *Icones plantarum Indiae orientalis*, vol. IV, No. 1281

[62] Lakshman Sarup, 1920, *The Nighaṇṭu and the Nirukta*, Delhi, Motilal Banarsidass, p.24.

[63] *Houben, Jan E. M. (May 4, 2003).* "The Soma-Haoma problem". *Electronic Journal of Vedic Studies 9/1a.*

[64] See Kalyanaraman, 2004, *Indian Alchemy: Soma in the Veda*. [Description: chapter 1: Gold and the grammar of money in antiquity; chapter 2: Indus: roots of alchemy; chapter 3: Yak\d{s}a: alchemical potential and transmutation; chapter 4: Soma and alchemy; chapter 5: Brahmana-s: aurifiction; chapter 6: Alchemy as a state enterprise; chapter 7: Political economy of alchemy; chapter 8: Siddha and Tantric alchemy; chapter 9: Apparatus, terms, and symbols; chapter 10: Conclusion; chapter 11: A survey of sources for history of alchemy."The book is an epoch-making work - a paradigm-shift in Vedic studies - which identifies soma as electrum (gold-silver metallic compound). Soma is referred to in the Rgveda as the soul of the yajña. The path-breaking identification is based on textual evidence and a penetrating analysis of the Indian alchemical tradition, spanning nearly five millennia. The author is also the discoverer of the integrating role played by the mighty Sarasvati river adored in the Rgveda as the best of mothers, best of rivers and best of goddesses. Sarasvati and soma are no longer mythology but relevant to present-day children, respectively, as the repository of groundwater sanctuaries in north-west India and the metallurgical tradition starting with the Bronze Age civilization, c. 3000 BC. Sarasvati and soma are the symbols of the great Indian

traditions of devi worship and personification and deification of natural, material phenomena. The tirthas along the rivers are reminders of the critical nature of water management problems all over India and soma as an integral part of the yajña process, is the embodiment of the scientific, technological and materialist temper of ancient India." S. Kalyanaraman, 2008, Sarasvati: Soma yajña and the Veda. The argument: *Ṛgveda* is a metallurgical allegory; soma is electrum ore.]

[65] David Stophlet Flattery and Martin Schwartz, 1989, *Haoma and Harmaline: The botanical identity of the Indo-Iranian sacred hallucinogen 'Soma' and its legacy in religion, language, and middle eastern folklore*, Berkeley, Univ. of California Press, p. 115-116.

[66] http://www.uni-koeln.de/cgi-bin/SFgate

[67] http://www.uni-koeln.de

[68] David Stophlet Flattery and Martin Schwartz, 1989, *Haoma and Harmaline: The botanical identity of the Indo-Iranian sacred hallucinogen 'Soma' and its legacy in religion, language, and middle eastern folklore*, Berkeley, Univ. of California Press, p. 22..

[69] A. Lubotsky, The Indo-Iranian Substratum, in: *Early Contacts between Uralic and Indo-European: Linguistic and Archaeological Considerations*, ed. Chr. Carpelan, A. Parpola, P.Koskikallio (Helsinki, Suomalais-Ugrilainen Seura 2001), pp. 301-317.

[70] http://www.nuffieldfoundation.org/practical-chemistry/turning-copper-coins-silver-and-gold

[71] http://www.valmikiramayan.net/aranya/sarga35/aranya_35_frame.htm

[72] See Bloomfield, The Legend of Soma and the Eagle, *JAOS*, 16, 1896, pp. 1-24). 'High is the birth of thee, the plant; thee being in heaven the earth received'. (RV. IX. 61.10). Yasna (X.4,10-12,17) places haoma on the high mountain Haraiti; it is placed there by a skilful god, wherefrom holy birds carried it everywhere to the heights where it grew both on the lofty tablelands and in the mountain valleys). (cf. H.D. Griswold, 1971, *The Religion of the Ṛgveda*, Delhi, Motilal Banaridass, p.217). *Ṛgveda* connects Soma with the mount Mūjavant: 'As draught of Maujavata Soma, so doth, the enlivening vibhīdaka delight me' (RV. X.34,1). Griswold notes: 'The mountain Mūjavant (if it was a mountain and not simply the name of a people), being closely connected with the Gandhāris (AV. V.22,5,7,8,14) must have been situated somewhere between Bactria and the Punjab. In the Tait. Samh. I. 8,6,2 and the AV. Passages referred to above the Mūjavants are taken as a type of

distant folk, to which Rudra with his fever-bearing bow is entreated to depart. In fact Mūjavant is as far off and mysterious as the river rasā. Possibly both embody dim reminiscences of the undivided Indo-Iranian days." (p. 217).

[73] http://www.fitzmuseum.cam.ac.uk/gallery/East-West/gallery/gallery_02.html
[74] http://www.bartleby.com

[75] W. Muss-Arnolt, *A concise dictionary of the Theyrian language*, Berlin, Reuther and Reichard, 1905.

[76] http://en.wikipedia.org/wiki/Chalcopyrite

[77] http://www.otago.ac.nz/Geology/features/gold/hard-rock.htm

[78] Alchemical treatise: *Rudrayamala Tantra*, cited in P.Ray, *History of Chemistry in Ancient and Medieval India*, p.157.

[79] *Encyclopaedia Britannica*

[80] Ball writes: "Gold is mined for, in quartz veins 3 miles to the north of kandahar city... The gold is sometimes chiselled out in pure granules and sometimes in large nuggets..." (V. Ball, Manual of the Geology of India, III, pp. 208-9).

[81] http://www.sacred-texts.com/ufo/vs/vs12.htm
[82] http://www.sacred-texts.com/ufo/vs/vs08.htm

[83] Geldner, Rig-Veda ubers, K.F.Geldner, Der Rig-Veda ubersetzt, Cambridge, Mass., 1951, III, p. 110.

[84] *Encyclopaedia Britannica.*

[85] http://www.mindat.org/min-1365.html

[86] http://www.thamesvalleyminerals.com

[87] http://www.mindat.org/picshow.php?id=5136
[88] These findings are further elaborated in the work: S. Kalyanaraman, 2004, Indian Alchemy: Soma in the Veda, Munshiram Manoharlal, Delhi.
[89] cited in Needham, Joseph, 1985, SCC, Vol. 5, Pt. II, pp.18-21

[90] Hopkins, AJ, 1967, Alchemy, pp. 103-104.

[91] Needham, Joseph, 1985, *Science and Civilization in China*, Vol. 5, pt. II, p.45.

[92] Smith, V., 1905, Indian Antiquary, pp. 233 ff.; loc.cit.Bharadwaj, H.C., Aspects of Ancient Indian Technology, Delhi, MotilalBanarsidass, 1979, p. 138.

[93] http://www.reshafim.org.il/ad/egypt/trades/metals.htm

[94] H.D. Griswold, 1923, *The Religion of the Rigveda*, London, Oxford University Press, p.217

[95] A.A. Macdonell, 1963. *The Vedic Mythology.* Indological Book House, (reprint) Varanasi, p.116.

[96] Staal, Frits. 2001. "How a psychoactive substance becomes a ritual: the case of Soma." Social Research, vol. 68.3: 745-778.

[97] cf. Identification of Mujavant, locus of Rigvedic soma - S. Kalyanaraman (2011) http://www.docstoc.com/docs/96601715/Identification-of-Mujavant-locus-of-Rigvedic-soma---S-Kalyanaraman-(2011)

[98] Gerd Carling, Georges-Jean Pinault, Werner Winter, 2008, *Dictionary and thesaurus of Tocharian A, Volume 1*, Otto Harrassowitz Verlag.

[99] Schwartz, Martin, 1974. Irano-Tocharica. In: Philippe Gignoux & Tafazzoli (eds.), Memorial Jean de Menasce. Louvain: Imprimerie Orientaliste. p. 409.

[100] Rau, Wilhelm, 1974, Metalle und Metallgerate im vedischen Indien. Mainz. Akademie der Wissenschaften und der Literatur. Abhandlungen der Geistes- und Sozialwissenschaftlichen Klasse, Jg. 1973, Nr.8. Wiesbaden: Steiner, pp. 18-24.

[101] (Sokoloff's *A Dictionary of Jewish Palestinian Aramaic*). http://cal.huc.edu/djpa.php?lemma=tgr+N In K. Veenhof's view, the basic meaning of tamkaru is 'traders, travelling or working abroad.' (Klaas R. Veenhof, Jesper Eidem, 2008, Mesopotamia, the old Assyrian period, Academic Press Fribourg Vandenhoeck & Ruprech Gottingen).

[102] Samuel Noah Kramer, 1979, *From the poetry of Sumer: creation, glorification, adoration*, Univ. of California Press, Berkeley, p. 51.

[103] E. Unger, Babylon: *Die heilige Stadt nach der Beschreibung der Babylonier*, 2nd ed., Berlin, 1970, 285, line 19; cf. AL Oppenheim, *Ancient Mesopotamia*, Chicago, 1964, p. 94.) (M.A. Dandamayev, The neo-Babylonian Tamkāru, in:Ziony Zevit, Seymour Gitin, and Michael Sokoloff, eds., 1995, Solving Riddles and Untying Knots: Biblical, Epigraphic, and Semitic Studies in Honor of Jonas C. Greenfield, Eisenbrauns, pp.523-530.

[104] PRU IV, pp. 103-105. Cf. M. Heltzer, *The Rural community in Ancient Ugarit,* Wiesbaden 1976, (n.5), pp. 57-58; Id., *Goods, prices and the organization of trade*

in Ugarit, Wiesbaden 1978, pp. 127-128; R. Yaron, Foreign Merchants in Ugarit, in *ILR* 4 (1969), pp. 71-74.

105 Akkadian Cylinder seal -- ca. 2334-2154 BCE --. Cuneiform inscription: 'S'u-ilis'u, Meluhha interpreter', i.e., translator of the Meluhhan language (EME.BAL.ME.LUH.HA.KI). The Meluhhan being introduced carries an antelope on his arm. Musee du Louvre. Ao 22 310, Collection De Clercq. http://www.penn.museum/documents/publications/expedition/PDFs/48-1/What in the World.pdf

106 http://penn.museum/documents/publications/expedition/PDFs/48-1/What%20in%20the%20World.pdf de Clercq, Louis. Collection de Clercq: Catalogue Méthodique et Raisonné: Antiquités Assyriennes, Cylindres Orientauz, Cachets, Briques, Bronzes, Bas-Reliefs, Etc. Paris: E. Leroux, 1888.

107 Satya Swarup Misra, 1999, *The date of the Rigveda and the Aryan Migration,* Pune, Centre of Advanced Study in Sanskrit, University of Pune http://vepa.us/dir8/Sanskrit%20ssmisra2.htm See Muir, OST, 2nd ed., II, p. 114; Kuhn, Beiträge z. P. Gr., p. 43; Davidson, ZDMG, XXXVII, p. 23; Eggeling, SBE, XXVI, p. 31, n.3).

108 Valdiya, KS. 2002. Sarasvati, the river that disappeared. Hyderabad. Academic Press.

109 Simo Parpola, A. Parpola and R.H. Brunswig, "The Meluhha Village: Evidence of Acculturation of Harappan Traders in Late Third Millennium Mesopotamia":*Journal of the Economic and Social History of the Orient* 20, 129-165.

110 Robert H. Brunswig, Jr. et al, New Indus Type and Related Seals from the Near East, 101-115 in: Daniel T. Potts (ed.), Dilmun: New Studies in the Archaeology and Early History of Bahrain, Berlin, Dietrich Reimer Verlag, 1983, p. 110.

111 J.D. Muhly, 1973, *Copper and Tin*, Conn.: Archon., Hamden; Transactions of Connecticut Academy of Arts and Sciences, vol. 43, p. 221f.

112 Muhly, JD, 1976, *Copper and Tin*, Hamden, Archon Books, pp. 306-7.

113 Moorey, 1994, opcit, p. 298-299). Meluhhan speakers had hieroglyphs for tin as demonstrated in *Indian Hieroglyphs* (S. Kalyanaraman, 2012.

114 Edwin Yamauchi, 1993, Metal sources and metallurgy in the biblical world, Oxford, OH 45056, Dept. of History, Miami University From: PSCF 45 (December

1993): 252-259. http://www.asa3.org/ASA/PSCF/1993/PSCF12-93Yamauchi.html) [See: G. Dossin, "La route de l'étain en Mesopotamie au temps de Zimri-Lim," *Revue d'Assyriologie* 64 (1970), 97-106. M. Heltzer, "The Metal Trade of Ugarit and the Problem of Transportation of Commercial Goods," *Iraq* 39 (1977), 203-11. A. Malamat, "Syro-Palestinian Destinations in a Mari Tin Inventory," *Israel Exploration Journal* 21 (1971), 31-38.

[115] James D. Muhly, 1995, Mining and Metalwork in Ancient Western Asia, in: Jack M. Sasson, ed. 1995, *Civilizations of the Ancient Near East*, Vol. III, New York, Charles Scribner's Sons, pp. 1501-1521.

[116] Muhly, JD, 1979, The evidence for sources of and trade in Bronze Age tin, in Franklin AD, Olin JS, Wertime, TA, *The search for Ancient Tin*, Washington DC: A seminar organized by Theodore A. Wertime and held at the Smithsonian Institution and the national Bureau of Standards, Washington DC, March 14-15, 1977, pp. 43-48.
http://en.wikipedia.org/wiki/Tin_sources_and_trade_in_ancient_times

[117] E.J.H.Mackay, Further links between ancient Sind, Sumer and elsewhere, *Antiquity*, Vol. 5, 1931, pp. 459-473.

[118] Potts, D., 1995, Distant Shores: Ancient Near Eastern Trade, in: Jack M. Sasson (ed.), *Civilizations of the Ancient Near East*, Vol. I, pp. 1451-1463.

[119] Serge Cleuziou, Dilmun and Makkan during the third and early second millennia BC, 143-155 in: Shaikha Haya Ali Al Khalifa and Michael Rice (eds.) *Bahrain through the ages: the archaeology*, London, KPI, 1986.

[120] Thornton, C.P.; Lamberg-Karlovsky, C.C.; Liezers, M.; Young, S.M.M. (2002). "On pins and needles: tracing the evolution of copper-based alloying at Tepe Yahya, Iran, via ICP-MS analysis of Common-place items." *Journal of Archaeological Science* 29 (29): 1451–1460.

[121] http://bharatkalyan97.blogspot.com/2011/11/decoding-longest-inscription-of-indus.html

[122] http://www.cngcoins.com/Coin.aspx?CoinID=23986 Anonymous. Period of Agathokles, ca. 185 to 170 BCE. AV quarter stater (2.34 gms). Humped bull standing left. Taxila symbol before fish-like symbol with pellet and crescents. Bopeerachchi –SNG ANS – MIG 163 (Pushkalavati); BMC India pl. 35,11. "Taxila-Gandhara formed an independent territory from the late 3rd to the early 2nd century BC. Its two important cities, Taxila and Pushkalavati, were situated on the eastern and western sides respectively of the upper Indus river. Each city struck its own coinage, almost exclusively in copper. During the wars of succession in Baktria, Pantaleon and Agathokles were expelled from Baktria and created their own kingdom in Taxila-Gandhara, ruling from circa 185-170 BC. This anonymous coin probably represents the final issue of the local coinage attributable to Taxila during the period of these Greco-Baktrian kings, as well as one of India's earliest native gold coins."

[123]Ta'anach (10th Century BCE): A Terra Cotta Cult Stand This 50cm tall terra cotta stand is decorated with images of human, animal and mythical figures. It may have served as an incense altar or a libation receptacle. http://cnes.cla.umn.edu/courses/archaeology/Taanach/TaanachStart.html

[124] http://www.springerlink.com/content/w72n363w6l078182/fulltext.pdf Ghada Ziadeh Seely, 2002, The archaeology of Ottoman Ti'innik – an interdisciplinary approach, in: A historical archaeology of he Ottoman empire, contributions to global historical archaeology, 2002, II, 79-91

[125] http://www.cais-soas.com/CAIS/Images2/Misc/cult.gif

[126]http://www.nationalgeographicstock.com/ngsimages/explore/explorecomp.jsf?xsys=SE&id=1002469 Cult stand from Taanach (Tell Ti'innik). Location: Jerusalem, Israel.

[127] http://concordances.org/hebrew/8590.htm Original Word: tanak תַּעְנַךְ
Transliteration: Tanak
Phonetic Spelling: (tah-an-awk') Short Definition: Taanach

[128] Tanaach citadel archive. From Sellin. Page 38, Plate 9 http://www.thefullwiki.org/Biblical_Libraries

[129] http://www.ancientsites.com/aw/Post/1210441 Shell plaque From Ur, Southern Iraq (c. 2,600-2,400 B.C.) Entwined in the branches of a flowering tree, two goats appear to be nibbling on its leaves. This decorative plaque, which was carved from shell and highlighted with bitumen, was excavated from the Royal Tombs of Ur.

[130] After Amiet, P., 1961, *La glyptique mesopotamienne archaique*, Paris: 497; Mundigak IV.3; 3.. Sumerian cylinder seal showing flanking goats with hooves on tree and/or mountain. Uruk period. (After Joyce Burstein in: Katherine Anne Harper, Robert L. Brown, 2002, The roots of tantra, SUNY Press, p.100).

[131] cf. http://bharatkalyan97.blogspot.in/2011/12/acarya-hemacandra-1088-1173-ce.html

[132] Dave Winter *Israel handbook: with the Palestinian Authority areas,* p. 644 http://en.wikipedia.org/wiki/Taanach

[133] Source: *Encyclopaedia Biblica/Trade and Commerce* http://en.wikisource.org/wiki/Encyclopaedia_Biblica/Trade_and_Commerce —

[134] http://press.princeton.edu/chapters/s9006.pdf (Page 12).Michael Hudson, *Entrepreneurs: from the Near Eastern Takeoff to the Roman collapse* July 19, 2010http://michael-hudson.com/2010/07/entrepreneurs-from-the-near-eastern-takeoff-to-the-roman-collapse/

[135] Source: Fig. 48. Kul Tarike, copper figurine from Iron Age burial (photograph courtesy H. Rezvani) cited on Massoud Azarnoush and Barbara Helwing, 2007, Recent archaeological research in Iran -- Prehistory to Iron Age, p. 222. http://bharatkalyan97.blogspot.in/2012/07/between-mesopotamia-and-meluhha-ancient.html

[136] Kleiner, Fred S.; Mamiya, Christin J. (2006). *Gardner's Art Through the Ages: The Western Perspective – Volume 1* (12th Edition ed.). Belmont, California, USA: Thomson Wadsworth. pp. 20–21.

[137] http://oi.uchicago.edu/OI/IRAQ/Images/strom/strom_fig019l.jpg

[138] http://arthistorypart1.blogspot.in/2011/01/sumerian-art-warka-vase.html cf. http://en.wikipedia.org/wiki/Warka_Vase
http://bharatkalyan97.blogspot.in/2012/05/hieroglyphs-on-warka-vase-read-rebus-as.html

[139] Period: Late Cypriot Date: ca. 16th–12th century B.C.E. Geography: Cyprus, Ayia Paraskevi; Cyprus

Culture: Cypriot Medium: Black-grey steatite

Dimensions: 0.63 in. (1.6 cm) Classification:

Stone-Cylinder Seal Credit Line: The Cesnola Collection, Purchased by subscription, 1874-76

Accession Number: 74.51.4325

This artwork is currently on display in Gallery 173 Said to be from Amathus, Cyprus. 1865–1872, found in Cyprus by General Luigi Palma di Cesnola; acquired by the Museum in 1874, purchased from General Luigi Palma di Cesnola. http://www.metmuseum.org/Collections/search-the-collections/30000037?rpp=20&pg=1&gallerynos=173&ft=*&pos=6

[140] Period: Late Cypriot II Date: ca. 14th–13th century B.C.E. Geography: Cyprus Culture: Cypriot

Medium: Hematite Dimensions: H. 15/16 in. (2.4 cm); Diam. 3/8 in. (1 cm) Classification: Stone-Cylinder Seal Credit Line: Gift of Nanette B. Kelekian, in memory of Charles Dikran and Beatrice Kelekian, 1999 Accession Number: 1999.325.222 This artwork is currently on display in Gallery 406

http://www.metmuseum.org/Collections/search-the-collections/30006507?rpp=20&pg=1&ft=1999.325.222+&pos=1

[141] A cylinder seal carved with an elongated buffalo and a Harappan inscription circa 2600-1700 BC Susa, Iran Fired steatite H. 2.3 cm; Diam. 1.6 cm Jacques de Morgan excavations, Susa Sb 2425 http://www.metmuseum.org/toah/works-of-art/1999.325.4 http://www.louvre.fr/en/oeuvre-notices/cylinder-seal-carved-elongated-buffalo-and-harappan-inscription

[142] Images courtesy: Maurizio Tosi in an international conference in New Delhi, November 2010 organised by Draupati Trust.

[143] References: Ernout-M. A. Dictionnaire etymologique de la langue latine, 2nd ed.; Walde-H. Lateinisches etymologisches Worterbuch, 3te Aufl., von J.B.Hofmann

[144] [http://www.people.fas.harvard.edu/~witzel/IndusLang.pdf Michael E. J. Witzel, The Languages of Harappa, provisional version dated 17 February 2000, intended for J. Kenoyer (ed.),Proceedings of the conference on the Indus civilization, Madison 1998.Mirror: Languages of Harappa - Witzel (2000)].

[145] Douglas Q. Adams, 1999, A Dictionary of Tocharian, Atlanta, Rodopi, p.80)

[146] http://en.wikipedia.org/wiki/Haoma

147

http://www.fas.harvard.edu/~iranian/Zoroastrianism/Zoroastrianism3_Texts_I.pdf (Zoroastrian Texts translated with notes by Prods Oktor Skjærvø, 2007, Page 11).

148 Angot, Michel, 2001, *L'Inde Classique, Les Belles Lettres*, Paris.
149 Excerpted from HW Bodewitz, 1990, The Jyotistoma ritual: Jaiminiya Brahmana I, 66-364, Brill, p. 203. http://tinyurl.com/9l5z8vl

150 http://content.answers.com/main/content/wp/en/d/d9/Melting_crucible.jpg

151 Source: Evans, George G. ILLUSTRATED HISTORY OF THE UNITED STATES MINT. New York, NY: Sanford J. Durst Numismatic Publications, New Revised Edition, 1977, page 27.
152 Payne, JR, 1987, Iranian languages in: Bernard Comrie (ed.), *The world's major languages*, OUP, pp. 514- 519

153 Ruhlen, Merritt. 1975. *A Guide to the Languages of the World*, Stanford, OCLC: 1940981; Philip Baldi, 2002, The foundations of Latin, Water de Gruyter, p. 24.

154 Gerd Carling, Georges-Jean Pinault, Werner Winter, 2008, *Dictionary and thesaurus of Tocharian A, Volume 1*, Otto Harrassowitz Verlag. http://tinyurl.com/cwzc4s7

155 R. Roth, 'Ueber den Soma, *ZDMG*, xxxv, 1881, 684). Renou's rendering is: '*Amśu- designe, aussi bien dans le RV. Que dans l'Avesta, le soma en tant que plante (et proprement la tige ou les fibres du soma)*' ('Amśu- means both in the RV and in the Avesta the Soma as a plant (or the stem itself and the fibers of the soma') (L. Renou, 'Les elements vedique dans le Sanskrit classique', *JA*, ccxxxi, juillet-sept. 1939, 341). Roth rendered *amśavah* as 'stengelglieder' (internodes of stems).

156 G.U.Pope, Indian Antiquary; loc. Cit. R. Swaminatha Aiyar, Dravidian Theories, 1922-23, repr., Delhi, Motilal Banarsidass, 1987, pp.11-12.

157 Johnson, Samuel, 1755, Dictionary of the English Language, J&P Knapton, London. http://www.bl.uk/learning/langlit/dic/johnson/drudge/drudge.html

158 John D. Kelly, 1996. Metadiscursive strategies in. Jan EM Houben, Ideology and status of Sanskrit: contributions to the history of the Sanskrit language, Brill. p. 101.

159 A. Weber, History of Indian Literature, pp. 67-68.

160 Personal communication from Prof. TP Verma, 7 May 2010.

[161] F.R. Allchin, 1959, Upon the contextual significance of certain groups of ancient signs, *Bulletin of the School of Oriental and African Studies*, London.

[162] See Boehmer (Boehmer, R.M., 1965, Die Entwicklung der Glyptik wahrend der Akkad-Zeit, Berlin: De Gruyter: fig. 47 no. 557) and Edzard (Edzard, D.O., 1968-69, Die Inschriften der altakkadischen Rollsiegel, AfO 22: 12-20:15 no. 33)." (Gonzalo Rubio, 2006, Shulgi and the death of Sumerian in: Piotr Michalowski and Niek Veldhuis, 2006, *Approaches to Sumerian Literature*, Brill, p.170).

[163] http://www.humanistictexts.org/sumer.htm#5 Praise of Gudea

[164] Leemans W.F., 1960, Foreign trade in the old Babylonian period: as revealed by texts from southern Mesopotamia, Brill, pp.11-12. Source: http://tinyurl.com/cvvs9zg

[165] Samuel Noah Kramer, 1963, *The Sumerians: their history, culture and character*, University of Chicago Press, p. 283.

[166] B. Landsberger, *ZA*, xxxv, 3, 1924, 217.

[167] I.J. Gelb, *RA*, LXIV, 1, 1970, 5.

[168] Leemans, Foreign trade in the Old Babylonian Period, Leiden, 1960, 164). Mleccha is mentioned in*śatapathabrāhmaṇa* (tr. J. Eggeling, SBE, xxvi, 32; ca. 600 BCE.

[169] John Hansman, 1973, pp. 574-7.

[170] Bailey,1973 in: John Hansman, *A Periplus of Magan and Meluhha*, 1973, pp. 584-6.

[171] see S. Levi, *Journal Asiatique*, XIe Ser., XI, 1, 1918, 123.

[172] For recent comments on mleccha, see Wackernage, Altindische Grammatik. Introduction generale. Nouvelle edition...par Louis Renou, 1957, 73; M. Mayrhofer, Kurzgefasstes etymologisches Worterbuch des Altindischen, 699, mleccha.

[173] http://www.adventurecorps.com/archaeo/centperiph.html

[174] *Strabo's Geography* in 3 volumes translated by H.C. Hamilton, ed. H.G. Bohn, 1854-1857 (vol 1, vol 2, vol 3 at Google Books)

[175] http://www.iranicaonline.org/articles/dahyu-

[176] M.B. Emeneau, Onomatopoetics in the Indian linguistic area, *Language*, Vol. 45, No. 2, Part 1, June 1969, pp. 274-299.

[177] Emeneau, M.B., "India as a Linguistic Area". *Language* 32 (1): 3–16.),p. 16, n. 28

[178] Fig. 96f: Failaka no. 260 Double antelope joined at the belly; in the Levant, similar doubling occurs for a lion.

[179] Cover image of: Hasan Al Naboodah, and Peter Hellyer Edited by Daniel Potts, Archaeology of the United Arab Emirates: Proceedings of the First International Conference on the Archaeology of the UAE, (Abu Dhabi, 15-18 April 2001, Trident Press, London.

[180] http://en.wikipedia.org/wiki/Kharosthi

[181] http://en.wikipedia.org/wiki/Kharosthi

[182] Easton's 1897 Bible Dictionary http://dictionary.reference.com/browse/harosheth of the gentiles

[183] http://bharatkalyan97.blogspot.in/2011/11/archaeological-mystery-solved-site-of.html B. N. Mukherjee. 2008 – Origin of Brahmi & Kharosti script, Kolkata. Progressive Publishers.

[184] Date: ca. 1st century Culture: Pakistan (ancient region of Gandhara) Medium: Silver with gold foil Dimensions: Diam. 3 1/2 in. (8.9 cm) Classification: Metalwork Credit Line: Gift of The Kronos Collections, 1981 Accession Number: 1981.460.2
This artwork is currently on display in Gallery 251

[185] http://www.abarim-publications.com/Meaning/Harosheth.html

[186] http://www.abarim-publications.com/Meaning/Harosheth.html#.TtGLS7K4q7s

[187] http://pursiful.com/2008/06/all-the-kings-horses-what-a-bronze-age-military-expedition-might-look-like/

[188] http://tinyurl.com/d7be2qh

[189] Covered with Prakrit inscriptions in the Kharoshthi script, the form of writing of acient north-western India. Between the two lions is a square crowning relief bearing auspicious symbols like the triratna,which stands for the veneration of the Buddha, his monastic order and dharma, the code of religious conduct that the Buddha professed. OA 1889.3-14.1 British Museum, London, Great Britain.

[190] G. Buhler, 1894, Dr. Bhagvanlal Indraji's interpretation of the Mathura lion pillar inscription. JRAS, July 1894, pp. 525-540. http://www.jstor.org/stable/info/25197209

[191] http://www.xtimeline.com/evt/view.aspx?id=170935

[192] *Journal of Indo-Judaic Studies*, Vol. 1, Number 11 (2010) -- The Bronze Age Writing System of Sarasvati Hieroglyphics as Evidenced by Two "Rosetta Stones" By S. Kalyanaraman (Editor of JIJS: Prof. Nathan Katz) http://www.indojudaic.com/index.php?option=com_contact&view=contact&id=1&Itemid=8

[193] http://www.freedomsphoenix.com/News/057335-2009-09-11-archaeologists-find-early-menorah-depiction.htm

[194] http://en.wikipedia.org/wiki/Goy

[195] Ahmad Hasan Dani, 1992, Significance of silk road to human civilization: its cultural dimension, Senri Ethnological Studies 32 1992, p. 22). http://ir.minpaku.ac.jp/dspace/bitstream/10502/658/1/SES32_004.pdf

[196] Monier-Williams, Introduction, Sanskrit-English Dictionary, p.xxv) http://www.sanskrit-lexicon.uni-koeln.de/scans/MWScan/MWScanpdf/mw010029.pdf

[197] Govindraya Prabhu in:http://www.forumancientcoins.com/india/kushana/kus_language.html

[198] E. Errington and J. Cribb (eds), The Crossroads of Asia: transf (Cambridge, Ancient India and Iran Trust, 1992)

[199] Andrew Glass, A Preliminary Study of Kharoṣṭhī Manuscript Paleography August 2000. http://andrewglass.org/ma.php

[200] http://www.scribd.com/doc/73963509/A-Preliminary-Study-of-Kharo%E1%B9%A3%E1%B9%ADh%C4%AB-Manuscript-Paleography-Andrew-Glass-2000

[201] http://www.jpost.com/ChristianInIsrael/Features/Article.aspx?id=180213

[202] Emeneau, Murray. 1956. India as a Lingusitic Area. "Langauge" 32: 3-16. http://en.academic.ru/dic.nsf/enwiki/113093

203 Berger, H. Die Burushaski-Sprache von Hunza und Nagar. Vols. I-III. Wiesbaden: Harrassowitz 1988] [Tikkanen (2005)]

204 [G.Morgenstierne, Irano-Dardica. Wiesbaden 1973]

205 The Munda Languages. Edited by Gregory D. S. Anderson. London and New York: Routledge (Routledge Language Family Series), 2008.

206 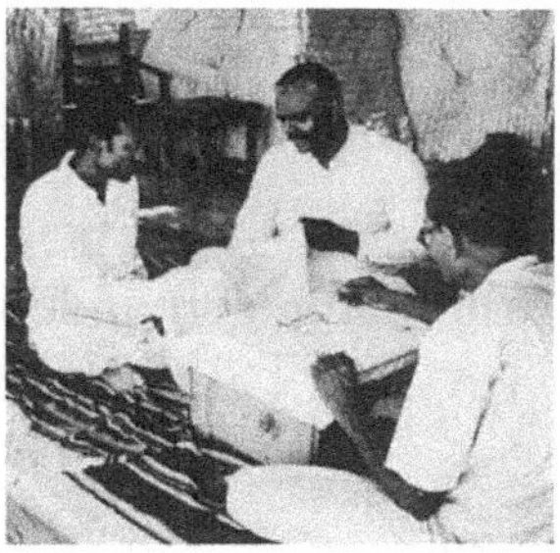

A pearl merchant of South India settling price for a pearl using finger gestures under a handkerchief. Cited in Karl Menninger, 1969, *Number words and number symbols: a cultural history of numbers*, MIT Press, p.212. http://tinyurl.com/26ze95s

207 After Fig. 2 in P.R.S. Moorey, 1994, Ancient Mesopotamian Materials and Industries, Oxford, Clarendon Press.

208 Source for the archaeological sites distribution maps: Current Science, Vol. 98, No. 6, 25 March 2010, pp 846-852; Spatio-temporal analysis of the Indus urbanization Kavita Gangal, M. N. Vahia and R. Adhikari http://www.ias.ac.in/currsci/25mar2010/846.pdf

209 Source: Magan and Meluhha See Steinkeller 1984, 265.

210 Jain, 1984, Life in Ancient India as Described in the Jain Canon and Commentaries (6th century BC - 17th century AD, p. 150.

211 Cowell, 1973, Jatakas Book II, p. 172 ff.

212 M.B.Emeneau, India as a Linguistic Area [Lang. 32, 1956, 3-16; LICS, 196, 642-51; repr. In Collected papers: Dravidian Linguistics Ethnology and Folktales, Annamalai Nagar, Annamalai University, 1967, pp. 171-186.

213 M.B.Emeneau, Linguistic Prehistory of India PAPS98 (1954). 282-92; Tamil Culture 5 (1956). 30-55; repr. In Collected papers: Dravidian Linguistics Ethnology and Folktales, Annamalai Nagar, Annamalai University, 1967, pp. 155-171.

214 Swaminatha Iyer, 1975, Dravidian Theories, Madras, Madras Law Journal Office

[215] Bryant, Edwin and Laurie L. Patton, 2005, The Indo-Aryan controversy: evidence and inference in Indian history, Routledge, p.197.

[216] Emeneau, MB, 1956, India as a linguistic area, in: Language, 32.3-16

•Kuiper, FBJ, 1967, The genesis of a linguistic area, Indo-Iranian Journal 10: 81-102

•Masica, Colin P., 1976, Defining a linguistic area, South Asia, Chicago, University of Chicago Press

•Franklin Southworth, 2005, Linguistic Archaeology of South Asia, Routledge Curzon

[217] F.B.J. Kuiper, 1948, Proto-Munda Words in Sanskrit, Amsterdam, Verhandeling der Koninklijke Nederlandsche Akademie Van Wetenschappen, Afd. Letterkunde, Nieuwe Reeks Deel Li, No. 3, 1948, p.9 http://www.scribd.com/doc/12238039/mundalexemesinSanskrit

[218] Aloka Parasher,1991, *Mlecchas in Early India,* Delhi, Munishiram Manorharlal. http://www.kushan.org/reviews/mlecchas.htm

[219] cf. K. Karttunen (1989). India in Early Greek Literature. Helsinki, Finnish Oriental Society. *Studia Orientalia.* Vol. 65. 293 pages. ISBN 951-9380-10-8, pp. 11 ff et passim. Asko Parpola (1975a). Isolation and tentative interpretation of a toponym in the Harappan inscriptions. Le dechiffrement des ecritures et des langues. *Colloque du XXXIXe congres des orientalistes*, Paris Juillet 1973. Paris, Le dechiffrement des ecritures et des langues. Colloque du XXXIXe congres des orientalistes, Paris Juillet 1973. 121-143 and Asko Parpola (1975b). "India's Name in Early Foreign Sources." *Sri Venkateswara* University *Oriental Journal*, Tirupati, 18: 9-19.

[220] Hirsch, H., 1963, Die Inschriften der Konige Von Agade, *Afo*, 20, pp. 37-38; Leemans, W.F., 1960, *Foreign Trade in the Old Babylonian Period*, p. 164; Oppenheim, A.L., 1954, The seafaring merchants of Ur, *JAOS*, 74, pp. 6-17.

[221] Scheil, V., 1925, Un Nouvea Sceau Hindou Pseudo-Sumerian, *RA*, 22/3, pp. 55-56

[222] Wheeler, R.E.M., 1965, *Indus Civilization*, Cambridge University Press, UK.

[223] Shendge, Malati, 1977, *The civilized demons: the Harappans in Rigveda*, *Rigveda*, Abhinav Publications. New Delhi.

[224] cf. Asko and Simo Parpola, On the relationship of the Sumerian Toponym Meluhha and Sanskrit Mleccha, *Studia Orientalia,* vol. 46, 1975, pp. 205-38). http://www.hindunet.org/hindu_history/sarasvati/html/vedictech.htm

[225] Massimo Vidale, 2004, "Growing in a Foreign World. For a History of the "Meluhha Villages" in Mesopotamia in the 3rd Millennium BC" http://www.scribd.com/doc/2566221/meluhhanvillage

[226] http://sites.google.com/site/kalyan97/mlecchitavikalpa

[227] Massimo Vidale, 2007, The collapse melts down, a reply to Farmer, Sprout & Witzel, *East and West*
Vol. 57, No. 1/4 (December 2007), pp. 333-366
http://www.jstor.org/discover/10.2307/29757733?uid=3738256&uid=2456270415&uid=2129&uid=2&uid=70&uid=3&uid=60&sid=21100968484243

[228] Massimo Vidale, "Growing in a Foreign World. For a History of the "Meluhha Villages" in Mesopotamia in the 3rd Millennium BC" in Melammu Symposia 4: A. Panaino and A. Piras (eds.), Schools of Oriental Studies and the Development of Modern Historiography. Proceedings of the Fourth Annual Symposium of the Assyrian and Babylonian Intellectual Heritage Project. Held in Ravenna, Italy, October 13-17, 2001 (Milan: Università di Bologna & IsIao 2004), pp. 261-80. http://www.mimesisedizioni.it/ The Melammu project: http://www.aakkl.helsinki.fi/melammu/

[229] Edwin Bryant and Laurie Patton. 2005. Indo-Aryan Controversy - Evidence and inference in Indian History. Routledge.
Source: http://www.scribd.com/doc/54128303/Bryant-Edwin-and-Laurie-Patton-Ed-the-Indo-Aryan-Cotroversy

[230] Trubetzkoy, 1928: 18 (italics his)] Trubetzkoy, N. S., 1928. Proposition 16. In: Actes du 1er Congrès international de linguistes, 17-18.Leiden: A. W. Sijthoff's Uitgeversmaatschappij.

[231] Burrow, T. 1973. The Proto-Indoaryans. Journal of the Royal Asiatic Society (New Series) April 1973 105 : pp 123-140
http://www.docstoc.com/docs/125553673/Protoindoaryanstburrow1973

[232] Thieme, P. The 'Aryan' Gods of the Mitanni treaties, JAOS, 60, 1960, 301-317.

[233] http://news.bbc.co.uk/2/hi/science/nature/334517.stm

www.ingramcontent.com/pod-product-compliance
Lightning Source LLC
Chambersburg PA
CBHW050453110426
42743CB00017B/3345
* 9 7 8 0 9 8 2 8 9 7 1 4 0 *